D1061784

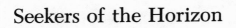

Seekers of the Horizon

Seekers of the Horizon

Sea-Kayaking Voyages from around the World

edited by

Will Nordby

The Globe Pequot Press ≈ Chester, Connecticut

The following selections in this anthology are reprinted by permission of the authors and/or their publishers:

Kaufmann, Paul. "Paddling the Gate." In *Paddling the Gate: A Kayak Trip on San Francisco Bay*. Santa Monica, Calif.: Mara Books Incorporated, 1978.

Lindemann, Hannes. "An Impossible Voyage." In *Alone at Sea*. New York: Random House, 1958.

Sutherland, Audrey. "The Canoe." In *Paddling My Own Canoe*. Honolulu: The University Press of Hawaii, 1978.

Black and white photo credits: Will Nordby pages xii, 10, 37, 85, 90, 245; John Bauman page 61; Chris Duff page 137; C. Bell page 156; Hannes Lindemann page 179; Larry Rice pages 268, 273; Greg Blanchette page 293.

Color photo credits: Joel W. Rodgers 1, 3, 11; Will Nordby 2, 8, 10, 12; Ben Davidson 4, 5, 7, 9; Peter Thomas 6.

© 1989 by Will Nordby

Library of Congress Cataloging-in-Publication Data

Seekers of the horizon: sea-kayaking voyages from around the world/
    edited by Will Nordby.—1st ed.
        p.   cm.
    ISBN 0-87106-634-3
    1. Sea kayaking. 2. Voyages around the world. I. Nordby, Will.
GV788.5.S44   1989
797.1'22—dc20   89-16782
                                                                 CIP

Manufactured in the United States of America
First Edition/First Printing

Contents

Color section follows page 128

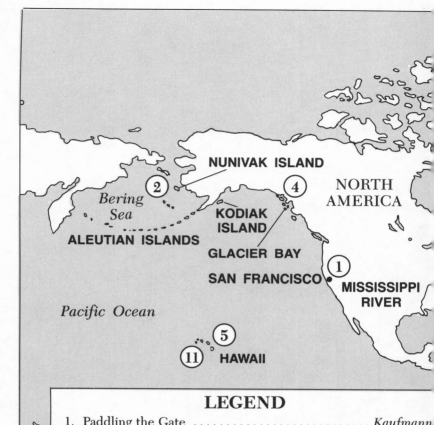

NUNIVAK ISLAND

② Bering Sea

④ NORTH AMERICA

ALEUTIAN ISLANDS

KODIAK ISLAND

GLACIER BAY

SAN FRANCISCO

① MISSISSIPPI RIVER

Pacific Ocean

⑤ ⑪ HAWAII

LEGEND

NOTE: *These map numbers correspond with chapter numbers and indicate the location of the voyages described in this book.*

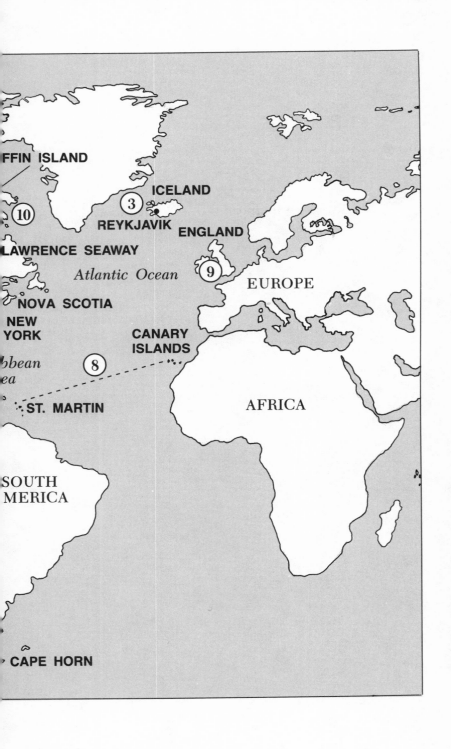

To my brother, Dr. LeRoy Nordby,
for introducing me to sea kayaking.

Foreword

Of the fact that the earth is round they were aware as a result of the following event: Their forefathers had sent out two baidarkas in which the travelers had set out young and had returned old men, and they had still not found the edge of the world. So they had concluded that there was no edge of the world and therefore it must be round.

—Koniag legend, as recorded by Hieromonk Father Gedeon,
Kodiak Island, 1804

From the viewpoint of a sea kayaker, the Earth's horizon lies barely two miles away. The kayaks (or *baidarkas*, in Russian usage) of Father Gedeon's time could paddle this distance four times within an hour, bringing the edge of the world—if there was one—within easy reach. Was Gedeon's account of a legendary round-the-world voyage pure fiction? Was it based on a circumpolar traverse rather than a true circumnavigation of the globe? Who knows? Sea kayakers are still setting out, young and old, in search of the edge of the world. In the pages that follow we find individual chapters of a paddling journey that began a long, long time ago.

Will Nordby brings us an anthology of sea kayaking emphasizing the individual whys rather than the collective hows of the modern sport. Drawn from all waters of the world, the contributions to this volume are more closely allied in spirit than they are in choice of destination or technique. And by choosing to pick up a paddle, we are, all of us, allied with a common past that underlies the whole subject of this book.

Whether sea kayaking goes back more than 10,000 years
remains conjectural; the prevailing evidence, however, does
point to sea kayaking as having been a popular activity as many
as 5,000 years ago. Most of the great kayaking adventures will
remain forever untold. Only by Gedeon's time, at least in the
Pacific Ocean, was the extent, if not the details, of sea kayaking
being recorded. A golden age of ocean paddling appeared in
outline as a result: At the close of the eighteenth century, the
Russian-American Company was organizing kayak expeditions
extending thousands of miles afield from its Kodiak Island
headquarters and involving as many as 800 boats. Under Russian administration, Aleut and Koniag baidarkas ranged from
Baja California to the islands off northern Japan, in numbers
that soon exceeded those of the sea otters on which they preyed.

The recent resurgence of sea kayaking in a modern context
reflects the equipment, the techniques, and, yes, even the moti-
vations of former times. After all, historical evidence suggests
that today's recreational aspects of sea kayaking were not without precedent among the paddlers of long ago. In past expeditions as in present ones, therefore, the discomforts were no
doubt balanced to a degree by the rewards: the excitement of
venturing into new territory, the companionship and solitude
of the voyage, and the stories to be told and retold afterwards,
much as we tell them today.

The paddlers of Father Gedeon's time are, significantly,
only a few generations removed from individuals still paddling
today. Living memory still tells the stories, and our own paddling experience allows us to perceive the unspoken details.
Regardless of the era, it is the days, months, years, and life-
times spent kayaking—one paddle stroke at a time—that
sharpens the senses, resulting in the degree of heightened perception that we find described by the authors of this book.
Paradoxically, it is the repetitive monotony of paddling that
frees the senses as well as the intellect to explore one's surroundings in detail.

Circumstances for today's paddlers may be quite different
from those of Gedeon's time, yet the burdens and the joys of the
paddle remain fundamentally the same. Each generation must
rediscover this for itself, inventing new excuses for the chance to
spend its time, productively or aimlessly, at sea. The craft that

was designed to put food on the table now puts a few moments of sanity into the urban kayaker's otherwise too hectic world. The arm that once held the spear-thrower now hoists a kayak to the roof rack at launching ramps around the world, then navigates city traffic with some of the same skills that may once again be applied to the spear.

Traditions are not so much extinguished as transformed.

—GEORGE DYSON

Will Nordby

Introduction

Adventure, self-discovery, a fascination for probing the mysteries of wilderness areas—these are some of the reasons why people sea kayak. There are many other reasons as stated in the journeys that make up this anthology. Whether paddling around San Francisco Bay or crossing the Atlantic, the questing spirit of man is revealed. Within each of us is the desire to explore; by so doing, we hope to understand and appreciate the complexities and mysteries of the world and ourselves. When that exploration is done from the seat of a kayak some truly unique perspectives result. My involvement with sea kayaking serves as an example.

I can clearly remember my first group outing in 1973 near Alert Bay on the northeastern tip of Vancouver Island, British Columbia. It seemed like the greatest adventure of my life. And it was. I have been sea kayaking ever since.

I, along with three others, planned a week-long outing. On one level, I felt comfortable anticipating the companionship, exercise, and camping. But, I was also uneasy. This would be the first time I would be dependent upon a kayak for my food, clothing, shelter, and transportation. It was my only connection with civilization. As such, the kayak seemed fragile and small against the vastness of the sea and surrounding forest. And what about my capabilities and limitations? Could I keep pace with the others? Would I panic in a rough sea? I would be testing myself and knew it.

Beyond these concerns was the adjustment to a new environment, a foreign culture, for Alert Bay was the domain of the Kwakiutl people. They had been living there for centuries before the white man arrived.

As our group prepared to leave, I noticed several elderly

Kwakiutl observing us, their dark eyes hinting of rapport. Perhaps they were reminded of youthful days when they paddled huge dugout canoes. Up until this moment they had seemed preoccupied and oblivious of our actions—always at a distance, never close. Then materializing from nowhere were a handful of children with smudged faces and runny noses. At first shy, they quickly swarmed around our kayaks and peppered us with questions: Where are you from? Where are you going? Why? How much does this cost (pointing to paddles, kayaks, and camping gear)? Can I go for a paddle?

All the while they darted among our kayaks touching the deck or looking inside. Their vivid imaginations bubbled with fantasies involving themselves and the kayak. The universal curiosity of kids had melted the cultural barrier, and we felt closer to the native community as a result. So, with the ragtag kids shouting and waving farewells, we stroked seaward in jubilant spirits.

Once into the trip, I gained confidence in handling my kayak, though I was still apprehensive. Aside from the intrigue of experiencing unfamiliar territory, the seeds for a deeper awareness were being sown. I found myself wanting to know more about: the Kwakiutls and their culture; the sea, the weather; vegetation, land and sea wildlife; even the perceptions my companions had about the environment. In short, I wanted to be able to read my surrounding like a book while actually experiencing it.

As the trip progressed, I was enchanted with the variety of new sights, sounds, and scents. Vivid in my memory are the ghostly multihued northern lights shimmering in a velvet black sky; the surge and gurgle of a rising tide among glistening kelp beds at dawn; and the pervasive redolence of a cedar log being carved into a totem pole by a native using hand tools from another generation.

At trip's end, my kayak had become a magical waterborne carpet. There was an unparalleled freedom in gliding self-propelled from one magnificent vista to another: passing fishing boats to orca whales to isolated native people's villages to islands to the open sea. Indeed, over the past fifteen years of paddling the North Pacific coast, my kayak has bridged worlds.

The act of moving quietly on the sea to approach and examine ancient native people's middens and overgrown pioneer homesteads enhances a feeling of timelessness and continuity. Present meets the past and I am part of it. To travel by kayak is to think about the past. An archetypal self emerges with the physical exertion of paddling from place to place. It is a reminder of ancient man's journey for survival and quest.

One of the gratifying results of sea kayaking is to contemplate the "why," the meaning of the activity. But it is difficult to express the meaning of sea kayaking because there is such a depth of experience to draw from. Rarely am I called upon to articulate my feelings. Like my fellow sea kayakers, I challenge myself physically and mentally and gain an appreciation for my growth in the activity. It is an area of private communication with the self. The self that confronts such heavyweight subjects as truth, identity, and existence. The combination of sea kayaking with this ongoing inner dialogue is what I call the Proteus experience.

According to Roman mythology, sea-dwelling Proteus was an elderly and elusive gray-eyed prophet employed by Neptune to tend his sea calves (seals). Being omniscient, Proteus knew and understood the secrets of the sea. For this reason, people sought his counsel. But finding Proteus was difficult because he had the ability to change his shape into any form he chose. Only by catching him asleep and binding him could one get the information one sought.

Allegorically, I interpret Proteus as a symbol of the sea's changing character. To know the sea requires "counseling" or being on it. As a result, knowledge gained from waterborne experiences allows a sea kayaker to recognize the many shapes or conditions the sea assumes and to develop skills necessary to navigate safely. In the process, the sea kayaker conducts a dialogue with the sea—an internal dialogue unique to each paddler. As unique as truth, identity, and existence. Proteus is repeatedly sought, caught, and bound in the eternal quest for meaning. In the same manner, as a sea kayaker arrives at a distant point on the horizon, he finds another distant point on the horizon to pique his curiosity. Thus he, like other sea kayakers, becomes a seeker of the horizon.

"It can be said of most small-ship wanderers that they voyage not to acquire money or status but to accumulate new experience. And beyond that, perhaps, bare points of contact when the beginning, present, and future connect somehow with a ship, sea, sky, and an individual, when for a moment the secret of it all will stand revealed almost within reach. It is these times past and present that give meaning to life."

Charles A. Borden
-*Sea Quest*-

PAUL KAUFMANN

Paddling the Gate
A Kayak Trip on San Francisco Bay

Opening my eyes, barely awake, and focusing fuzzily, I look at the clock: 4:30 A.M.? I doublecheck the message of the clock's hands. Oh, time and tide don't wait. . . .

I really must get up to meet the current schedule! The numbers I wrote down on my little tide card as dry calculations last week are now a part of me, and those figures convincingly urge my getting out of bed. After years of paddling on San Francisco Bay, the times and strengths of ebb and flood precisely describe the changing face of the moving waters. I picture the current patterns for the hours ahead, anticipating the reactions of an old friend. If I can only get up now, I'll have time to prepare leisurely, embarking before sunrise, about an hour after maximum ebb.

However, before acting on any plans for the trip, I carefully listen. Last night's weather report predicted small-craft warnings for this afternoon, but now I hear nothing, only the comfort of silence . . . not a flutter of the shutters by the open window. So I get up, walk downstairs, and open the front door: what encouragement—the leaves of the bamboo in the tub on the porch barely flicker in the early morning stillness. Such gentle air movement suggests very light winds on the bay a block away, reassurance of ample time for an easy launch.

*Eskimo words: *Naoyak*, "Sea gull"; *Natsek*, "Seal"; *Sirinek*, "Sun"; *Taktik*, "Moon"; *Taktuk*, "Fog."

Now I listen for fog horns—there are none. Though I love to paddle in the fog, that usually means cold west winds. So today at least the start will be calm. Being this intent on the weather, I almost forget to look up at the clear, dark purple sky with the barely perceptible twilight of dawn an hour and a half away: and there's *taktik*,* large and full, setting in the west. Noticing that the moon and earth and sun are all lined up, I immediately understand the predicted low tide a couple of hours after sunrise. From the clutter of city life I'm tuning in to the deeper forces controlling my trip: the wind, the tide, and the current. All these seem auspicious for a Golden Gate paddle, so I decide to go.

First for a shower. Why have I never gone on a trip without this initial ritual? It certainly isn't needed for waking up, as anticipation of the journey already has me very much at the ready, alert, and even a bit tense—with my wits about me, awaiting the experiences to come. Standing under the hot water I wonder about this necessity. Is it some sort of ceremonial cleansing, removing the protective coating against the incessant inputs and trivialities of city living? Or possibly a purification, a preparation for the temple of Asclepius on the bay? After drying briskly with a towel, I shave carefully. Might this, too, have similar symbolic meanings? But it's also useful to have a clean-shaven face for sensing wind direction on foggy days. Some alcohol-based suntan lotion finishes the skin preparation.

Now I get dressed. A string undershirt creates a layer of warm air beneath my freshly laundered shirt, and it also prevents me from feeling clammy if I get a bit wet. I appreciate this gift from the Norse fishermen who found that fishnet gave protection from wet and cold, and I like feeling connected to those veterans of the sea. I pull on heavy wool cutoff pants, which make for comfortable sitting. Wool doesn't mat or feel cold when wet, and bare legs are easier for landing in the surf.

In the kitchen I start a large pot of coffee—not just for breakfast, but for the thermos gas tank needed on the trip. From the refrigerator I take some sliced cheese, an apple, hardtack, beef jerky, and pack these in a tiny orange nylon zippered bag for brunch at sea.

Leaving the coffee to brew, I go to the garage, open the door, and then drive the car out. The tiny boat hanging from the ceiling on two pulleys can now be lowered. It's a two by fourteen-foot, fifty-three pound, fiberglass kayak, with a cherry red deck and white hull. Its name, *Naoyak*, is in black reflecting letters on the port bow. The hull, made in Germany by Hans Klepper, is a standard touring design. And the trade name, *Bummler*, on the foredeck means just that—to bum around.

Now the paddles. Any defect here would really put me up the proverbial creek. But overnight soaking has expanded the laminated spruce shafts tight in the ferrules; so today the two-piece double blades can be joined at the water. On my thumb joints I paint some aromatic tincture of benzoin, a sticky protective undercoat to secure the patches of moleskin, which serve as bearing surfaces where the paddle shaft turns over the bone. Bare skin had not lasted an hour my first trips.

By now the coffee is ready, so I eat a light breakfast of orange juice, granola, and milk. This is also a time for running through checklists in my head—an automatic process for each trip—just to be sure nothing is left out before leaving the house. Once I forgot the paddles, once the dock key; those mistakes cast a shadow on the trips much greater than the brief jog back home for retrieval.

The thermos filled with the remaining coffee goes into the equipment pack that I put in the front of the boat along with the paddles, the radar reflector, and the Coast Guard approved cushion. This weight in the bow balances the kayak for carrying, and the bumper guards taped to the cockpit rim serve as shoulder pads. I wind and set my watch, check that the house and the dock keys are in the pockets of the jacket worn only until the launch, and I am ready for the second hour of the trip.

I grip the angular edges of the cockpit coaming through padded leather mitts, take a deep breath, and then lift. Balancing the kayak is a bit tricky as I hoist it to my shoulders. But once up, this boat-shaped hat rides easily for the portage to the bay . . . past the silent houses . . . down the quiet streets. The stillness of the sleeping city is a balm. What a contrast: crowded highways and vacation travelers searching for solitude and wilderness—and here I've found it within a few minutes' walking distance. I wonder what will be in store today? After three hundred trips in the past ten years, might this be my first time to meet another kayak out the Gate?

The five-second sweep of the Alcatraz Light greets me at the corner. A very clear day on the bay! And from the west, where the orange lights of the Golden Gate Bridge sparkle this morning, I'm gently touched by a cold sea breeze.

In recent years jogging has become popular, so even at this predawn hour I can usually hail a runner on the Marina Green to come and open the gate to the dock. A dry launch is much easier than cold feet in the surf.

After handing the key on a cork float to a confused jogger, I point to the gate, and then carefully walk down the tide steepened gangway. The jogger hands back my key, the gate bangs shut behind, and I'm suddenly aware of another world, sensing the sea beneath the wet boards of the ramp. Among the rows of boats floating like race horses tied in their stalls, I look for an empty berth. There is just enough glow from the moon, the lightening sky, and the dock lamps to reveal an unoccupied slip for the launch. After dropping down the bumpers at the correct positions to serve as cushions for the boat, I set the kayak down . . . gently. That's a relief.

Before packing, I briefly survey the scene. The early morning glow on Mount Tamalpais is pink and mauve. Already a smoggy layer of haze over the Berkeley Hills separates them from Mount Diablo in the distance. The only navigational light seen from here, the Alcatraz beacon, sends its friendly welcome; the necklace of blue lights around the shore of that deserted prison are, in fact, grim floodlights on a chain link fence topped with barbed wire and footed with coils of concertina wire—an ugly barrier erected after the eviction of the Native Americans.

Packing the kayak is a precise routine; everything has to be stowed in exactly the right place, to be reached automatically when needed. The emergency flares and orange smoke signal are stored with rubber bands in front of the footrest. Anything farther forward is attached to a colored plastic dog leash so it may be recovered from in front of my feet: The coffee on a red one, and the bailer with emergency food on the yellow. Water-activated CO_2 cartridge air chambers are placed in both bow and stern. These are in addition to the permanently inflated air bags at both sides and ends. To the right of the seat are my gloves and a dayglow HELP sign; to the left a nylon emergency line and a small towel for landing use.

Under the deck, on the left, I hang a small utility bag filled with rarely used necessities: bandages, aspirin, antacid, caffeine pills, a compass for map reading, a mariner's compass on a suction cup for the fog, spare moleskin pads, a tube of cleansing cream for oily beach feet, dimes for the telephone, a tide and current book, a comb, and plastic bags for urinating. My watch hangs from a snap hook on the bag. Inside the cockpit on my right are the brunch bag and its holder. And there is a sack of soft things for final dressing after I'm in the boat.

When everything is stowed, I put on my life jacket, then the spray cover with its shoulder suspenders, and finally the international orange dayglow vest that the Coast Guard once asked me to wear for visibility. In the vest pocket is a horn, my last resort to warn sleepy motorboat operators—my panic button. Today my life jacket is underneath, because it's a thin, uninflated, CO_2 cartridge–activated type. On extremely cold or rough days I may wear a French kayak jacket on the outside—the kind with permanently inflated air cells.

In the east, over the Berkeley Hills, the purple sky is turning a deep blue; and just north of Mount Diablo is an orange tint, subtly expanding. I move the boat to the edge of the dock with the stern overhanging the water, lift the bow, and launch as the colorful sky puts a yellow blush on the sea.

What a good feeling to step into the kayak, onto a soft plush black rug. *Naoyak* floats motionlessly next to the dock as I finish dressing, the roomy cockpit allowing this easily. Sitting on a red Navaho wool blanket, I put my city sneakers and socks into a plastic bag and change into wool terry cloth-lined socks and down booties. My heels rest on a piece of sheepskin over the footrest sling of conveyor belt material, and my rubber knee pads are also lined with wool. The seat is made tight by inserting rubber hip pads faced with wool. Now the kayak is no longer just a boat, but has become a piece of special clothing covering the lower two-thirds of me, padded with wool everywhere, snug and warm and comfortable—a perfect fit.

Is that a cold westerly starting up so soon? I get out my gloves—gauntlet-length mitts with pigskin palms and wool liners. Mittens are warmer than gloves, and nothing between my fingers makes it easier to grip the paddle. Though coldness is rarely a problem in this cozy kayak dress, wind can change that rapidly by blowing away body heat. So I've learned to use gloves early when there's wind, for once my fingers are numb, it's usually too late to regain circulation. This west wind opposing the ebb may mean chop, or even an overfall, for a rough paddle going out; but the same wind might be an assistance on the return trip, supplying a push, and perhaps waves to ride.

Even more than the warmth and security of all this equipment, there's my need to feel psychologically comfortable, totally at peace with safety precautions, with nothing extraneous to think about so I can just be myself at sea. All the time and care of accouterment sometimes seems a bit contradictory to my wish to escape from trivial details; but it's just this precise and shipshape preparation that now allows me to forget all about this paraphernalia when out on the salt water. It's not just stowed in the boat, but in my subconscious—in both places for instant retrieval.

The elastic edge of the spray cover is attached over the coaming, sealing out every drop of water up to my armpits. Now I pick up the paddle; the line tied to the center of the shaft runs to a suction cup, which I secure to the deck. Finally, after pulling on my gloves, I push off from the dock.

Now I'm in a different world, the world of the sea: the firm realm of land and dock has been exchanged for the realm of the depths—far less secure, but infinitely more peaceful. The soothing calmness from the water flows right up through my body, and I can feel the sea inside, nourishing some hungry spaces.

Sitting exactly at sea level is unique to kayaking; in no other craft is the water so close—close enough to touch. Just dangling an arm wets my hand above the wrist. And at this distance I can read the words of the surface waters.

The color of the sea changes with the reflection from the sky: the dull gold sea hints at the coming sunrise. As I head toward the point of the jetty, the surface speaks about current flow. Small whirlpools and larger round areas of upwelling show where the ebb from the bay and the harbor confront, pile up, and form a place of excess water—a dimly shaking surface, like ripples of obesity. Paddling over this feels eerie, as if the paddle and rudder were touched by foreign hands.

The aches of the first stint of paddling are taking away the stiffness of a long dry week. How good it feels to grasp the wooden shaft. What delight seeing how far the kayak coasts with but one paddle dip—such a small bite of the sea. The spooned blades have a raised spine of laminated wood that helps them pull comfortably without much tendency to flutter or turn. I never have to look at them, sensing precisely how they enter and grip the water . . . leaving behind two whirlpools each . . . as footprints following the boat. The resistance of a paddleful of water, such a tiny mass in the vast expanse, is a sensuous pleasure: with gentle strokes it's lovely pliant softness; with stronger pulls, the water responds hard and firm. Through the paddle I learn the mood of the sea. Here it feels indecisive, as the currents argue, but soon they agree to cooperate and join forces, building toward the awesome power flowing out the Gate.

I paddle out the harbor past the tip of the breakwater. Here the ebb catches the bow for a bouncy ride through the rip . . . I don't think about the foot-controlled rudder. It's become quite automatic, allowing rhythmic paddling without constant concern for directions when wind or waves push the boat. My feet enjoy taking care of the course for me. Rudderless river kayaks are much more maneuverable, but making headway in such a confused sea would be impossible. I remember the first time that Willi used his new single kayak. . . . That day there was a huge following sea causing us both to surf. . . . But the rudder he'd ordered hadn't arrived, and Willi had to use his paddle so much for controlling direction that he couldn't make it to the restaurant at Mission Rock Resort. So, the goal was changed; my emergency food supply was needed for the first time; and we shared a dry stale snack on the calm water between two piers along the Embarcadero, right under the Bay Bridge.

If it hadn't been for Willi, I doubt I'd ever have confronted the advantages of kayaking alone. What a fateful meeting that day ten years ago when both of us were strolling on the beach near the St. Francis Yacht Club. Mr. Sorensen, the old German who fishes from his kayak along the shore, was just landing through the surf. Several people walked over to greet him. Willi inquired if someone might paddle farther from shore, as his father had done in Germany, on the North Sea. Mr. Sorensen knew of one person who did just that—who was standing right there. So, after astonished introductions, I invited Willi to go as front paddler for a demonstration trip around Seal rocks the next week. Then, for years afterwards, with Willi in an identical double Klepper Aerius, there were four of us on the bay each weekend. And after we both graduated to singles, we continued paddling together for several more years. It was all those shared trips, those special learning experiences, that now permit the risk of going solo.

My dayglow vest is dazzling these minutes before sunrise, so I have little concern about not being seen by the fishing boats heading out for the day. Though some ridiculously early pre-dawn paddles were extremely beautiful, they have been my most frightening trips: from the blackness on the bay, the lights on the shore were thrilling, but I never knew if my flashlight would be seen by an approaching boat. So today I can just relax . . . and take it all in. . . .

To the west the sky remains purple; to the east it's baby blue tinged with orange. It feels like the sun should arrive momentarily; yet with so many lights still visible, there's time to enjoy the drama.

Before being doused by the sun, the lights of man are startling. The Golden Gate Bridge is a chain of gold extending up the Waldo grade into the tunnels. Farther west, at the northern entrance to the Gate, on the tip of land the shape of Pluto's nose, the Point Bonita Light sends its gentle on and off Morse code "A," dot then dash, as it calls out, "I'm heeeere, I'm . . . heeeere, I'm . . . heeeeeeeere." Its ancient Fresnel lens imported from France polarizes the light along the plane of the horizon; this is one of the last large navigational lights on the bay not yet replaced by the rotating police car type.

Along the Marin headlands the Point Diablo Light is but a flicker at this distance. At the base of the north tower of the bridge is the brief rotating flash from the floodlighted white-washed building at Lime Point. At this angle the Yellow Bluff signal is difficult to distinguish from the lights of Sausalito directly behind. The south tower pier has a flashing red light; and to the southwest the rotating, bright, instantaneous beam of Mile Rocks stands out clearly, as the cove of South Bay comes into view.

The last time I looked, there was a rapidly spreading orange over the Berkeley Hills, but now the blinding yellow sliver turns out to be the ball of *Sirinek* himself. It must be near summer solstice with the sunrise behind Yerba Buena Island. How beautiful! The orange glow comes right through my eyes, into my head, down into my body, filling me with warmth. The sun pops up from the hills; the entire scene changes as everything is colored brilliant gold, as the bay boils in the light. The waves, previously so clear toward the east, are now one mass of glaring yellow and orange. No longer can any lights be seen in the city, the distances suddenly elongate, and somehow I'm left much more isolated, more alone, separated from the life in the city that the lights had represented like a candle in the window.

Having drifted far from the jetty, it's time to concentrate on my destination and route. Going out the Gate is physically easy, the current doing most of the work. But it's technically complex, and emotionally very stimulating—the power of the sea experienced so much more intensely in the ocean than here inside the bay. With small-craft warnings for westerlies, a Seal Rocks circuit seems prohibitively dangerous. So I decide on a favorite breakfast spot in the lee of Point Diablo, on the Marin shore, where the cliffs form an excellent protection from the west. But first I have to paddle across the bay . . . before attempting the Gate.

From the feel of the intimately known skyline I sense my position and am constantly oriented. Foggy trips have forced my recognition of the shoreline from the smallest, most indistinct, or even briefly seen segment. So, on a clear morning like this, the map in my head works like a computer with but glimpsed awareness of the surrounding lands as sufficient programming.

In a way I almost miss those early days with the new joys of first learning the Marin shore, the Sausalito hills, Point Cavallo, Yellow Bluff, Strawberry Peninsula, Belvedere Island,

Paul Kaufmann

Peninsula Point, Angel Island, Brooks Island, and on and on past Yerba Buena Island . . . the San Francisco skyline . . . to the hills of the Presidio.

My heading is across the current to get close to the north tower where I can then let the ebb take me out under the bridge. Because of the oil spill from the tanker collision of 1971, the Coast Guard has painted an imaginary white line between Alcatraz Island and the center of the bridge span; ships keep to the right, as on a highway. Previously, most traffic, both inbound and outbound, passed in the channel between Alcatraz and the city. But now the shipping lanes take up much of the bay. And though my peripheral vision does an automatic job, I carefully look west after passing the south buoy of the Navy degaussing range, while crossing the incoming channel. All remains clear . . . out toward the sea. Then, after crossing the line from Alcatraz, my attention turns east.

An oil tanker rounding Point Blunt! it will probably head west, so I decide to wait. If I went farther, unsure of the ship's route while she's still turning, I wouldn't know what direction to paddle out of the way. It takes a long time. But I relax and enjoy the view, feeling confident the tanker will pass well north of me. With the sun higher, there is less glare on the bay; but the still low angle makes the waves to the west stand out sharply. The sea is quite rough here over the Alcatraz Shoal. The west wind has a cold bite—a disadvantage for resting right now—but it has produced sparkling clean air, turning the San Francisco skyline into a cardboard cutout stage setting in the morning light.

The tanker passes a few hundred yards north. How easily I could have paddled ahead before the ship arrived. But when in doubt, I doubt! I paddle to meet the tanker's wake: first are the large bow waves, fun to float over . . . and then the central wake itself . . . churned-up swirls and eddies that give a strange sensation, as if my paddle and rudder were responding to forces trying to trick them. I paddle hard to overtake the other side of the expanding wake and catch a ride by surfing on a few waves.

Closer to the Gate the sea suddenly becomes rough with turbulent waves topped by a noisy breaking rip. Now I know exactly where I am: this is caused by the eighty-nine-foot nee-

dle, an undersea geologic formation rising as a pinnacle from
the bay floor hundreds of feet deeper. This pinpoints my position—not far from the north tower. I wonder if the shape of the
thing under me is related to the Needles rising above the surface
in Horseshoe Bay close by? It takes extra care paddling through
the huge caldrons of upwelling water that form circular eddies
momentarily stopping my progress. The wind had whipped up
enough chop to obscure this tricky area; I hadn't seen it in time
to skirt around. But I know from experience that calmer water
is not far to the other side.

I am sobered by the memory of Harry Flower, who almost
lost his life several years ago when he capsized at this very spot.
His accident has increased my caution about lightly discussing
bay kayaking.

Here's the story. We were driving together to a peace rally
at Port Chicago. Harry had questioned me all about kayaking
on the bay. But he had asked too much . . . and I was later
chided for being so rude to him. Somehow I sensed that he was
too turned on, and I was fearful that he might try paddling
without further knowledge and preparation. He did! After
renting a Sierra Club slalom kayak, he practiced once at the
Berkeley Marina—his first kayak trip. For his second trip he
attempted to cross the Gate from the beach at the St. Francis
Yacht Club. It was in this rip over the eighty-nine-foot needle
that the agitated sea frightened him; he lost control of the boat
and capsized. When the kayak filled with water, the stern sank
first; but he was able to hang onto the upended craft, the air
trapped in the bow his only flotation. The ebb current carried
him all the way out the Gate to Point Bonita. He was wearing a
wetsuit, but by then was so cold he could barely hang on. As he
was being carried out to the open sea, fortune remained close
by. Sighted by a fishing boat, he was barely hauled out in time
to save his life.

Now it's time for the Gate. I feel a new quality in my
alertness, a quiet but sharper attentiveness, a more earnest caution. Once under the bridge, carried on tidal waters augmented by river runoff, there is no turning back. I couldn't
make headway paddling against even an average current of 4.7
knots (5.4 miles per hour); and today, with the full moon, the
flow is stronger still. All the decisions leading to my present
position are now irrevocably set. I can do nothing but trust the

judgments that have placed me on this mass of water returning to the sea. There are no choices left until I'm outside the Gate . . . in the ocean.

Looking up at the deck far overhead, I feel very small. I'm passing under the tallest bridge towers in the world, on the largest volume of water for such a narrows in the world, riding out to sea on three hundred feet of water. I feel an urgency come to all this liquid trying to get out through the restricted one mile passage, fighting up into the air for enough room, forming a rip of haystacks. And then, as the Gate passes behind, and as the strait broadens into the two-mile entrance, the rip decreases to but a surface marking perceptible on the faces of the massive ocean swells moving in from the west. Inside the bay, after crowding through this entrance funnel, these swells had dissipated when their width expanded to four miles. But here, outside the Gate, they are like mountains of moving water. And what seems like an optical illusion is really true: the waves are coming toward me, yet the current pulling me is flowing out, right through them.

Even after countless trips, going out the Gate is again a deep experience. I well remember the first time! Were the swells especially huge? Or was it the newness of the confrontation? It felt like suddenly coming into a moving desert of great dunes, and I repeatedly wondered if *Naoyak* would rise up the wall to the next crest. But now it's a delightful roller coaster ride—a lovely feeling of tininess . . . floating along with that enormous volume . . . over the power of storm-born seas.

What joy! The sea here is a giant's Jacuzzi bath; the upsurges from the changing bottom show on the surface as smooth circles, like boiling mush, like a mountain spring of gigantic proportion—merely a clue to the mysterious turbulence of unfathomable force caused by the three hundred-foot bottom rising to half that depth beneath me. The sea is like a living thing. The swells are the heaving chest from storms blowing far at sea; the breaking rips are the groans from flowing over a rocky shoal; and the noisy little haystacks marking the backeddy are the friction pain where opposing currents meet.

In a strange sort of way I don't feel I'm paddling a kayak, but that "it" is being paddled. If someone asks me if I've been paddling *on* the bay, *in* a kayak, I obviously answer yes. But in another sense that really isn't true, because on looking back on a trip, I simply remember nothing about the boat or the equipment. Long ago I began to feel I wasn't *using* a kayak, but *wearing* my boat. And in time even that intimacy grew into feeling the kayak as a prolongation of the lower half of my body, like a merman. Now even the paddle isn't *used*; the blades are merely elongations of my arms. The rudder *is* my feet, determining direction as in walking. The differences between my body and these extensions have faded; I'm unconscious of kayak or paddle or rudder; I'm just experiencing the bay, conscious only of being at sea.

My mind is quiet and empty, yet fully active. I'm concentrating more than ever in my life, all the time, yet on nothing cognitive—extremely alert, but with no thoughts. My head is full of the now, with no sense of time passing . . . no past . . . no future. All the ships, boats, horns, lights, and waves aren't really *out* there, but sort of inside my head—we are all inseparable. It's an indescribable feeling, an experience of being where it's at, at one with the cosmos, a meditative experience of the universe . . . without ever thinking about meditation.

But a stomach growl tunes me back to earthly time. And as the tide carries me out, I keep away from the easily seen backeddy already beginning in Kirby Cove, a countercurrent caused by the vacuum from the water flowing past the north tower. It's a clearly marked line of junk—flotsam and jetsam forming a debris-filled demarcation with bubbly foam. Where does that Champagne bottle come from? That strange single walnut? That not too withered yellow chrysanthemum? Is any really flotsam—evidence of a wreck? Is any really jetsam— cargo cast overboard to lighten a boat in distress? It's mostly questionable jetsam—garbage jettisoned for reasons far from nautical safety.

Drifting out to sea . . . a mind trip . . . in touch with the seashores of the world . . . distant ports and cities . . . far away islands and continents . . . ships connecting to all the oceans . . . the seven seas . . . salt water tasting of the entire planet . . .

A few hundred yards outside the Gate is a huge container ship bearing down on me. But I know it will turn far south in the inbound shipping lane, so my only concern is for its ugliness. Container ships are made for efficiency, not beauty. Its deck is piled high with potential truck trailer bodies; its bridge overhangs the bow so that the pilot can have at least some visibility over the massive deck load. It's a ship without the esthetics of one pleasing line, an excess of practicality over grace, like much of the culture back on shore.

Though I've been paddling for over an hour, I wonder why I'm not very tired? Maybe it's my intimacy with *Naoyak* and the sea, a kind of oneness that makes paddling quite effortless because I then don't have to work so hard. Strange, but sometimes it feels as if I don't have to work at all, when in fact I might seem to be doing a tremendous amount. But is that really true? Possibly it only appears that way. Perhaps it's all being done for me by the boat, and by the sea. A recent winter experience felt just that way.

It was after a long, cold, and especially windy early morning paddle to visit friends in El Campo, eight difficult miles up the bay on the east side of the Tiburon Peninsula. On arrival I absolutely *had* to land. I was much too cold and exhausted to go on; I couldn't stay in the boat to rest or eat because the chop was too rough; the north wind across San Pablo Bay was draining my warmth away dangerously; shivering had begun; and my numb hands could barely feel the paddle through wet gloves.

Now the ability to land is one of the special advantages of kayak over most other craft. But how could it ever be done here? The breakers looked too big! The beach felt too unknown! And even the launching ramp that sloped down into the sea had waves crashing right through the spaces between the boards—a totally unexperienced threat! However, that unexplored landing site seemed wiser than a strange beach in such large surf. So, damn it, it just had to be . . . And it was!

The truth is I can barely remember landing. In a peculiar sense perhaps I didn't land at all. "It" landed me. It just happened so nicely . . . at precisely the right time . . . with exactly the right wave—something I never could have planned. The boat and the waves and the quay and I simply experienced this all together. And I didn't even get wet: I just stepped right out of the sea onto the ramp in the crashing surf, lifted the boat, and walked up the boards to rest *Naoyak* on the lawn of a beautiful home. My friends escorted me off for a hot shower, their blazing fireplace, and steaming coffee.

But it's time to stop drifting. With a half hour more ebb until the tide turns at the point, I want to be secure in the lee calmness before being swept out too far. Along the cliffs is a lone pelican apparently riding a black and white line, as if on a wire above the sea. But I remember. Close up that's a remnant of the oil spill above a layer of white barnacles. I paddle toward the cove, cross the rip marking the outer limits of this sanctuary, nod to the fishermen waving from the promontory, and then pass through the rough water and white foam from the swells turning around the projecting rocks. Now I enter onto the flat and windless sea below the steep cliffs just east of Point Diablo, the one reliably sheltered spot of the entire outer Gate.

What a welcome sense of relief, having left the Gate behind. Though I was relaxed out there, it's nothing like the restfulness here by the shore. The sea sometimes feels a bit large, the swells a mite powerful, the shipping lanes of one of the world's great ports a little dangerous. But now I'm in one of my favorite breakfast rooms, where buttresses of layered red Franciscan jasper guard a small bay of unusually peaceful sea. The surge gently sweeps me back and forth close to the starfish-decorated walls. Watching how close a piece of floating debris comes to the rocks with each swell, I may safely allow *Naoyak* to drift within inches of the steep cliffs . . . and if that floating stick doesn't hit the rocks, then neither will I. When there isn't a twig, then a little spit does the trick. So I can relax here for as long as I want, with just an infrequent slight paddle dip to keep from floating too close to the cliffs or too near the surf on the shingly beach.

Returning here over the years I've developed a very personal relationship to this cove, animating many of the rock shapes. So I greet my old friends, enlivened by more nostalgic memories each trip: the profile of the young boy's face on the point; the man with the green beard, clean-shaven chin, and bloody nose whose hair ends above a cave on a tiny rocky beach a few yards away; and the large turtle guarding that beach, the one rock formation that's a perfect likeness, requiring no extra imagination. Because of low tide, today these rock forms are dressed in a hula skirt of glistening sea lettuce, waving with each surge. The colors vary from lime green to wine, olive green to purple, and kelly green to gold. The red rock crust alga beneath is a blushing pink, as if the bareness needs the green dress as protection from the bright morning sun. The surge exposes that nakedness, and then the floating seaweeds are modestly brushed down by each receding swell. This marine vegetation was once used by a large leopard shark to scratch his chin, presumably removing irritating parasites; I enjoyed watching him, but his dorsal fin cutting through the surface kept my fingers a wee bit farther from the sea.

Even the waves are alive! On the rocky beach they beat on the shore with anger; and then, feeling guilty, try to soothe the rocks with white, tender foam, feeding the starfish, the barnacles, and the seaweeds, as if to make up for the recent slapping thud. I sense the moon and wind spirits behind each wave, giving life to the sea. High above, where the cliffs slope back, the songs of birds in the trees make this refuge friendly after the loneliness and distant fear of the sea. On a high ledge there sometimes sits a stately hawk as my sentry. What an idyllic spot to set about breakfast tasks.

After drying off the spray cover, I roll it back. Inside, the kayak is all toasty and dry. How I appreciate the luxury of the large cockpit where my knees aren't cramped under the deck as with a competition kayak, not only making it very comfortable on long trips, but allowing for relaxed eating in the boat. First I need coffee, and it's reassuring to have the thermos arrive on the end of the red leash. Oh, how hard I laughed that day, years ago, returning from a Seal Rocks trip with Willi in another single kayak. We were resting on some broad swells at Deadman's Cove; and when Willi reached for his breakfast he accidentally pushed it farther away, beyond reach, completely unobtainable, the ultimate in frustration. But my contribution to our mutual laughter ended abruptly when I realized we must share my food, and that I would eat but half a meal.

I recall so many memories of laughs with Willi: screaming ourselves hoarse at the aircraft carrier *Coral Sea*, as if we might deter it from returning to Vietnam; shaking our fists at nuclear subs as they caused the water to vibrate right through our hulls. But nothing like that time at Point Blunt after a visit with the lightkeeper and his wife. I had launched alone into the moderate surf and was watching Willi and his friend carefully launch their double; they did well and were sealing themselves in with their spray cover—only to discover they had forgotten their paddles! There, back on the beach leaning against a willow bush were the two sets of blades. I got a stomachache laughing as they paddled by hand, got soaking wet in the surf, and then had to go through it all over again. Why do we laugh when a friend is up a creek?

I hang the brunch bag on a little wooden rack that fits across the front of the cockpit. Over a rubber nubbin on the end of the rack I hook the key chain from the handle of the coffee cup, thus balancing it on the deck. Now I pour my first cup of coffee. The cheese goes on a napkin on the folded spray cover, a sort of table over my knees, and I eat in this glorious tabernacle. Somehow, so close to the sea, a simple cup of hot coffee is a remarkable gift . . . and the cheese is absolutely delicious—the plain cheddar of the city changing to a rare delicacy out here. Food has a new meaning of thanksgiving, compensatory to the thoughts that usually intrude during kayak trip meals—thoughts about the suffering in Southeast Asia and the hunger in many lands.

I eat up the view with my eyes. The light patterns on the water are geometric yet never the same, hypnotically fascinating, with rapidly changing colors, shapes, and brightness. Closing my eyes, the glare from the moving ripples comes through my eyelids, producing a light show with fantastic shapes augmented by the colorful afterimages from whatever I've just been looking at. When not so close to shore I sometimes do this for longer periods, the visions reminding me of psychedelic effects. The light shows at rock concerts seem pallid in comparison.

The wall a couple of feet from my dining room table is a contorted and twisted layer cake of upturned sedimentary rock. The lower layers are highlighted by wetness in the cracks where numerous starfish cling, a few shore crabs scurry away, and several rock lice scamper about. The starfish are curled up to avoid too much dryness while waiting for the flood tide; most are a bright international orange, some a deep purple, and one tiny star a glowing pink. Just above my head is a white band of barnacles, a base for the black oil layer that from the sea had looked like a pelican tightrope. And just below the surface of the water are rows of sea anemone, green and red, like pimento-stuffed Spanish olives.

On the cliffs above the cave, several seeps glisten in the sunlight. One has a moss bed that is bright malachite green. A larger seep, black with wet lichen that shines like leaking oil, forms a treasure niche of lustrous golden iron oxide. How I relish the isolation of this secluded spot. The faraway roar of cars on the bridge is such a contrast to my solitude; that constant background noise can still be faintly heard, making the silence here an even emptier quietness.

Across the Gate the sun distinctly marks the great face at Deadman's Cove. It's so clear I can see the sandy shore at Bakers Beach and Phelan Beach—the China Beach of my childhood. Even the rocks near Lands End can be distinguished: Pyramid Rock, Black Head Rock, Lobos Rock, Little Mile Rock, and the five Seal Rocks. What a contrast this distant view is to the *taktuk* trips. . . .

Though every paddle is individual and different, the foggy crossings are my favorites. Just a couple of weeks ago there was a lovely experience, the fog a thin layer right on the water. Though the dock was sunny and warm for the launching, I could hear the symphony of horns and see the dense gray over the bay. The fog began abruptly and, so much quicker than today, I was immediately away from civilization, quite alone in the fog. It was suddenly a dream world, the water the same gray as the fog; the horizon disappeared, blending with the sea; and it felt like floating in space.

I didn't bother with a compass, knowing my bearing and position by balancing the Alcatraz horns and the high-pitched double scream from Lime Point. The other horns of the Gate have become so familiar that I didn't have any concern about where I was going . . . by their sound alone I was quite sure of my route. And I didn't even feel such an alert concern about shipping; just one new sound in the background would immediately direct attention to a motorboat, a steamship lane problem, or even a *natsek* breathing. The set of the waves, the wind on my left cheek, and the feel of the warmth from the sun through the fog on my other cheek helped confirm my direction. Changes in the height of the chop checked my location when I passed over the Presidio Shoal, the Alcatraz Shoal, and the eighty-nine-foot needle.

In a special sort of way I can relax more in *taktuk*. Using sounds inside my head feels less active than having to look; ears seem to pick up things that eyes might miss, and they do so more reliably. The sound of a liner's steam whistle is quite shaking, but they move so slowly in the fog that I can paddle out of the way. That day there was a delicate white rainbow on the port beam that accompanied me all the way across the bay. It was dark gray under a glowing arch, with the barest hint of pink outside and purple inside. That radiant white gateway into the distant fog gave a false impression of orientation as it just moved along with me, a weird companion for the crossing.

Then, when the midspan diaphone was on the port beam, and the south tower deep bass single horn passed the port quarter, it was safe to turn directly toward the Lime Point whine. I soon saw the revolving light at the point where the fog thins in the lee of the Marin hills. It's the horn-announced Gate that makes the most profound crossings of the bay. Each fog signal is like a friendly old guide calling out specific instructions; each tone reassures that I need not fear being lost in the fog. And sometimes I wonder what meanings, if any, these same sounds have for a listener on the shore.

Finishing brunch, drinking my last cup of coffee, I feel very alone. The populated city isn't so very far away in miles. In another sense, it's exceedingly distant from this natural world at the shore. Perhaps just this contrast of my serene cove and the metropolis across the Gate touches on a universal polarity—the individual and the collective—opposites constantly in need of rebalancing. But which way does it work? After a week in the city, each trip weights the individual end; yet the collective end is also weighted, though in a transpersonal, more natural way. No wonder a trip is heavy. Why am I so lucky in this increasingly crowded world to have such exquisite, peaceful solitude? Has another kayak ever been here? Does that matter? Does the pride of discovery add any meaning? And is that discovery in the sea, or in me? But enough questioning, it's time to prepare for the return home.

Checking watch . . . backeddy now returning all the way

to the north tower . . . stowing breakfast things . . . readying for the shore hugging start toward home . . . warmer but still windy . . . taking wool liners out of mittens . . . thanking sheep who keep fingers warm . . . don't forget geese for down around toes . . . and pigs for paddle palms.

With the spray cover again sealing me in, it feels good to get under way, to pull the water with each blade. Such a thrill looking up from the tiny boat, moving by the vertical cliffs; and at this angle, a gliding gull against that craggy background is soaring beauty. The point ahead looks snow covered; but where are the usual cormorants today? Not a single bird to explain that guano source. Oh, but what's up ahead, on that offshore white-frosted rock?

Several necks in alignment! White-breasted brown pelicans! Closer I count eight or ten, with a couple of cormorants next to them on the rock. And the two yellow-billed birds more streamlined than gulls must be terns, but I'll have to check the bird book at home. Drifting very near, I love watching how each species takes off so differently. The cormorants are swimming birds, barely getting off the water by beating their wings on the sea to gain the needed air speed. It's easier with the ungainly pelicans who merely open their broad wings, give a slight hop, and are immediately airborne—flying away with a magnificent slow rhythm. And the terns just swoop away, as if pulled by an invisible string, riding imaginary hills in the air. Being at such intimate range is a treat, and one pelican stays on the rock for a three-foot close-up . . . as we stare at each other.

I've had such friendly experiences with other bay animals over the years. There's a small dog-faced harbor seal that lives on Yerba Buena Island and has met me on the beach for lunch. On the Alcatraz Bell Buoy a California sea lion often sleeps in the sun, apathetically waking up as I drift close by, almost waiting to be touched before diving off with a grunt. In the semitropical growth imported to the east side of Angel Island lives a great blue heron, occasionally found fishing in the shallows. And I'm embarrassed to remember shocking a lone black-tailed deer on the Angel Island beach just west of Point Campbell; being upwind, I floated to within a few feet before the frightened deer saw me and bounded away in panic. On the grass at Ayala Cove there used to be an entire herd of black-

tailed deer when I paddled there for breakfast; but that was
before so many overnight sailors had civilized that Angel Island
anchorage. There even was one rare, brief encounter with a sea
otter off the south beach of Angel Island. On the rocks just off
Point Blunt lives an entire family of vocal harbor seals who are
charming to talk to. And Seal Rocks trips are especially delightful when thirty or more inquisitive Steller's and California sea
lions swim and dive around the kayak.

Right near my present position at the entrance to Kirby
Cove I once was startled by the sound of breathing behind the
boat. Being so flustered I couldn't figure out why that huge,
brown, barnacle-encrusted, flatheaded fish breathed! It
dawned only after the trip that fish don't breathe—that it must
have been a baby whale. In the papers the next day I read with
satisfaction that the sight-seeing boat had discovered a whale in
the bay.

Though such exotic animal experiences are exciting, the
common animals are my best-known acquaintances. Gulls and
seals almost always cross my path. Jumping fish sometimes
surprise me, especially if one hits the deck! Frequently I meet
murres and grebes decked out in their black-and-white formal
dress. I love to watch the shorebirds, sandpipers and dowit-
chers running in the backwash of the waves on the sand . . . to
laugh at the coots and scoters with their funny lack of grace.

But now I'm moving nearer a different sort of animal
life—the human kind. Paddling through the white foamy back
rush from the waves smashing on the cliffs a few yards away, I
go inside some larger rocks to enter Kirby Cove, enjoying the
lovely sea stacks here as evidence of the sea eating away at the
headlands. And there, eating away at the natural scene at this
new state park development is civilization, with tents in the
background and kids on the shore. I reluctantly decide to drift
past this one beach at a less interesting but safer distance because, as expected, a couple of kids start throwing rocks at me.
Oh, what is that unthinking urge that seems so common as I
paddle by? Hey kids, there's a life in this boat!

I also have pleasant memories of landing at this noisy
beach. The reddish brown sand is like chocolate, alternately
covered by the whipped cream topping of sea-foam that reflects
the light with a pulsating rhythm, which feels funny in my

eyes. The sound of the salt water rushing back over the graveled shore soothes somewhere down deep inside, the cliffs of the cove adding an acoustic quality, something like listening to a seashell held to the ear.

The shoreline between Kirby Cove and the north tower is truly beautiful: high sheer cliffs broken in a few places by small coves with sand beaches; and a couple of hanging valleys, one with a waterfall cascading down onto the shore. I'm anxious to hear from my favorite caverns this morning, as certain heights of the tide can make them quite boisterous. The sea has washed several tunnels into the walls. By the inflow of a swell of just the right size, the surge generates blowholes, spewing out saltwater mist when the built-up compressed air suddenly escapes. How I cherish these places where the rock speaks. Each orifice has a different gruff bellow. Here, at the foot of the high cliffs, the tones are very low; deep groans belch as if from infinite depths in the bowels of the earth. In contrast, the grottos of Alcatraz have fissures that produce a higher timbre with more vibrato. And because there the covering rock is thin, even the air seems to vibrate along with the entire north end of the island as the long caves fill and then are burped by the sea.

Nostalgia has softened these sounds whose first hearing was frightening. Perhaps familiarity plays a large part in all my enjoyment of the sea. Early years were sometimes scary; dealing with unknown reefs and currents was a lot of work. But now most of the covered snags have been seen many times, all those experiences filed away, and now only the simple pleasure remains. The surface darkness of seaweed over a rock is just a friendly reminder, instead of being a fearful shock as on beginning trips. And with these sea caves, I now know where an unexpected roar from the walls might be heard, so today I can talk back. On virgin paddles the shock of being yelled at had left me speechless.

On the beach next to the north tower an abandoned wreck of a fishing boat disintegrates more each year and brings to mind the attraction of other shoreline ruins. How amazing, so close to current life, to see these relics from the past. All along the entrance to the Gate are the bunkers and barbed wire from World War II, defenses against a Japanese invasion. But more pleasant are the antiques from still earlier times. Bonita Cove has a rotting dock and branching tracks that converge and run into the sea for the rapid launching of lifeboats. I picture those rugged men manning oars and going out on a rescue mission. Tennessee Cove and Lands End have remnants of shipwrecks. Of course there are the many old buildings on Alcatraz and Angel islands. At Point Knox sits the large old fog bell that Harold Gilliam wrote about in his book about the bay. From the water, at such close range, these dead remains from long ago are food for fantasies about the life they once involved.

In contrast, many recent experiences are unvarnished sagas. One cold morning, in a pea-soup fog right under the sound of the Point Blunt horn (on Angel Island), a powerboat encountered me, and the skipper asked where in the world he was! One time, going out the Gate, a panic-stricken sailor was caught in the ebb on a windless day; he frantically waved me over, merely to ask when the tide would turn. He didn't have a tide book and assumed a kayak would know. Another day, in Bonita Cove, three fishermen in an outboard had motor failure and were drifting toward the surf. They asked me for help—a lone kayaker! All they needed was a little knowledge; I didn't even use an emergency flare, but merely the international distress signal of raising and lowering both arms at the side. My trust in seamen was renewed when a cabin cruiser immediately headed over and upon hearing the story had the Coast Guard called. They arrived in time!

But help doesn't always get there soon enough. Returning from a trip to Seal Rocks, I heard kids yelling from Fort Point and pointing to a body in the water! The Coast Guard soon roared up to pick her out of the bay—another Gate Bridge suicide. I cried in that beautiful spot, thinking how morbidly incongruous a death wish seemed from such a sunny place on the sea.

Another tragedy? Near Kirby Cove on a return from Fort Cronkite, Willi and I saw a fisherman presumably fast asleep in an anchored outboard from Mission Rock Resort. We went by quietly to avoid awakening and frightening him. In the papers the following day was news of a fisherman who disappeared. Parts from a rented Mission Rock boat were found strewn from Point Diablo to Point Bonita. I reported my experience to the Coast Guard. It was a year later that the insurance adjuster called to ask more questions. A massive double indemnity insurance had been taken out the day before the "accident," and mysteriously the body had never been recovered. The way the boat was found just didn't fit my concepts of what changing tides could possibly do. I wonder how he is living now?

Help unfortunately also arrived too late to save the Mile Rocks lighthouse. On early Seal Rocks trips it was such a delight to be hailed by a keeper, when the light was manned by the Coast Guard. But now it's a sad and lonely trip with nobody living there—the light has been automated and resident personnel are no longer needed. The forlorn shape leaves my eyes wet; merely a decapitated stump for a helicopter pad is all that remains of that once classic lighthouse at the southern doorway to the Gate.

Though these experiences bring me back to the human level, they also intrude on my communion with the sea. Yet just that attachment, my sense of special possessiveness, once led to trouble when the Native Americans were occupying Alcatraz. I was just sitting and eating an apple on a very choppy day as they were having a difficult time unloading the contents of a pitching boat onto the dock. When they yelled at me to get away, I was flabbergasted that someone would treat me as if the bay didn't belong to us all. Was I the recipient of their projection of a white man looking at them as in a museum? Or did it bother them to see me acting as if I, too, were experiencing the Great Spirit through nature? Empty quart bottles were thrown, landing very close to the kayak. I quickly paddled away, filled with fear and anger.

But there have also been gratifying encounters on the bay. One of the nicest meetings was with Elinor and Dick Nickerson, authors of *Kayaks To The Arctic*, a chronicle of their trip down the Mackenzie River from Great Slave Lake to the Arctic Ocean. After reading the book, I phoned to ask them to join me for a bay paddle. Amazing, but even after that remarkable feat, they felt the bay itself too difficult. So we agreed on the Oakland Estuary. What fun! I paddled from San Francisco and, at precisely the prearranged time, their kayak emerged from the Norwalk Marina, the first launching spot in the Oakland Inner Harbor. After vociferous introductions we paddled together, up the estuary, to a restaurant for lunch. And that still remains my longest paddle—a twenty-two mile round trip.

Today, resting in the shadow of the last precipitous cliff, which rises to almost touch the deck of the bridge, such thoughts are fleeting images of past experiences on the bay. From this shady place on the sea my view is strange. The bridge, almost directly overhead in the bright sunlight, looks like somebody made a mistake and put the wrong backdrop in the picture. All that man-made structure seems too much in opposition to the seashore a few feet away, where the beach vibrates safety and dryness, light and firmness in contrast to the dark and impersonal waters. What an ancient atmosphere here at the edge of the ocean, imagining the beginnings of life, and what the quietness and security of a sandy beach felt like to the first creatures leaving the sea. Maybe that has something to do with the reluctance I feel paddling from shore, rounding Lime Point, and preparing to cross the Gate toward home.

Hugging the base of the north tower, I paddle into the sunlight. Across the bay, with *sirinek* higher, the city skyline is softer. Oh, but the ugliness of the Bank of America building, a black monstrosity so out of proportion; the plastic shimmer of the Transamerica pyramid impaling the heavens—they are just too much. How they overshadow the spires of Saints Peter and Paul's Church. What could the Transamerica pyramid be reaching up for, so far above the church spires? And now there's that gigantic Mount Sutro television tower, loftier still. It looks like something from outer space as my drifting causes it to move stealthily behind the Pacific Heights homes. Maybe such a messenger from another planet is needed in all that crowded and busy concrete city; but is that other world really up higher and higher or perhaps down much lower, right here at the seashore?

It's been a big trip, and I'm tired. Though forty-five minutes remain before slack water under the bridge, perhaps I can cross right now if the light west winds counterbalance the falling ebb. To test this, I paddle out from the sheltered inlet at Lime Point. In a few seconds, using the south tower as a range like a gun sight, the fort behind remains motionless—proof I can cross easily. The shipping lanes are quickly checked out in the crystal-clear air. There's no traffic in this usually busy port.

I'd really prefer seeing a ship or two. The channels are so

definite under the bridge that I can get close safely; and being next to a large ship is a very special experience. Once, in just this midspan position, in a pea-soup fog, I heard the tremulous blast of a ship's horn out the Gate in the inbound lane. It was so loud and deep that I suspected it would turn out to be a P&O passenger liner. Sometimes it's easier to judge the size of a ship from the sound in the fog than from visual sighting on a clear day, when distance and perspective can be deceptive. I waited at this spot, right under the diaphone at the center of the bridge, as the one-minute blasts came closer. And there she appeared, suddenly, mysteriously, emerging as if newly formed right out of the fog, the *Arcadia!* As the huge ship passed by, many passengers waved from the decks. Oh, how far from the sea they seemed, having taken their city with them on their ocean voyage.

Though experiencing a ship pass in the fog is relating to civilization and not to nature, it's still confronting something quiet in the nature of life. From my tiny boat, such a view of the forces of the collective puts me in the proper perspective for returning to the city.

For a while I remain in the shadow of the bridge, the view being much clearer without the sun in my eyes. But it's dangerous right under the deck: Any falling object, even a penny, could be deadly. So I cross the Gate a short distance east of the span inside the bay. Do walkers get up so late? Not a single person is by the bridge rail at this hour, thus canceling the need to keep a suicide watch. Over the years there have been three suicides within minutes of my paddling near the Gate.

Nevertheless, I decide to cross under the deck two more times, rounding the south tower to my port, around its west side, just because the water is so delightfully slack and calm; and I can then catch the early flood close to Fort Point. The football field-size caisson around the tower base welcomes me, a familiar pivot for many bay paddles. How unique to find ease and quiet water around this concrete buffer against usually powerful currents. I paddle to catch a few short rides on the ends of the combers that turn around the point like spokes of a wheel. How beautiful to ride a crest that's breaking just a few yards away. I pass close by the frightening rock that rises above the surface in the trough before each wave, only to hide from the unwary beneath each seemingly innocent swell. In winter, after a storm, the large surf here will attract daredevil surfers, who skim by these rocks shouting with excitement.

In the lee of Fort Point I can now rest, enjoying the handsome stonework of the old seawall as I'm carried along the Presidio shore by the gentle flood.

I drift under the dock of the Army Motor Pool and then paddle by the Fort Point Coast Guard Station. What lovely old buildings with their turrets, towers, and individually shaped dormer windows. And if that doesn't date them, the garage doors open onto unused tracks that lead into the bay from the main house. How long ago were those used? When was this a lifeboat station that launched oared recovery boats instead of the present forty-foot motor ships and two Hovercraft? I like having the reassurance of these more speedy guardians of the bay.

The hills of the Presidio have blocked the wind, and I become too warm. So, I take off my gloves . . . then my life jacket . . . and even my booties; now I'm comfortable for the coast home. I meet a rower from the Dolphin club in his elegant old lapstraked hull. We complain to each other about having to stay two hundred yards from shore because, just east of the Coast Guard Station, the Presidio Rod and Gun Club has started skeet shooting over the bay! The first Harbor Tours sight-seeing boat passes by; it must be shortly after 10:00 A.M.; I'll be arriving back just before the strong winds begin.

Along Crissy Field the beach changes with each season. The sand is broad in summer, but the winter storms tend to wash it away. I float past the beach by the St. Francis Yacht Club where I used to launch into the surf. The current is bringing me quite close to home, ending my trip. Oh, how can personal problems and trivia mean much of anything when the rocks of my breakfast room were curved and twisted millions of years ago, laid down at the bottom of the sea an inconceivable time before that? And the feelings from the mass of water I've just crossed—how long will they persist in my body? I round the end of the harbor jetty, the flood still taking me in. The wind is just picking up; the sun must be warming the Central Valley air causing an updraft, and thus sucking in the usual late morning summer wind. Perhaps that will create fog by this afternoon. I like to picture all that warm and humid Pacific air being cooled by the upwelling of the icy bottom waters offshore and forming the sea fog that will bring ocean coolness during the next several days' fog cycle. The valley had cooled enough last night so that this morning there was little onshore breeze.

There's the dock, the sailboats and cabin cruisers, and a couple of boat owner friends waving, "Good morning!" I've returned to man's social world. I find an open berth but am reluctant to leave the sea. The tranquility of the water here is like an opiate. The sun on my shoulders has become an anodyne, its heat penetrating sore muscles, its visible rays pass through the salt water, illuminating the seaweeds thick on the styrofoam floats. Nevertheless, slowly, dallying, I undress the kayak. Then, trusting my stiffness won't produce too unbalanced a finale, I step out . . . Ah, how quieting to feel the warmth of the wood deck after the exertion—a special sensation of firmness underfoot, which is restored after each trip.

On the dock I wash off the boat and the paddles. And while I'm packing up the gear, a stranger asks, "Did you go out the Gate in that thing?" I barely mumble a stereotyped answer . . . But how could anyone know where I've been, so alone, in real wilderness, healed by the sea. I'm holding onto an inner secret that I'll take with me after the dock gate closes behind, and I carry *Naoyak* home. During the week in the city, foghorns will kindle memories of forgotten trips; weather reports will speak of the changes in the sea; and a ship's blast will awaken a part of me still rocking out there on the swells.

The walk home is tiring after the trip. I'm ready for a long afternoon nap, with the experiences of my voyage to digest, to muse about, to put me to sleep. When everything is unpacked, I finally pull the boat back up to the garage ceiling where it comes to rest. And on the wall, alongside the cleats where I belay the pulley lines, is a tile with the outline of a lighthouse, and the words:

> Oh God, thy sea is so great
> and my boat is so small.

PAUL KAUFMANN began his solo wilderness experiences during high school with hikes in the San Gabriel Mountains behind Pasadena. In college and medical school he became a charter member of the Stanford Alpine Club, worked as chef for the Sierra Club High Trips, and made many long, solo cross-country–backpack trips. His interest in kayaking started when cooking for the first Sierra Club trips down the Yampa and Green rivers.

With a growing family, a busy psychiatric practice, and a home but one block from San Francisco Bay, he wondered about sea kayaking. So, after reading the British books on sea canoeing, studying the Bay Model, and learning about tides, currents, charts, and navigation, he started ocean kayaking twenty-five years and eight-hundred trips ago.

SUSAN MEREDITH

Alaskan Remembrances

The landscape near our ship was spectacular. To the west rugged snowcapped peaks thrust toward leaden-gray clouds. Far below, tidewater glaciers calved icebergs thunderously into the sea. To the east in Prince William Sound, mountainous Montague Island rose like a crown jewel above a cluster of lesser islands. Ahead on a low bluff overlooking the sheltered bay we entered, were the native houses in the village of Chenega. And everywhere danced the snowflakes of early November.

Bundled against the cold, I stood at the ship's railing and absorbed the view. I was aboard the *Hygiene*, a one hundred-foot public health vessel taking a medical program to the far-flung coastline of Alaska. Chenega was next on our schedule.

After the crew dropped anchor, I waited for the usual buzz of a skiff's outboard motor coming to greet us. But there was only silence. Looking toward the distant village, I spotted a slim, elegant-looking craft being propelled through the icy waters by a man with a single-bladed paddle. This was the first kayak I'd seen, and I knew it was the boat for me. Because I had had polio as a child and was left with weak legs—and very strong arms—rowboats, canoes, and small sailboats had been my favorite forms of transportation, but never had I seen any boat that moved as cleanly, efficiently, and gracefully through the water as this sealskin-covered kayak. It was nearly twenty feet long, a little over two feet wide, and had three cockpits.

The bow swept boldly upward, and the stern terminated in a slender point.

After the paddler (later identified as the village school-teacher) had boarded the ship, and the official business had been taken care of, I cornered him and bombarded him with questions, "Is the kayak hard to paddle? Does it tip easily? Are there any more around?"

Laughingly he answered, "It's called a baidarka. Feels quite tippy at first, but is very easy to paddle."

"I noticed you use a single-bladed paddle."

"Yes, double-bladed paddles weren't common in this area. And yes, there are still several baidarkas here. In the early days they were used for hunting and transportation, but the natives now prefer skiffs and outboard motors."

"How much would one cost?"

"Well . . uh, I think I could find you an old one for about $40. I'll let you know when you come ashore."

Great. I could hardly wait. My next task was to convince the captain that it was a very small boat and would stow nicely on the upper deck next to my bike. The captain was a slender, rather nervous clean-shaven man of about forty. He was not very popular with the crew. He was nice to me because I volunteered to stand wheel watches with him when we were short a deckhand—which was often. He was interested in poetry and would read me poems by the hour while I was on the bridge.

Upon hearing my request, the captain regarded me through narrowed eyes for a minute then reluctantly said, "OK. But it doesn't look very safe to me."

I had trouble sleeping that night as I thought of all the wonderful adventures I could have in that little boat. I certainly wasn't daunted by the dire predictions voiced by some of my crew mates, "You'll tip over." "You'll meet an early demise." "We won't have anyone to run the X-ray machine."

Their concerns made me laugh. Handling the baidarka would be a breeze. However, the next day, after I paid the teacher and walked down to the beach to get my new boat, I had to admit it looked a lot narrower than I remembered. My first surprise came as I got in and sat on the floorboards only to find there wasn't room for my feet between the deck and the bottom of the boat. This meant I had to sit on my heels, which gave me a sensation of great instability. With everyone watching, I felt obligated to give a paddling demonstration. Reassuringly, one of the crew said, "We'll stay right behind you in the dory."

It was about a ten minute paddle to the ship, and by the time I arrived, I had a little more trust in the baidarka. But my feet and legs were completely numb, and it was all I could do to lift myself onto the ship's ladder. Becoming proficient with the kayak was going to be a challenge.

I'd been reading Chevigny's *Lord of Alaska*—a fascinating history of Aleksandr Baranov's exploration and development of the fur trade on the coast of Alaska. His principal tool was the baidarka. I marveled as I read about how the Aleuts, in fleets of four to five hundred baidarkas, crossed the treacherous Gulf of Alaska in search of sea otters. Now, with my baidarka, I could paddle the same waters, imagining myself an explorer scouting for the ideal outpost location. But first I had to learn to sit on my heels for hours at a time and balance this narrow tippy boat. I smiled, remembering my priorities only a few months earlier.

The year was 1946, and it was the beginning of a new era in Alaska's Public Health program. Unaware of this program, I'd written the Territorial Health Department in Juneau asking if they had any positions available for a bacteriologist in one of their coastal towns. All I knew was that I had been trapped in a hospital lab in Seattle while all my friends were in far-flung places. I was ready for action.

My hopes fell when I read the first few words of reply from the Juneau office. They were sorry to inform me there were no lab jobs available, but they were putting a public health ship into service to visit most of the coastal villages in Alaska. Would I be interested in being part of the medical team? Would I? That sounded better than anything I could have dreamed.

So there I was, working as a bacteriologist/X-ray technician on the MS *Hygiene*, a freight supply ship used in Alaska during World War II and now converted into a floating clinic. In addition to the crew, the ship carried a doctor, a nurse, a secretary, and, periodically, a dentist and a dental technician. We worked year-round, spending the winters in southeastern Alaska and crossing the Gulf of Alaska to work around the

Aleutian Chain and Bering Sea during the summers.

Living on board ship, seeing the coastline of Alaska, and meeting the people who lived there was as exciting as I had envisioned, but I had developed a great desire to explore the many little bays and coves that abounded there. The kayak seemed ideal for that purpose; it was light enough to be lowered from the *Hygiene*'s deck and small enough to be stowed.

Getting into the kayak from the ship's side ladder was difficult, especially if there was a swell. I had to time my drop into the cockpit quite carefully as the two craft rose and fell. Playing it safe, I never let go of the ladder until I was in the kayak cockpit. A couple of time I was left hanging for a few seconds and was most thankful for the crew's strong arms keeping my baidarka lined up below me by holding onto the fore and aft ropes.

Getting out was easier as I could wait and grab the highest rung of the ship's ladder then work my way onto it. Naturally a chorus of advice erupted from the deck above me whenever I hesitated too long before attempting the tricky move.

In southeastern Alaska, skiffs with outboard motors had replaced native log canoes, and many of the villages had docks. However, around the Bering Sea the villages were isolated except for one or two freighters a year. There were no docks and often the anchorages were completely unprotected or so far out that land wasn't visible. This inaccessibility was part of the reason that a program such as ours was necessary. It also made the kayak useful in that area; it was so easily deployed.

During the early settlement of Alaska, only a handful of dedicated doctors, nurses, teachers, and missionaries were available to combat diseases introduced by the white man— particularly tuberculosis and venereal diseases. But it was a losing battle. Our primary medical purpose was to conduct an X-ray survey of Alaska's native coastal population to determine how many were afflicted with tuberculosis. Tuberculosis appeared among the native population just twenty-nine years after the first white man set foot in Alaska in 1728. Two hundred years later, it was estimated that four out of every one hundred people had the disease and there were only forty-six tuberculosis hospital beds available in the territory. During that period the main treatment for tuberculosis was bed rest—there were no drugs. By 1943 the beds had been increased to one hundred.

In 1941 the war made legislators in Washington, D.C., aware, apparently for the first time, that Alaska was a part of the United States and strategically important. This came after seventy-four years of ignoring all problems and failing to pass, until recently, even the most fundamental laws needed for orderly development of resources and people.

When the government and particularly the U.S. Public Health Service did become interested in this neglected territory, the problems were staggering. If there were going to be hospitals, it was necessary to know how many beds were needed, what they would treat, and where they would be most effective. That tuberculosis was prevalent was general knowledge, but there were no specific figures. Our job was to provide them.

A survey of eleven southeastern Alaska villages in 1943 showed that 13 percent of the native Americans had tuberculosis and, in some of these communities, more than one fourth of the population had active and, heretofore, unrecognized cases of the disease. These figures proved shocking enough to cause both the territorial legislature and the U.S. Department of Public Health to take action. Thus in 1945, for the first time, money was appropriated for a full-time commissioner of health in Alaska. A system of mobile units was designed to discover the magnitude of the problems in the remote villages as well as the larger towns; to take to the isolated areas, in particular, a health/education program stressing prevention and home care of tuberculosis and venereal disease; and to provide urgently needed medical care. Our medical group was the first full-sized mobile unit in this ambitious program.

After a few months' shakedown and program organization in southeast Alaska, we headed north stopping in Prince William Sound, where I purchased my baidarka. We then circled Kodiak Island and worked a portion of the Alaska Peninsula. I didn't see any skin boats in those areas. This was a surprise since Baranov had described huge fleets of kayaks that originated from Kodiak Island.

The following year, after working in southeast Alaska for the winter, we headed north again, this time bound for the Bering Sea, St. Lawrence Island, and the Aleutian Chain with its many islands. Here we would totally be on our own. Even radio contact with the outside world was minimal. Here, too, we came into the land of the midnight sun and Eskimos—those people most associated with igloos, dog teams, and seal hunting from kayaks. This was the way of life I had studied in school many years before. And as far as I could see, nothing had greatly changed—except for the dwellings. Now they were wood-frame houses instead of the well-known igloos.

One night after I had finished my work about 9:00 P.M., I went for a short paddle to explore the shoreline of Golovnin on Norton Sound—the first of our Eskimo villages. The evening was clear and calm with just a little surf rolling along the curve of the flat beach on which the village was located. There were no trees anywhere, and the town was surrounded by ocean, marsh, and grass. The whole effect was of a vast and lonely space that made man and his works very small. About twenty-five unpainted houses stretched in a row on the long, flat sandspit. At the top of the beach were rows of oil drums and a few racks with well-crafted kayaks. Some kayaks were covered with canvas and others with *oogoruk* (bearded seal) skins tanned snowy white. Later, one of the young men who spoke English explained, "We tan 'em white so they won't show against the ice and snow when we use 'em for hunting in the winter. We don't use 'em much now."

While looking at the kayaks, I noticed that the sleds on the beach were smaller than those traditionally pictured. Again my friend explained, "They're used with the kayaks and carried on the deck. Good for moving large loads over the ice."

It was impressive to see how these people, with none of our modern equipment or techniques, had adapted so well to one of the harshest and least-friendly climates in the world.

During the summer, people in these villages did much of their living both on the beach and tundra just above it. Fishing was going on constantly. Even young children in rowboats helped set the nets.

The fish were split open by the women and put on racks to dry. Once dried the fish were stored to feed the dogs through the winter. The women sat on the ground near the racks chatting and laughing as they worked. And all around children ran and jumped, mixing games with fishing. Seeing this happy

Susan Meredith

community life reminded me how so-called civilized people walled themselves from one another in cities. I didn't think I'd be lonesome in an Eskimo village.

I went ashore whenever I could to talk to people and see things up close. At times, when our ship was anchored off exposed beaches, I would have used my baidarka, but I didn't have enough confidence to go through surf; the baidarka still felt very long and unstable. I had to content myself with simply learning to handle my boat. I first tried paddling from the stern, then the middle cockpit. Of the two positions, it was much easier to handle the kayak from the middle. But it was more difficult to travel in a straight line and required constant paddle shifting from one side to the other.

Once when I returned to the ship, a crew member said he wanted to go for a paddle. I moved to the stern, and he jauntily dropped into the bow cockpit. After a couple of paddle strokes he wildly flailed his outspread arms and called in a panicky voice, "Help, help! Throw me a line. This damn thing is going to tip over."

Later, I tried the bow cockpit with another crew member in the stern and found I, too, felt unnerved. There was so little boat in front of me that whenever it tipped, which it did a lot, there was no reference to what it was doing. My admiration for Baranov and the Aleuts went to even higher levels. It was hard to imagine how they could paddle over rough seas, out of sight of land for forty or more hours, and with little chance to straighten their legs or sleep.

The weather was warm and sunny, and our biggest problem was lack of sleep. The sun didn't set until 10:30 P.M. and was up again at 1:30 A.M. It never got dark, and the sunsets and sunrises melded in varying shades of beautiful pink clouds through the twilight period. One night I took pictures every hour of spectacular rose and pink cloud formations that lasted three hours instead of the fifteen- or twenty-minute sunsets seen farther south. The villagers didn't keep any sort of formal hours, and I could hear and see children playing on the beach all night. During the day they often curled up beside a boat or an oil drum on the beach and slept until they woke up. Meals also seemed to be very impromptu, and they ate when they were hungry. We urged them to use local berries and greens instead of candy bars and soft drinks, which destroyed their teeth.

For a month we were fortunate to have the schoolteacher's wife acting as our secretary. She had been living in the area for a number of years and was well known by the people in the villages. She explained many mysteries, especially the system of people's names. Villages had a list of census names, but the people didn't use them or recognize them. They went rather by totally different villages names. The people were more open when she was around. They also allowed us to take pictures, which we had been warned not to do without permission. Apparently too many outsiders with cameras had made the villagers feel exploited.

Between storms we were able to work in the village of Elim. It was similar to Golovnin only the beach was more exposed. There were kayaks on racks on the beach, dog sleds, and teams of hungry dogs tied around posts. In addition, there was an airfield and some of our patients were brought in by plane. These people had never seen a car or a bicycle, but airplanes were fairly common. Luscious-looking vegetable gardens abounded, but we were a little too early to sample them.

The growing season was very short, but with nearly twenty-four hours of sunshine growth was rapid and luxuriant.

When we reached St. Lawrence Island we found that skin umiaks with outboard motors were used almost entirely. The umiak was a seaworthy boat with high sides. It was made of a light framework of branches covered with walrus hide. Standard equipment aboard the umiak were ropes made of walrus hide and sealskin pokes. A poke was a complete sealskin with all the openings closed, blown full of air, and tied off like a balloon. It served many functions: as a bumper between two boats, as a life preserver, as a float to tie onto spears in walrus hunting, and also as a roller to roll the boats up on the beach.

Our captain was uneasy about taking us ashore in the ship's launch because it wasn't designed to negotiate surf. It was arranged that we'd go ashore in umiaks.

The umiak that took us ashore had a crew of twelve men with paddles, two in the stern and five on each side. When in the open ocean they used one of their outboard motors—they always carried two—but when landing and taking off from the beach they used their paddles. Heavy surf constantly boiled up the steep gravel beaches.

Our first landing was an unforgettable experience. It was easy stepping into the big skin boat with many hands helping and no worry about tipping over. Nurse Kitty and I were placed in the middle. We knew the men were competent so we enjoyed our ride on the waves, feeling as though we were riding a big duck. But that feeling of security changed when we were fairly close to shore where the waves were beginning to break. Suddenly the motor cut out, and the boat swung sideways. The men grabbed their paddles and spoke in an excited babble. It was terrifying because we couldn't understand a word that was said. We were still sideways on the crest of a huge wave being swept rapidly toward a surf-pounded beach. I feared the worst and had visions of being smashed by the icy breakers. Of all things, I even worried my new camera might get wet. I noticed Kitty was nervously clutching her nurse's bag.

The Eskimos continued shouting and paddling as we flew sideways atop the wave. In a twinkling we were high and dry and right side up on the beach. And as the wave rolled back, the still shouting Eskimos jumped out and quickly pulled the

umiak away from the surf. We later learned this was standard
procedure among the Eskimos. The constant yelling was the
decision-making process to determine which was the biggest
wave to ride in on. It might not have been so scary if we could
have understood what they were saying, but the language barrier in a situation like this gave us a feeling of complete help-
lessness.

Just before we left Gambell, the *Square Knot*, one of two
large freighters that came into the Bering Sea during the summer to bring the year's supplies to the villages, showed up with
a load of freight. We were able to watch an interesting mix of
ancient and modern cultures. Among the things to be delivered
was a caterpillar tractor. This had to be moved from the *Square
Knot's* anchored position a quarter mile offshore onto a surf-
beaten beach. A relatively calm sea was the first necessity, then
the natives took two of their largest skin boats, fastened them
securely together and built a plank platform on top—large
enough to hold the tractor. This contraption was then tied
alongside the freighter. Using the ship's winch, the deck crew
carefully lowered the tractor onto the fragile skin boat platform, and the whole assembly was gently moved to shore by
outboards on the stern of the boats, where another tractor
stood ready to pull it up a ramp to dry land. While watching
this procedure, I wondered how they had gotten the first tractor up the beach.

Mekoryuk, on the north side of Nunivak Island, was one of
the most primitive villages we visited. It clearly resembled the
mental picture I had from books I'd read as a schoolgirl about
Eskimos. Typically, the village was located on a flat grassy
landscape barren of trees or shrubs but surrounded by a profusion of colorful wild flowers. The people lived in barabaras,
which were mostly underground. These igloo-shaped structures had earth roofs, no windows, and one small opening for
entering and exiting. I was amazed at the number of people
who apparently belonged to each small structure. The cooking
was done outside in large pots hanging over an open fire.

On the beach, which was in a relatively protected bay,
were the usual racks with kayaks. One of the kayaks was pulled
up on the beach where I could examine it closely. I realized this
shorter, wider boat with a single cockpit would be far easier to

manage than the baidarka. A big plus was the fact that there was room for me to sit on the bottom with my legs extended instead of kneeling.

On our first calm day off since entering the Bering Sea, several of us went ashore to talk to people and take pictures. I asked one of the men about the kayaks but he just smiled, shook his head, and put his hands together while making a tipping motion. Just then our Eskimo deckhand came along, and I said, "Johnny, can you help me? I'd like to ask if I might try this Nunivak kayak." Johnny nodded his head and proceeded to talk with the men. After a long conversation with much head shaking, he came to me. "They don't think you can do it by yourself. But I'll borrow two so I can go with you. I don't think I know anymore than you do, but it will be fun, and they'll feel better."

The men helped me launch with much head shaking and conversation, which I couldn't understand, and then stood around waiting for me to capsize. They didn't know about the much tippier baidarka I'd been practicing in.

Johnny and I had a wonderful afternoon paddling up a small river in the warm sunshine. The banks were covered with wild flowers, and reindeer horns littered the ground. We even met two reindeer swimming across the river.

Johnny was an interesting companion, and this was the first time I had a chance to chat with him on a one-to-one basis. He had joined us at St. Michael, a village east of the Yukon River's entry to Norton Sound, and he was to act as deckhand and interpreter. He had been educated at the Sheldon Jackson school in Sitka.

At first he was not well accepted and had a difficult time as the crew didn't like having to associate with a native. I was surprised at the race prejudice they exhibited. Johnny, although only in his teens, handled the situation diplomatically and soon was respected by all. He was a very intelligent fellow and was as interested in the different customs and villages as we were. The fact that he was having increasing trouble interpreting the farther we got from St. Michael embarrassed him greatly. Each village had its own dialect, and some were quite unique.

Johnny's prior boating experience had been in outboard-powered skiffs, but he had no trouble with the kayak. When we returned, we paddled along the shore, and I realized that this boat would make it possible for me to fulfill my dreams of paddling like the Aleuts—even if the boat was a slightly different style, and I had no ambitions to cross the Gulf of Alaska in it. Compared with my baidarka, this kayak was very stable and comfortable. Even in the short time I paddled it, I felt the kayak was an extension of myself, and I could easily go anywhere in it. I'd definitely been limited in using the baidarka, both by my own feeling of instability and by the worries of my shipmates. I asked Johnny to find out if there might be a local kayak for sale. Again there was a long conversation and much head shaking.

Returning to me, Johnny asked, "How much can you pay for it? Could you offer them $80?" I quickly nodded. Then he explained.

"They're worried because they don't have any wood to make a new framework. Driftwood is scarce around here, and there are no bushes to provide branches. But if you pay them enough, they'll part with it."

I felt guilty taking something away that would be hard to replace. But when I said something to that effect, the man who owned the boat smiled, nodded his head, then handed me the paddle. In turn, I gratefully handed him the $80. Later Johnny said he thought the fellow was hoping to get enough money for a skiff and outboard motor. This village was in transition— from a native culture to a more modern way of life. Adding to this process was the opportunity for Eskimos to earn money at a newly built reindeer meat packing plant nearby.

I paddled my new acquisition proudly out to the *Hygiene* where the captain checked it out with a look of resignation. After I had convinced him that the kayak wouldn't take up much space and was a lot safer than my baidarka, he said, "Well, OK, but you know anything that small can't be safe." This attitude was also reflected by most of the crew in spite of my quotes about Baranov.

The Nunivak kayak was similar to the baidarka in that it was a wood frame fastened together with leather thongs and covered with sealskin, but there the similarity ended. It was considerably shorter, wider, and deeper. Prominent features included a single large and comfortable cockpit, a circular opening in the bow, and a stern with a built-in handle. The coaming around the cockpit was quite high and thongs were laced across the forward and stern decks for holding spears and paddles. Unlike my baidarka, I felt secure and stable in this boat.

We finished the work in Mekoryuk on Monday and then headed north to Scammon Bay. All Tuesday morning was spent hunting for the channel and, as we couldn't find it, we proceeded to Hooper Bay. We dropped anchor there about 1:00 P.M. Kitty and the doctor went ashore where they had to walk about six miles across the tundra before finding the local village.

I'll never forget Hooper Bay. For it was there that I saw the ultimate in kayak transportation. A man was paddling a large single-holed kayak. Nothing unusual about that except behind him, in the cockpit, facing the stern, was his wife. In front of her on the deck, in order of decreasing size, were three small children, each with his arms around the one in front. Two older children were on the deck in front of the paddler. The kayak was so low in the water we prayed no wave would come along. Later, when the ship had moved closer to the village, I saw another kayak with two people in the single cockpit. As with the previous kayak, the woman was sitting facing the stern, and the man was facing the bow. It looked considerably safer with only two people. I never did see any women or children out in the kayaks by themselves. They seemed to prefer using the skiffs.

At Tanunak on Nelson Island, we had to anchor a long way out in an exposed bay, so I didn't try to take my kayak shore. Instead, a resident native took us ashore in his small boat.

I regretted not having my kayak because the village was beside a lovely stream and, finishing my work long before the others, I had time to explore. The local schoolteacher was most helpful in finding a kayak for me to borrow. Fortunately it was similar to mine, and I felt comfortable in it. After paddling past a few bends of the slow-moving stream, I was totally away from all signs of civilization. Each curve brought a new vista as I slid quietly along the edge of the stream sneaking close to feeding birds ignoring my presence. Wild flowers covered the banks in a profusion of reds, yellows, blues, and whites. I recognized wild iris, snapdragons, buttercups, daisies, and what I guessed to be alyssums. The fragrant wind blowing through the grasses was also bringing more and more huge puffy white clouds. It was such a joy to feel the push of the paddle in the water and the responsiveness of the little boat as it slid along so easily and quietly.

I felt integrated with the unfolding scene and wanted to keep going. But the wind was steadily increasing, and I knew the others would start to worry about me if I was gone too long. Reluctantly I headed back. The solitude and quietness, after the constant noise of motors and bustle of people on the ship, was hard to leave.

By the time I reached the village, the gentle breeze had turned into a full-blown gale making the sea too rough for our return. As a result, the poor schoolteacher was stuck with four unexpected guests for dinner and the night. Apparently not an uncommon occurrence.

While wandering about with this welcome bonus of free time, I found a store of sorts. It was owned and run by a most interesting native family. The three sons all had the same congenital deformity: Their legs were bent back double at the knee, and they had to walk on their knees. The two older boys had adjusted very well with leather kneepads and were strong and agile in getting around and helping in the store, carrying boxes, climbing in and out of boats, and up and down ladders, or anything else they needed to do. They were jolly and full of confidence, and it was a pleasure to be around them.

The youngest boy had been sent to Children's Orthopedic Hospital in Seattle where they operated on him and straightened his legs. However, for whatever reason, he was quite helpless, weak, and fearful.

The store had the usual canned goods, cigarettes, candy, and soft drinks but what caught my eye were the many items woven from the grasses and reeds growing in the marshes around town. I bought some mats, rugs, and baskets and then spotted a pair of very long light mukluks way back in a corner.

"Can I try them on?" I asked one of the boys.

"Sure," he replied, "They are water mukluks and will keep you dry above your knees. We need 'em on the mud flats round here."

Just what I needed for getting in and out of my kayak, I thought. The mukluks came above my knees and didn't weigh more than a couple of ounces. Footwear had always been a problem in the kayak. Shoepaks kept my feet warm and dry, but were stiff and heavy to wear in the little boat. Regular mukluks were light and flexible, but didn't work too well when they were wet. So now I felt I had the ideal solution. On finding they fit, I examined them more closely. They were made of seal gut and were absolutely waterproof. There were broad straps tied around the ankle, just below the knee, and above the knee. The mukluks cost $7.50, and I bought them as well as a parka, which was also supposed to be waterproof—but not until the seams had been treated with seal oil. It was just a rain parka and not designed for the boat. It, too, was made of strips of seal gut sewn together in a special manner so water going through the needle holes would come out on the outside surface. These seams were all sewn by hand but the fur trim around the hood, cuffs, and bottom were machine sewn. Deciding it would be fun to return to the schoolteacher's house dressed in my new native garb, I put the items on and grandly made my appearance, only to be rapidly ushered back outdoors until I had removed it all. Unfortunately I had a bad cold and had lost my sense of smell. The mukluks, as I was soon made aware, had been tanned in urine and were extremely foul smelling.

The next morning it was still too rough to return to the *Hygiene*, so the teachers took us across the tundra to an ancient village to look for artifacts. The gravel looked as though it had been pretty well picked over by other visitors. In poking among the rocks I found a smooth one that seemed to have a design scratched on it. The doctor looked it over and said, "Come on Susie, that's just the nature of the rock."

"But," Kitty and I protested, "It looks like a sun with rays coming out of it—rocks don't come naturally with pictures."

The doctor shook his head, but I put the rock in my bag. Out of the corner of my eye I noticed the others began to search a bit more vigorously.

Fall approached, and the storms became more severe and frequent, forcing us to leave the Bering Sea. Sometimes, as we pitched and rolled for days, unable to sleep or get a hot meal, my mind would go back to the job I had in Seattle where I routinely rode back and forth on a bus, worked eight hours in a pleasant lab, and always ate on time. However, a couple of hours' rest and a hot meal would wipe those cushy urban thoughts totally from my mind.

Labor Day found us at Akutan on the Aleutian Chain. From here on we could look forward to anchoring mainly in sheltered waters instead of the vastly exposed and windy Bering Sea.

It was good to see foliage-covered hills displaying fall colors instead of the endlessly flat landscape. Interesting and different as the Bering Sea was, I hadn't realized how much I missed a well-defined shoreline until I was next to one again. The first night there was a full moon, and as I paddled my kayak across the bay to an abandoned whaling station, shadowy and mysterious in the moonlight, I envisioned how happy those old whalers must have felt when they rounded the point into this peaceful calm bay. Again I enjoyed the physical exercise of paddling as well as the freedom to go where I wanted. Experiencing the silence and being part of the scene in my kayak was blissful.

One of our first stops along the Aleutian Chain was Sanak, a small island with a partially protected harbor, where we dropped anchor shortly before dusk and waited for someone to come out. When no one came, Dr. Swanson asked the captain to put a boat in and take him ashore to get the census and inform the people of our plans. The captain refused, saying he and the crew had started work at 4:00 A.M. that day and were weary. The crew would take the doctor first thing next morning.

After the captain went to dinner, Dr. Swanson began moaning that we'd be delayed at least half a day. So, I piped up, "If you can put my kayak in the water, I'd be happy to paddle in and get the census and deliver the needed information. That would be a useful adventure don't you think?" He and the dentist quickly lowered the ship's ladder and set the kayak in the water. There wasn't much surf breaking so I thought it'd be a great paddle.

By the time I was settled in my cockpit it had become quite dark. I must admit it didn't appear to be such a simple paddle after all—particularly as I moved a short distance from the boat and heard waves crash close to me. The crew were all eating and unaware of what was going on.

I had to paddle about a third of a mile to the beach. In that space were several submerged rocks, which waves broke over. Usually I could make out the white foam and hear the noise where they were breaking, but occasionally I'd be frightened by one erupting unexpectedly next to me. I began to realize how foolhardy I'd been in volunteering to do this favor. The captain really did have a sound reason for refusing to go in. But I decided to keep going as someone had built a fire on the beach around which people were milling. I called for help to land, and several flashlights pointed to a spot on the beach. By now, rocks were scattered everywhere, and I was afraid I might puncture my kayak. Voices directed me to the proper channel, and as I reached shore many willing hands pulled me up on the beach. The two schoolteachers, an older woman and a handsome young man, were there to greet me. They had just arrived the day before.

"We haven't had a chance to read our mail and didn't know who you were," they explained.

The woman looked at me and shook her head, "I don't believe it. A blonde young lady. And you paddled a kayak here in the dark? I was sure you were an Eskimo fisherman. I just don't believe it."

We sat around the fire for a few minutes while I answered their questions. "Where did you get the kayak? Were you afraid paddling in the dark?"

"Yes," I had to admit, "I was."

The young man, Dick, arranged for one of the natives to take us all back to the *Hygiene* in his boat, which had an outboard and searchlight. My little kayak was towed along behind.

On my return, the captain sternly took me aside and gravely admonished, "Susie, I've trusted you with your kayak and you've been very cautious. But this episode was just plain stupid. From now on you're not to take your kayak off the ship without my permission. Is that understood?"

Feeling like a teenager being grounded, I had to admit my poor judgment, "I realized when I was halfway in I was doing a dumb thing. I got scared but . . . well, I had to keep going. Thought it would be safer than turning back."

"Did the doctor ask you to go?"

"No, it was my idea. I was just trying to be helpful and . . . well, I always like an excuse to go for a paddle."

Only later did I learn that when the captain came out from dinner and found out what was going on, he was so furious he started a fight with the dentist, and they had to be forcibly separated. Kitty told me that as I disappeared in the darkness even the doctor had some qualms about the whole escapade. They all seemed glad to see me back. I really hadn't meant to cause any trouble and decided that in the future I wouldn't volunteer that type of service again.

About a week later we arrived at Kanatak. Ashore we found only sixteen people. It was a ghost town. Oil had been discovered there about ten years earlier, and an oil company had moved in and eventually capped a number of wells. But now, the area was overgrown. Buildings were in all stages of collapse.

With so few people to examine we were finished by noon. Being a sunny Saturday, we all took the afternoon off.

I returned to the *Hygiene* to get my fishing gear and kayak. As I paddled toward the beach, the wind unexpectedly started blowing and created breaking surf. I figured I'd probably get wet in landing, but what the heck, I'd give it a try.

I rode in on the crest of a wave that must have been about three feet high. It broke and white froth boiled all around me. The water was filled with sand, and I could feel its motion through the thin skin of the hull. I rode the wave onto the beach and almost capsized when it swung me sideways. I thought I was going over for sure. But that little kayak popped back up leaving me high and dry. I hopped out fast and pulled it above the water before the next wave came in. What a thrill, especially knowing the crew members were watching through binoculars and were convinced I wouldn't be able to land without capsizing.

Three native boys ran up to me apparently fascinated by the kayak. They poked their heads inside to see how the boat was put together. The oldest boy turned to me with wide eyes and asked if he could paddle it. Thinking I might learn something, I asked him if he had gone out in his father's kayak.

"No," he replied, "he don't have one like this. This is the first kayak I've seen."

As I told him I wouldn't be able to let him use the kayak, one of his companions chimed in, "Our fathers tell us stories about the old days and hunting with kayaks, but no one uses them anymore."

I was sad to be in a place where I could have talked to someone about kayaks but the men of the village were all hunting inland. Two hundred years before, in Baranov's time, each of the Aleut villages in this area depended largely on baidarkas for their survival. Now there were few people, and baidarkas were rare.

After a rough crossing from Kodiak Island to Cook Inlet—another of Baranov's haunts—we spent the day at Port Chatham getting organized. It was a scenic, but windy location. That afternoon I launched my kayak and went exploring with a deckhand, Dell, who used the baidarka. The seas were choppy so we lashed the two kayaks together. We hoped we did it in the same manner as the Aleuts when they got in rough water. I'd read that when they were crossing the gulf in storms, they'd lash two or three kayaks together, being careful to cushion the hulls with sealskin floats so they wouldn't bang together. With this in mind, Dell and I went ashore in a protected bay and found a couple of smooth sticks, which we laid across the kayaks fore and aft. We secured them with our bow lines under and around the hulls. It was a rather messy arrangement. I'm not sure how effective it was, but Dell felt safer.

Again my mind went back to Baranov and the difficulties he had in establishing outposts here. He had to be on guard against raids from rival Russian companies and the unfriendly Kenaitze. I thought of how he paddled from Cook Inlet to Kodiak Island through breakers that froze on his face, paddle, and boat. The Aleuts were acclimated to these rough conditions but here was a man who learned all of this when he was no longer young. Yet, he was able to lead his fleet of hunters in their own techniques under the worst conditions.

Sometimes when we sat around our warm galley table drinking hot coffee and, with plenty to eat, complained about our difficult working conditions, I marveled at the strength and courage of the men like Baranov, who endured almost unbelievable dangers and deprivations. Against that adversity, they built an empire known around the world.

As fall turned to winter there was less and less weather suitable for kayaking. We were working our way south eventually returning to Chenega in Prince William Sound—the village where I bought my baidarka.

Because I was collecting quite a few large items, such as my bike, skis, and reindeer horns, I decided to sell the baidarka back to the schoolteacher, as he wanted it, and I hadn't used it since getting the Nunivak kayak. I sold the baidarka for $40, the same amount I had paid for it. I had learned what features I didn't like in the baidarka. I didn't like paddling from the kneeling position. I didn't like the long skinny, tippy boat as opposed to the more stable, comfortable Nunivak kayak, and I really didn't like three cockpits, which might have been useful under some conditions, but not for me.

During the spring of 1948 I had to leave Alaska and return to Seattle to take care of my invalid mother. I shipped my Nunivak kayak home with the intention of paddling on Puget Sound. But I was doomed to disappointment. That summer turned out to be very wet and warm. My kayak simply rotted in that climate. First the skins deteriorated, then the leather thongs binding the wooden framework. The resulting stench wasn't very pleasant. With much pressure from family and close neighbors, I sadly took the remains of my faithful friend to the dump.

My Alaskan kayaking experience left such a definite impression on me that when I discovered a small group of foldboaters in Seattle in 1950, I immediately joined them. As a member of the newly formed Washington Foldboat Club, I was among kindred spirits who loved adventuring in kayaks.

For our initial outings, we made what we called "scouting trips" to various Northwest wilderness areas. These trips were exciting because we were the first people to paddle those particular waters in modern times. We had no idea what to expect regarding the currents, wind patterns, or wildlife we'd encounter. The only people we occasionally saw were Native Americans in their fishing boats. We gradually worked our way north keeping ahead of the creeping population growth on Vancouver Island.

To get up in the morning and take off not knowing what experiences the day would bring; not knowing where I would camp that night was the height of living to me. I savored each minute, observing the changing sunlight on the mountains, the billowing clouds, the island-studded bays, tidal pools carpeted with varicolored seaweeds and starfish, the myriad beautiful shells covering the shoreline.

Seals swam by curiously looking me over. Seabirds filled the air with haunting cries. And oh those orcas! I used to greatly fear them but now I watch them with awe and admiration—up close in my kayak.

As those halcyon paddling afternoons waned, and sea winds freshened, I automatically looked to sun-washed beaches or protected coves, searching for the perfect campsite. It wasn't always sunny. But even when it rained, a mysterious beauty veiled the surrounding forested hills. I especially liked being snug in my tent listening to the cheery pop and crackle of a campfire radiating tantalizing dinner odors. Such times could be even more satisfying than a sunny camp—if the rain didn't last too long.

The people I've kayaked with have had such a broad variety of interests and knowledge that my horizons have expanded greatly. There has hardly been a facet of the natural world that I haven't explored with an expert who happened to be on the trip. There have been engineers who built sandcastles and then dams to protect those delicate structures from the rising tide, or worked complicated lever systems to move gigantic logs. There have been geologists who explained the development of the land formations we paddled along and through. Once there was a doctor who insisted on making his fires by rubbing two sticks together.

There have been musicians who formed our group into a wonderful singing unit (at least we thought so). There have been artists who drew our pictures, and several excellent photographers who captured our smiles as well as the seascapes. And finally, there have been the gourmet cooks who worked wonders over the campfire and shared their delicious concoctions with everyone.

Kayaking has been a magic carpet taking me into the world of adventure and camaraderie of adventurers. When I was young and unable to get around, I spent many hours reading and vicariously living stories where the heroes and heroines were strong, composed, and able to endure any demanding situation. I've discovered, as I've traveled with some of my friends who've done what I considered major feats, that I too can be calm under difficulties—that I can endure hardship and even enjoy it. I love the wonderful feeling of being warm and dry in my boat with rain gear and spraydeck defying the wind and sea. I'm glad to know that I have the strength to keep going even when I have reached the point of numbness, and that I can still come out with a cheery word or smile. I'm particularly glad that I can travel through this wonderful world in my kayak as it has been done for thousands of years, quietly, slowly—savoring everything around me.

Everytime I put my kayak atop my car for a wilderness trip, I have that marvelous feeling of leaving material things, everyday pressures, and world problems. I can look forward to exploring new waters and remote islands. With only the bare necessities, I delight in the communal life on the beach. Such experiences take me back to the Eskimo villages on the Bering Sea where life was lived along the shoreline, and I recall the warm sense of community among the natives. Loneliness doesn't seem to exist.

While sea kayaking, my Alaskan experiences spring vividly to life triggered by an event such as landing on some deserted beach or lagoon. I nostalgically remember paddling in that Alaska unknown to so many. My mind goes to that native culture in the north—those areas where the kayak was once the predominant means of survival and transportation. To have paddled a skin boat in those areas where the ancient Aleuts and Eskimos hunted from kayaks is to feel a link with history. I'm privileged to have fleetingly touched the lifestyle of that old culture and to have helped carry it forward in paddling with a new generation of kayakers.

SUSAN HULL MEREDITH was born in 1918 in Seattle, Washington. It was during her two years aboard the health-ship *Hy-*

giene, which brought medical care to coastal villages in Alaska, that she was introduced to kayaking.

In her forty years of kayaking, Meredith has watched the sport develop from its early foldboat days to the present boom, when thousands are paddling sleek, highly engineered craft in just about every corner of the world.

Susan and her husband, Jim, retired to the San Juan Islands in 1981. They live in a log cabin built, with the help of kayaking friends, from logs that were hauled from the water by kayak.

JOHN BAUMAN

Icelandic Odyssey

"Now tell me again what your plan is," inquired Hannes from behind his neatly organized desk. His raised eyebrows and doubtful tone threw me off guard and gave me a sickening feeling that all was not well. Had I not already answered this at our initial meeting earlier in the day? My mind was racing as I spoke, and I constantly had to remind myself to be diplomatic at all costs. As head of the Icelandic Lifesaving Association, Hannes Hafstein had the power to put an end to our trip. It was incomprehensible that the time, effort, and money that went into planning this trip could be all for naught. If need be, Harry and I would sneak off on our own to paddle, but we knew the advantages of having the journey sanctioned by Hannes.

"We want to circumnavigate Iceland in our sea kayaks," I spoke with forced conviction.

"Do you have any idea how dangerous that is? Why, even huge fishing boats capsize in these treacherous waters." Hannes stared at us in disbelief and disapproval. "I really don't think I can allow such a hazardous trip," he continued as he scrutinized us.

How could I convince this man that we were not insane, that we knew what we were doing? Although Hannes didn't know it, Harry and I were both harboring thoughts of potential failure. To project confidence and win Hannes' approval, I spoke of past trips and experiences, especially in Alaska where extremes in water and wind conditions are similar to Iceland. But Hannes remained unconvinced.

"We can roll our kayaks upright using the paddle. It's called the Eskimo roll. All competent paddlers know the technique. We wouldn't even think about going out onto the ocean without this skill," I casually replied hoping to project an impression of expertise. "Besides, we'll be close to shore," I heard myself say, knowing that some of the bays and fjords we were to cross would put us quite far from the coast.

"Do you have a radio with you?"

My heart sank. "No," I said uneasily. "But we do have an ELT (Emergency Locator Transmitter) that operates off satellites in case of an emergency," I quickly added. I had the feeling we were at a pivotal point in the conversation so I continued. "All the other paddling trips we've taken in the past were in remote wilderness areas where a radio was useless." I held my breath in anticipation.

"I wish that you'd contacted me in advance about this trip. I would have required you to have a radio. Do you have all the navigational charts for Iceland?"

"Yes. We have both nautical charts and topographical maps," I said confidently.

"You can fit everything you need for camping in the kayaks?"

"We can carry nearly a month's worth of supplies in the boats if need be. But we'll be buying food in villages along the way."

Hannes fell silent for a moment, looking intently first at Harry then me. "Tell you what. If you'll report to the harbormaster upon your arrival at each port so I can keep track of your progress, I'll let you go. But you'll have to report whenever possible." He paused again, then added with fatherly concern, "I'm still very worried about you two."

As I left the meeting, I felt relieved at having won Hannes' approval. Yet, my private doubts seemed more exaggerated now that I had both a responsibility to Hannes and a challenge to my integrity.

Sea kayaking in Iceland would be both a wilderness experience and a cultural experience. The 3,700-mile coastline of mountains, fjords, sea cliffs, and secluded bays is dotted with communities ranging from only a few inhabitants to the capital city, Reykjavik, with a population of 85,000 people. The introspection induced by the isolation of the uninhabited shoreline and the necessary, but enjoyable, socializing that might occur in the villages could create a mix of paddling that would be unique in contrast to the nature of a purely wilderness excursion.

Iceland, being so close to Britain where modern sea kayaking has been a sport for years, has attracted many English paddlers. The most noteworthy journey was a circumnavigation by Nigel Foster and Geoff Hunter in the mid-1970s.

My reasons for repeating this feat were manifold. As a youngster in geography class, I perceived Iceland as simply a dot on the globe. Little time was devoted to studying this island nation. Yet, the scant knowledge the teacher imparted about volcanoes and boiling hot springs was fascinating and helped to create a mystique for me. Adding to this mystique was my reading of the famous Jules Verne novel, *Journey to the Center of the Earth*, an adventure tale set in Iceland.

I've always been greatly intrigued by the more northerly and southerly latitudes, where remoteness seems synonymous with exploration. It is in such regions of sparse human population and inclement weather that I have found the most pristine wilderness abundant with wildlife and natural beauty. To sense the delight of discovery, such as the first explorers probably experienced, is what fascinates me as well as Harry. So, the lure of exploring Iceland's volcanoes, fjords, glaciers, hot springs, and inaccessible bays surrounded by the beauty of a mountainous landscape, compellingly drew us to kayak around the island nation.

Our ocean journey began on a sunny summer day, June 4, 1986. We hauled our gear to a secluded rocky beach on the outskirts of Reykjavik, carefully packed three weeks provisions in the boats, and quietly pushed off from the rocky shore for our first taste of the North Atlantic. No one, except Hannes, knew of our intent, so our departure was without fanfare or audience.

Across the fjord, the green pastured hillsides of farmland illuminated by the sun beckoned us on. Turning in my cockpit to glance back at the receding skyline of Reykjavik, I wondered what type of journey this would be. Was our goal lunacy? Were we being foolhardy or would we be able to handle the nasty conditions of open-ocean paddling? I couldn't help thinking back to the Aleutian Islands and a few of the harrowing moments we had experienced paddling the rough and unpredictable waters of the North Pacific Ocean and Bering Sea. Would we encounter as severe conditions on this adventure? Could we overcome these dangers when they inevitably appeared? These concerns and uncertainties arose as the bows of our kayaks dipped into the cold waters off Iceland.

Another concern was my kayak. I was paddling an experimental take-apart. It was a full-size, sixteen-foot Eskimo model cut into three equal sections complete with bulkheads. This allowed me to transport it on a commercial flight as excess baggage instead of paying exorbitant fees to have a regular hardshell kayak shipped by air freight. But would my three-piece kayak, joined with bolts, stand up to the rigors of the North Atlantic for three months? It would be a hellish nightmare to be a victim of a kayak breaking apart in heavy seas.

Only twenty miles out of Reykjavik, we encountered our first ocean hazard as we approached a rocky point of lowland pasture—"boomers." Twelve-foot swells, generated from a recent offshore storm, were washing across submerged reefs near the point and creating huge hydraulics capable of crushing our kayaks. With boomers lurking everywhere, I constantly peered over my shoulder whenever I heard a thundering crash nearby. After hours of this forced alertness, I was convinced Harry and I would sooner or later have a major incident if this typified the entire coastline. Seeking shelter on the lee side of an island brought us temporary refuge from the crashing swells and our frightening introduction to Icelandic paddling.

The coastal pastureland slowly transformed into steeper and more rugged hillsides as we progressed. Bad weather dogged us from the very beginning. The constant drizzle gave a dull gray cast to the mountain slopes and sea.

Out of the first fifteen days, we were only able to launch on six. On June 10, to our surprise, it snowed followed by a three-day blow. We didn't have enough fresh water to last through the storm so we walked 4 miles to the nearest farmhouse for water. We were greeted suspiciously by a swarthy, red-faced farmer. This was understandable; we appeared from nowhere and were unable to speak Icelandic. Fortunately Erna, one of his daughters, was home from college and could speak fluent English.

Soon we were seated at the kitchen table for a lunch of freshly baked sweet breads and a large pot of steaming coffee. This was the first opportunity for Harry and I to experience the rural culture of Iceland. We spent the remainder of the day talking with Erna about the customs, the philosophies, and the idiosyncracies of Icelanders.

The most valuable aspect of our interchange was the grammar lesson we received. Harry had bought a small Icelandic dictionary in Reykjavik, which helped a bit, but we had no idea how to pronounce such letters as "d" or "ae" or "b." Erna was able to answer all of our questions about the thirty-three-letter alphabet and the language. When she informed us that a good dictionary cost nearly $250 (U.S.), we quickly decided our mediocre dictionary would suffice.

The native language is as close to the original Viking as exists today. Instead of using the root English words for the new computer lingo, entirely new Icelandic words are created to keep the language pure. Even the Danes, who ruled Iceland up until 1944, have a difficult time with Icelandic. Thus, when Harry and I tried deciphering their perplexing language and failed miserably, we didn't feel too defeated.

I remember the time I purchased dry milk, labeled *mjol*, at a market. Upon arriving at our campsite that evening, I began to mix some of the newly purchased milk. For some reason, it wasn't dissolving well. One large gulp of the translucent liquid had me spitting it out and gagging. It definitely wasn't milk. In checking the dictionary more carefully, I found that milk was *mjolk* and flour was *mjol*! Hereafter, we purchased baby formula, our only source of dry milk.

Three days after the farm visit, nearly seventy miles into the trip, we arrived at Hotel Budir on the west coast. The proprietor, a most gracious woman, immediately offered us a campsite and shower in the luxury hotel for free.

Unexpectedly, a storm moved in and stranded us for two extra days. Our idle mornings were spent in the hotel dining room where we drank copious quantities of strong coffee and wrote lengthy letters. On one of these mornings, a waiter inexplicably offered us a tray of whole wheat bread and homemade soup. When we tried to pay the man, we were flatly refused. This type of open, unquestioned, hospitality was to follow us throughout our entire trip.

During our forced layover spent at the hotel, I thoroughly studied our charts. By cutting across the entrances of the larger bays and the multitude of deep fjords, some stretching 40 miles inland, I calculated we had to paddle about 1,400 miles to reach Reykjavik. When the storm finally passed, we left Budir most anxious to cover this vast distance.

Ahead of us projected the largest peninsula in Iceland, some fifty miles long and notorious for huge upwellings and powerful riptides, which form at the tip. The entire southern side of this peninsula has steep volcanic cliffs of black rock that serve as a nesting site for the huge population of marine bird species native to Iceland. I was amazed at the variety and profusion of birds circling above us as we paddled beneath the mossy, thousand-foot walls. Fortunately, the seas were calm—ideal for wildlife photography.

I paddled my kayak into flotillas of guillemots, murres, puffins, and razorbills. But each time I'd come close enough for a photograph, the birds would hastily disperse no matter how quietly or slowly I approached. My frustration was mounting as I chased after these birds for that perfect shot. The only thing I captured on film was the tail end of several unidentifiable marine birds.

To add to my frustration, I ran out of film and had to take time to retrieve a new roll from inside the cockpit and load it into the camera. During this operation I was oblivious of anything else. Upon completion of the film exchange, I looked up to find I was completely surrounded by a huge gathering of razorbills and murres that were curiously regarding me. I had to laugh at the situation and wondered who was observing whom?

While the waterfowl were plentiful, we only had a few sightings of seals and porpoises. For some reason, the seals we saw were never inquisitive enough to come close to our kayaks. In most cases, upon detecting us, they immediately dove under-

John Bauman

water and disappeared. And, despite our expectations, we still had not seen any whales.

In the two days after leaving Budir, the calm seas allowed us to paddle 53 miles, most reassuring after sitting out several stormy days. Having now traveled 120 miles from Reykjavik, we made our first phone report to Hannes. He was anxious to hear from us and inquired about sea conditions and storms since our departure. I could sense Hannes' displeasure due to the long period of time with no contact, so I vowed to call whenever possible. I knew that Hannes was still not thoroughly convinced of our expertise and judgment, but I hoped his attitude would change as we continued our journey.

"The three things you can't count in Iceland," Hannes told us in our first meeting, "are the mountains in the north, the lakes in the center of the country, and the islands along the west coast." Now that we had reached the area of islands, we realized how right Hannes was. Islands were scattered as far as we could see. Because our progress was being slowed by the frequent storms, we chose a shorter route through the complex concentration of islets that was far from the coastline. An amazingly flat, calm day put us in the center of the islands on a tiny spot of land that was serving as a bird rookery for fulmars, the most common marine species found in Iceland.

Because of the fulmars abundance, Icelanders consider it a national sport to use them for target practice and shoot them out of the sky. At campsites we later occupied during our journey, we were astonished and distressed at the large number of dead fulmars scattered about the ground.

On the other end of the spectrum, the gyrfalcon is a protected species. This fact came to us in a strange manner. That evening, while camped at the fulmar rookery on a tiny island, we heard distant gunshots. Apparently, fishermen were shooting fulmars. Soon a small, yellow boat appeared and approached the island we inhabited. The five men aboard the vessel rowed to shore in a cramped inflatable raft. It looked like an excellent situation for a cultural exchange and, we hoped, some fresh fish. None of the five could speak English so we had difficulty in verbal communication and immediately resorted to sign language and gestures. One scruffy fellow kept saying, "*polish, polish,*" which was very confusing. He certainly didn't appear to be Polish.

The outward friendliness that I had expected from this group was nonexistent. They were a rather belligerent lot ranging in age from teens to one individual who looked to be about sixty years old. I couldn't interpret their intent, though their gruffness was most apparent. Showing them our American passports seemed to change their attitude. Upon further exchange, the youngest one finally revealed he could speak some English. They claimed to be wildlife officers, though they were dressed in common fishing attire. The "*polish, polish*" must have been their attempt at "police." They thought we were Germans there to steal gyrfalcon eggs to sell at a huge profit to sheiks or sultans interested in falconry. Apparently this lucrative type of theft has contributed to the demise of this raptor. All of us got a chuckle out of that one, and their departure was accompanied with grins, smiles, and repeated head nodding.

I thought it rather strange that no badges were produced to verify their status, and it was odd to envision wildlife officers shooting the fulmars despite the traditions of their countrymen. Later we found that there are no gyrfalcons in the lowland islands. Furthermore, there are no wildlife officers in Iceland. The locals must have gotten a good laugh out of spoofing the unsuspecting foreigners.

We left the island the next morning and had paddled for only half a day when another storm beset us. Blowing rain, driven by fifteen-knot head winds, pelted us in the face and restricted our visibility. We had to battle the stinging rain for five miles before we found refuge on a larger island with a small fishing village. Upon landing in the surf, I slammed the right side of my rudder against shoreline rocks. The impact produced a tiny crack in the rudder bracket but nothing to worry about.

Again the perpetually foul weather was working on my mind, casting doubts as to the sanity of our circumnavigation. I was exasperated at how infrequently we were able to paddle. Was our goal truly realistic? Was this weather pattern normal or were we just experiencing an unusual summer?

I called Hannes to check in and ask him about the strange

weather. I was apprehensive to speak with him; our location would indicate we had not paddled along the shoreline but had gone far out into the ocean.

"Where are you calling from, John?" Hannes asked jovially.

"Flatey." I waited the dreaded question about our position so far from shore. He could cancel our trip.

"Flatey, the fishing village of Flatey?"

"Uh, yes," I stammered. For a moment there was silence.

"That's wonderful! How's the weather been?"

"Terrible," I blurted, somewhat dumbfounded at Hannes' enthusiastic response. I suppose his surprise at our progress was because he knew how stormy the weather had been. I had the feeling Hannes was still apprehensive about our trip. He wasn't sure what type of ocean conditions our small boats could safely handle.

"You and Harry are making fast progress. How many miles can you paddle a day in those kayaks anyway?"

"Well that all depends on the seas. On a good day we can cover anywhere from twenty-five to thirty miles."

"That much, hmmm. Where are you headed to next?"

I had to smile before answering. Hannes always asked that question, and how long it would take us to reach a particular port. This was a most leading and difficult question to answer. If the estimated time of arrival was surpassed, Hannes would worry and possibly send out a search party. This might cause him to cancel the trip so, to play it safe, I always padded our projected arrival by a healthy margin. Our next port was a major town of five thousand people, nearly 150 miles along in the far northwestern section of the country.

"Isafjordur. It'll probably take us ten to twelve days, weather permitting," I told Hannes. "By the way, are there usually this many storms this time of year?"

"No, our weather patterns have been unusual. It's been one of the worst summers we've had. With any luck you should see an improvement soon. You be careful now."

The following day, the seas were still huge from the strong north wind, so we wandered about the small village, leisurely passing time. We stopped to chat with a resident of Flatey and soon had an invitation for coffee and bread with the fisherman and his family. Little English was spoken, and sign language became our major form of communication.

Rows and rows of large wooden drying racks were erected about the village for curing some type of fish. Harry and I were very curious about these man-made forests of racks. Upon questioning the fishermen, we discovered that the fish were called lumpfish. The female is marketed for the roe, which is sold in the Orient as caviar. Our curiosity earned us an invitation for lunch and the opportunity to taste the lumpfish. Our hosts told us that many people dislike the meat but most local fishermen think it's quite good.

A huge platter of the boiled white fish, which looked much like halibut, was set before us. With the thought of enjoying an authentic Icelandic dish, I eagerly dug in and placed several hunks on my plate. The smell of the fish from the hot steam rising off the flesh surprised me. It was quite pungent and unappetizing. I warily placed a forkful in my mouth and . . . ugh! I nearly choked on the foul-tasting fish. It was absolutely unpalatable, and I am not a "picky" eater by any standards.

I self-consciously glanced at my hosts to see if they had observed my displeasure and then at Harry to see how he was surviving the ordeal. Everyone, including Harry, was carrying on as if they had just eaten a delightful dessert, talking and laughing about other matters. No one else was having difficulty consuming their portions. I force fed myself as much as was humanly possible without gagging, attempting to cover my distress gracefully. When Harry reached over for another helping, I whispered that he was more than welcome to the last piece on my plate.

"Did you enjoy the lumpfish?" asked one of my hosts.

"Oh yes, it was very good," I lied. "I thoroughly enjoyed the meal." What was really going through my mind was that I would forever remember that first awful mouthful of lumpfish and the mere sight, smell, or thought of lumpfish would undoubtedly cause me to gag.

Away from our guests, I thanked Harry for coming to my aid in a time of crisis. Harry admitted the fish was a bit on the strong side, even though he *truly* does eat anything.

Back at the village harbor we watched a small fishing boat

land. It had just come in from a storm. A dead seal was tossed onto the wooden dock.

"Why did they bring the seal back with them instead of dumping it overboard?" I asked a nearby onlooker.

"For the bounty," he said emphatically.

"Bounty? There's a bounty on seals?" I asked in astonishment.

"Yeah, fishermen hate 'em. They kill the cod."

My later research helped me understand the issue. Cod is the most lucrative fish for the Icelandic fishing industry, but seals serve as a host species for a parasite that infects the cod. The fishermen go after these seals with a real vengeance. No wonder the seals we saw were reclusive. In fact, all the marine mammals we anticipated observing on the trip were few in number and limited to an occasional porpoise or seal. Icelanders hunt whales for "scientific purposes" taking about thirty of the leviathans each year. Not surprisingly, we neither heard nor observed any whales during the entire trip.

Aided by a week of fair weather, we glided by the butte-shaped mountains of the west, arriving in Isafjordur well under the estimated time. With over three hundred miles of paddling behind us, we had completed a fourth of our circumnavigation.

"Which fishing boat did you get a ride with John? You must be cheating." Hannes was quite impressed with our headway and didn't hide his amazement and enthusiasm. This was the first time the elements of doubt and persuasion did not pervade our telephone conversation.

"We finally had the weather on our side."

"Speaking of the weather, you may have trouble ahead. Sea ice has broken off the Arctic ice pack and has been pushed near the north shore by strong winds," Hannes warned. "It's so extensive that even the larger trawlers can't find a route through. You might want to wait a few days to let the ice clear out."

If the ice was that massive, I wondered how we would manage. My first experience with an ice floe was in Alaska where calving glacier ice had closed a fjord. I assumed that the ice would part at the bow of my kayak as I paddled through the floe. After all, the chunks of floating ice were rather small.

Wham! The bowling ball-sized chunk I hit nearly tore off my bow causing me to pitch forward with such force that I almost capsized. Glacier ice, as I learned, is simply more dense and heavier than regular ice. I was lucky it didn't puncture my thin fiberglass hull.

Now Harry and I were faced with the obstacle of a huge ice floe. Even if there was an open lead near shore, we could get crushed between minibergs wedged against the land by wind. I hoped a change in wind direction would occur to ease the ice jam before we reached the critical area. If not, our accelerated progress would come to a grinding halt.

It wasn't long after setting off that the seas began to build. Soon we were battling six-foot waves and surfing along on a stiff tail wind. I had brought small spinnakers along to take advantage of such conditions. Aided by steady winds, we could cover fifty to sixty miles in a day. Now the spinnakers were deployed, and we surged ahead. Since we didn't use our paddles, except to brace or balance, the wind and cold water quickly cooled our bodies causing us to shiver—the first warning signs of hypothermia. We donned extra clothing to keep warm.

I could not believe how fast we were moving. At times, while surfing down the smooth wave faces, our bows would dig in and throw icy spray in our faces. This "bow plowing" was unnerving and pushed the limits of sane sailing. After several bow plows, both Harry and I reefed the spinnakers to rest from the adrenaline coursing through our bodies.

Suddenly, to the north, I spotted something glistening white near shore. Pack ice! We dropped the spinnakers to see if there was an ample lead ahead to pass through. A wrong decision could mean getting our kayaks crushed and splintered between mammoth blocks of drifting sea ice. We cautiously approached, apprehensively assessing the situation. There seemed to be open water near shore so we slowly paddled forward. To our relief, a long narrow channel enabled us to squeeze by an ice mass. We hoisted sails again and went speeding off.

Overhead the sun disappeared behind thick gray clouds, and the air turned bitingly cold. To our astonishment, giant wet snowflakes fluttered from the sky. With a stiff wind at our backs and surrounded by sea ice and falling snow, we had little choice but to keep moving. The lead was open for the entire four kilometers where the ice abutted the shoreline. Having covered thirty-one miles in little over five hours, we felt quite justified in putting ashore to camp after passing the main ice floe.

The weather dramatically improved enabling us to make good progress. I was able to paddle shirtless in the warm sun down the mountainous forty-mile fjord to Akureyre—the half-way point in our trip.

The few storms we encountered were shorter in duration than the frequent two- and three-day blows experienced on the first segment of the trip. Many of the winds were ideal for sailing because they built to a certain velocity then remained constant for the remainder of the day. The miles began to slide by quickly, and our final goal seemed much more attainable.

After a fifty-mile paddling and sailing day, Harry and I arrived quite exhausted at a large peninsula on the northeast shoreline. We were surprised to find a small green tent pitched on barren ground near a cement lighthouse. It belonged to a Swedish couple who had hiked in from a nearby road. We hadn't encountered any backpackers or campers along the coast before so it was a delight to have company.

The northernmost point of the peninsula we were near was only a mile and a half from the Arctic Circle. Harry and I wanted to paddle across this imaginary geographic line so we unloaded our kayaks and pushed off into stormy seas. It was a thrill to maneuver our empty boats in a eight-foot waves. Being tossed and jostled about, a feeling that was frightening for us at the journey's beginning, had become routine after nearly eight hundred miles of paddling.

The two Swedes looked on in amazement as we bounced around in the steep waves. Upon our return, they told us our kayaks looked incredibly tiny amid the turbulent seas—like two pieces of straw tossed into rapids. They had no idea kayaks could withstand such hydraulics, and they cordially invited us over for a celebration of fresh green cucumbers and canned shrimp on Swedish brown bread (supposedly the Swedish tradition for anyone crossing the Arctic Circle). This culinary treat was a welcome change from our standard fare of dried food.

The Northeast Cape of Iceland was our next goal. A major split in the arctic currents at this peninsula results in some very confused seas. During periods of stormy weather, huge boils and upwellings begin to form. The cape is composed of black volcanic rock with precipitous walls along its entire length; rebound or "clapotis" waves add to the currents, compounding water turbulence. Knowing this, we decided to paddle around the cape in the best weather possible.

We made camp on the last landing site before the sea cliffs, eighteen miles short of the peninsula tip, with the hope of rounding the treacherous point the next day. Stormy weather moved in that evening and, for two days, Harry and I anxiously waited for better conditions. On the morning of the third day, we became impatient and tempestuously pushed off to paddle the cape in adverse conditions. The closer we came to the peninsula's tip, the worse the seas became. Huge waves rebounded from the towering rock walls with no predictable rhythm or periodicity. It was a bucking bronco ride all the way.

The stern of my boat would rise on a ten-foot wave, then suddenly slam down into a trough simultaneously as the bow was forced up on a huge rebounder. These violent seas created intense paddling conditions, and Harry and I found ourselves constantly bracing to keep upright. After what seemed like hours, we finally entered calm waters on the southern side of the peninsula. We reveled in having put a major obstacle behind us.

We were now nearing the one thousand-mile mark of our journey and were headed for the town of Neskaupstadhur on the mountainous eastern coastline. Paddling across the six-mile mouth of a deep fjord along this coast, I had unexpected rudder problems. It was a quartering sea of large size, so the sudden erratic behavior of my kayak was quite apparent. Peering over my shoulder, I saw that one of the two brackets that secured the rudder to the stern of the boat was severed. I cursed myself for my present plight. I had neglected to repair the tiny crack in my rudder bracket caused by my bad landing early in the trip. Now I was paying for my negligence.

We were two miles off a point with a lighthouse and adjacent farm so we steered in that direction hoping I could somehow fix my rudder. Upon beaching the boats, we found three young women pitching hay into a barn loft. Their English was quite passable so they understood my rudder problems. The husband of one of the women was driving his wagonload of hay to a barn and would be arriving shortly. In the meantime all work was stopped, and we were cordially invited in for fresh coffee and bread.

The woman's husband, Marizibil, soon appeared and he obligingly located a piece of metal in his shop. But the temper of the metal was just too hard for a drill bit to penetrate, and it was impossible to drill the required holes. A cutting torch was then pulled out and by repeatedly heating the spot for the hole to molten metal, then using a drill press, Marzibil was able to finally punch a rough hole through the tough steel. By the time the second hole was drilled, a full two hours had passed. I was most grateful for the time Marzibil had spent on manufacturing a rudder bracket for my boat.

"How much do you want for fixing my rudder?" I asked.

"No no, I want nothing. I'm sorry I couldn't do a better job," he apologized.

"Well thanks, but I really must give you something for it."

"No, I don't want anything," he said. Then after a moment's hesitation, he smiled, "But you could do something for me."

"What's that?"

"Write me a letter in English." My puzzled look prompted him to continue, "I speak English very poorly, but I read it very well."

Icelanders are an insular folk. With only 242,000 of them, they're very concerned with preserving their Viking heritage. Most Icelanders stay in Iceland all their lives. Very few embraced an adventurous spirit, which made our journey seem all the more incredible and surprising to them. Though being a reserved people, those we encountered were curious about our trip. Their curiosity broke down the reserved demeanor almost immediately.

The broken rudder incident is representative of that wonderful Icelandic hospitality. They interrupted their work unquestioningly and devoted their time and concern to us, be it our need for help, for directions, or just for conversation. Compared to the fast-paced world of the United States, we found this selfless attitude most charming.

None of the ocean conditions thus far encountered were a surprise. The North Atlantic Ocean has a reputation of being one of the worst seas in the world. Strong winds, cool weather, and cold water, in combination with swift ocean currents, create extremely hazardous conditions. During bad weather, major peninsulas become areas of confused seas with boils, upwellings, and rebounded waves from steep sea cliffs. Forty-degree water makes hypothermia a constant threat. All these conditions add up to the most demanding and potentially dangerous paddling I have encountered. No wonder the Icelanders were incredulous when we told them of our plans. One fellow remarked, "Icelanders go out onto the ocean to work, not to play."

The southern coast of Iceland is 250 miles of virtually uninterrupted black sand beach. If the weather deteriorates along this stretch, there's no place to land other than possibly at the river mouths, which empty into the ocean along the coast.

There are three tiers of sand beneath the ocean's surface at the shoreline. In extremely bad winds, all three tiers will create huge hydraulics, forming a surf zone that will sometimes stretch for several miles offshore. To attempt a landing under these treacherous surf conditions could severely injure body or kayak.

The entire coastal area has a notoriously bad record for fishing boats getting stuck when traveling too close to shore. Once a boat is pushed inside the first tier of sand, there is little hope of saving it, let alone the fisherman. Scattered along the coastline are orange emergency shelters outfitted with stoves, clothes, food, and a radio, which is monitored twenty-four hours a day.

With the introduction of radar, navigating this treacherous shoreline was thought to be eminently more safe for fishing vessels. Such was not the case. The low profile shoreline is backed by mountains, and the radar rebounds off of them, not the shoreline, thus giving boats a false reading as to where the actual shoreline is.

With all of this in mind, Harry and I cautiously embarked for the town of Hofn on the southeastern coast where the sand beach begins. We packed extra clothing and double lunches just in case we had to sit out bad weather offshore.

A sudden brisk wind out of the west stopped our progress

seventeen miles short of Hofn. Two small rocky islands offered refuge from the blow, so we spent most of the afternoon and early evening waiting out the wind.

The islands are a nesting site for fulmars. Having time to pass, I thought it would be fun to photograph the chicks snuggled in shallow burrows. A close-up of one of these cute feathery creatures would make a great picture. Approaching an occupied burrow, with the sun at my back, I pushed my lens to within three feet of one of these helpless chicks. Much to my surprise, the chick regurgitated a putrid orange liquid nearly hitting me in the face. So much for the illusion of vulnerability. Later, I discovered that another name for fulmars is "foul gulls."

Around 8:00 P.M. the winds began to calm, so Harry and I pushed off for the final paddle to Hofn, which has a protected harbor. Unfortunately, we encountered strong tidal currents and soon found ourselves in darkness thirteen miles from our destination. The weather improved, and the seas continued to settle making our night paddling less threatening and almost enjoyable except for the fact that we didn't reach Hofn until 4:00 A.M. By that time, we were both extremely tired from the long night and swore we would never paddle at night again.

A low-pressure system moved into the area, and Hofn became our home for the next three days while it rained. Only fifteen miles to the north lies a small NATO base run by the U.S. Air Force. Out of sheer boredom, Harry and I decided to take a trip to the base to see if they might give us a tour.

Surprisingly, formal clearance at the entrance gate of the NATO complex was nonexistent. We were left standing in the middle of this military installation surrounded by an assortment of gray buildings, totally lost and confused. No uniformed personnel confronted us. After inquiring, we learned there was no visitor tour. We were welcome, however, to use the base facilities and could eat in the mess hall for a slight fee. After ten weeks of dried food, the invitation to eat in the mess was most welcome.

We were standing in line to eat when one of the kitchen help approached us. "Are you military," he asked with a straight face.

Military? I almost laughed aloud. There we stood with

full beards, and I with shoulder length hair. For a zany moment I was tempted to squint and mumble something about special forces but the slightest provocation might cause us to lose an opportunity to indulge in the buffet laid before our eyes.

Before I had time to answer, however, the soldier standing behind me condescendingly replied, "Aw come on Mark. Get serious. Take a look at these guys!" Mark merely shrugged and charged us $2 (U.S.) as guests for the all-you-can-eat affair that consisted of Cornish game hen, breaded hamburger, and steamship round roast beef.

The fourth time through the line, Mark asked in disbelief, "Are you guys putting that food in a backpack or something?"

"No," I smiled, "we haven't eaten in eight days. How much dessert can we have?"

This put Mark over the line. "I don't care, take it all," he retorted in surrender as he threw his arms skyward.

The weather in Hofn finally broke. Reykjavik lay nearly three hundred miles ahead of us. From Hofn we wanted to paddle thirty-five miles to the mouth of the Jokulsa River, the shortest river in Iceland. Its source was a small lake only a half-mile upstream from the ocean that is fed by a calving glacier. We arrived at the river entrance at about 8:00 P.M. in fairly heavy seas.

All along the shoreline waves were noisily pounding the beach. From the heavy rains, the river had risen and the torrent of water was carrying ice chunks, some half the size of our boats, into the ocean. A sand and gravel bar, created by the rushing waters, formed a spit, which ran perpendicular to the shoreline just under the water's surface. Surf was surging across the submerged spit at right angles to the shoreline surf and mixing with the rushing river water. This created some very confusing hydraulics. Harry tried to enter the rivermouth close to the shore across the sandpit, while I took more evasive action and paddled around the mouth of the river beyond the bad hydraulics to check the opposite shoreline for a safer landing. It was chaotic on both sides so I returned to Harry's side of the river and found that he had already penetrated the entrance and was on the riverbank waiting.

As I headed in a direction that would take me across the

sandspit, I noticed Harry waving his arms. It was too late to alter my course so I pressed on, punched through the sandspit surf. Suddenly I found myself struggling with the strong river currents while trying to avoid ice chunks. When I finally pulled alongside Harry, I discovered why he was so surprised at my choice in landing. Harry had hit the sandspit too close to shore, and once the wave passed over the spit it left him high and dry on the gravel pit only to be inundated and flipped over when the following wave hit. Upside down with his back on the gravel, and no water under him, Harry had to wait for the next surge to float him before he could roll up. My course across the spit had been out from shore just enough that I did not bottom out on the gravel bar.

The Jokulsa River landing taught us much. No way could we count on any river entrance to be a sanctuary. On the contrary, if the Jokulsa was representative, the entrances were to be avoided, at least at the high water levels we were experiencing. With this knowledge, Harry and I were even more concerned about the next 220 miles of unprotected water that lay ahead.

Twenty-two miles farther west of the Jokulsa River there is a rock outcrop that juts onto a sand beach. Our plan was to paddle just that far and hopefully find some calm water on at least one side of the promontory. Again we packed so that extra clothes and food were accessible from the cockpit. We left the Jokulsa River under fair conditions. This didn't last long. A light westerly tail wind in the early morning gradually strengthened and only a few hours after leaving, the seas increased to ten-foot waves. Our only hope was that the rock projection would give us some shelter on the west side.

Upon reaching the rock "haven," we were dismayed to find that this was not the case at all. It looked suicidal to attempt a landing anywhere. At this point, we realized we might be in for a prolonged paddle late into the night. No longer were we paddling to cover distance but merely to keep warm—hoping to save as much energy as possible for long hours in the heavy seas that lay ahead.

The tail wind increased, and the seas grew worse. We began to surf down the front of twenty-foot waves, which curled and broke with a deafening roar. I constantly peered over my shoulder to see how big the waves were, and if they were going to surge over my kayak's stern.

The speeds at which we were propelled forward were so tremendous that it required total concentration to maintain control of the boats, using the paddle blades to help rudder. Ironically, we could see the orange survival huts on the beach every fifteen miles or so but, for our purposes, they might as well have been on the moon. Calm waters were our only hope for deliverance. We prayed this would happen before darkness enveloped us.

At all costs we had to avoid the extensive surf zone along the shore. As darkness fell, we turned our boats out to sea and began to paddle a perpendicular course away from shore for several miles to give us some distance from the threatening surf. With five hours of total darkness to paddle through, we had to stay close together both for safety and camaraderie. But there were problems. The waves were large enough that only one wave separation was sufficient to hide us. If we were side-by-side on the same wave, we could slam into each other and capsize in the pitch blackness of night. A capsize in these cold waters would be decisively fatal. Despite knowing how to roll a kayak upright after flipping in such severe conditions, our fatigue from the extended paddle and the immersion in the cold sea would surely promote advanced hypothermia. Just staying awake would be a problem.

Several unanticipated events occurred during our night paddle. The lighthouses on the shore were a blessing. They were navigational references that kept us out of the surf zone and helped us gauge our progress. More importantly they gave us psychological security. Merely seeing a light in the darkness was uplifting.

I knew that fighting sleep would be a problem, but it soon proved to be the most dangerous aspect of our paddle. Because the seas remained rough throughout the night, concentration and alertness were mandatory. Dozing off was simply out of the question if we were to survive. We kept the boats as close as sanely possible to facilitate conversation, but even with this ploy, keeping awake seemed insurmountable. I was continually splashing icy sea water in my face to stay alert.

I have always experienced an unspoken communication

with long-time climbing or paddling friends when hazardous situations have arisen. Here it was no different. In discussing this episode later with Harry, the thoughts passing through our minds were identical. Both of us knew how real the potential for a fatality was and that whatever assistance could be offered in an emergency would unquestionably be attempted. We also knew that if one of us did succumb to the sea, there really was very little the other could do without putting himself into an identical crisis, which would result in death. This is a strange realization to accept, but when pushing the extremes, there comes a point when you are really on your own despite having an experienced partner who is willing to risk his or her life for your sake.

Dawn finally came after the seemingly endless night and with it calm seas. Because we had lost our horizon line through the five hours of night paddling, both Harry and I were extremely seasick.

Another insult came when we were within sight of a small harborless coastal village. A three-knot current greeted us, and the final ten miles were a long, hard pull. After twenty-two hours of paddling, it was a Herculean effort to undertake.

When we finally collapsed on a surfbound beach, a few miles past the town of Vik, we had covered a total of 110 miles—aided in part by tail winds and surfing. I swore I would never again take on such a long coastline paddle without some sort of stimulant in my medical kit.

At this point in our trip we felt as if we were on the home stretch. The next goal, the Vestmannaeyjar (Westmann Islands), located several miles off the southwestern coastline, was 39 miles away. More importantly, Reykjavik lay only 135 miles before us.

Iceland is situated along the mid-Atlantic Ridge, where two oceanic plates are being pulled apart, creating one of the most active volcanic regions in the world. On the average, there is a major volcanic eruption every five years. Much of Heimaey, a village of five thousand people in the Westmann Islands, was destroyed during an eruption in 1973. There were no fatalities because of expedient evacuation following the incident.

Even more famous is the island of Surtsey, also in the Westmann archipelago, which erupted from the sea in 1963.

This was a unique laboratory for both geologists and biologists. The latter believed that careful studies on this virgin terrain would reveal which plants and animals were pioneer species and how long it would take to establish breeding populations. Thus, the island was deemed off limits to all but scientists. Even with the decline in the biological and geological studies over a twenty-three-year period, Surtsey was still off limits when we arrived in the Westmann Islands.

Knowing this background made a journey to Surtsey all the more enticing. Local police told us we could paddle to the volcanic island as long as we did not tell anyone. Early the following day we left for Surtsey—an eighteen-mile paddle—before the authorities changed their minds.

It was an odd feeling to step onto Surtsey's sandy shore, a land that was so new. Vegetation was sprouting in circular patterns over some of the volcanic ash and rock, but for the most part the island was barren. There were some tiny steam vents in the area around the two craters, located on the north side of the five hundred-foot rise in the center of the island. By scraping away the top inch or so of rock in some spots, the earth beneath was so warm I had to lift my hand away after only half a minute.

Harry and I spent the entire sunny day walking around the small island, exploring the craters and steam vents, and just enjoying the feeling of creation that hung in the air around us. This unique place exuded an ineffable aura of primordial newness.

Returning to Heimaey, I informed Hannes that we were departing for the final leg of our journey and would be in Reykjavik in a few days. He was most anxious for our arrival because he had plans, too. The Icelandic Lifesaving Association gets its funding from the government each year, and it is necessary for them to justify their budget requests with concrete data. Hannes could use us an an example of yet another area for potentially expensive rescues.

This was not the sole reason Hannes was excited. Through the course of our trip a real friendship and respect had developed. Hannes had an appreciation for what we were accomplishing. He was a ranked captain and had fished for many years in the same waters we had paddled.

Rounding the last headland on August 28 to catch our first
glimpse of Reykjavik was an incredible thrill. Excitement
stirred in our hearts as we approached the harbor entrance.

My thoughts drifted back to the land and the ocean we
had explored and the people that touched us with their kind-
ness. The reason for our journey, so often lost amidst the routine of endless paddling, was once again extremely clear and
intensified. The events, experiences, and memories that Harry
and I shared over the previous three months would stay with us
a lifetime.

Suddenly we were in the harbor and surrounded by newspaper, radio, and television crews pushing microphones in our
faces, shouting out questions and blinding us with lights and
camera flashes. I was confused and a bit stunned by the sudden
flurry of activity and the palpable intensity emitted by the
people around me. What did this all mean to them and, more
importantly, to me? The daily paddling, exploring, and camping was a life unto itself. Our needs and demands centered
solely on these activities. Consequently, our values were oriented toward wilderness survival. Now I found myself immersed in an encounter with civilization. I was in a state of
limbo—somewhere between a wilderness and civilization mind
set. It was as if I wasn't part of the whole scenario but dis-
placed, an outside observer watching it all unfold. This became
even more evident when a television crew had us repeat our
arrival three times so they could get the scene just right. It
meant everything to them and so little to me!

Harry said it all too well, "If this is what you have to deal
with when a trip is funded, I'm really not very interested."

It was bad enough at the journey's end to encounter the
press, but visions of people and camera crews descending from
all corners in the midst of pristine wilderness, to catch you "in
the action" on videotape or film, is bordering on sacrilege.

Our moment of glory had passed quickly, but this was
most insignificant in comparison to the experiences Harry and I
shared. Nowhere, to my knowledge, do stronger bonds of
friendship develop than when two people share harrowing
times and come to realize that they are putting their lives in
each other's hands. An ultimate trust develops, and that trust

revolves around the fact that you know you will risk your life for the other person just as they would for you.

The shared experience of exploring new terrain and seeing spectacular scenery adds more emotional interchange, and bonds draw even closer. Much of my personal security lies in my friends and knowing that they would do whatever necessary if I had to turn to them in a time of physical or mental need. Through all my outdoor experiences, be it climbing, skiing, or paddling, I have managed to draw and tie these bonds with my compatriots. This bonding has contributed immensely to my character and my positive attitude toward life and what it has to offer. Consequently, I shall live and die a happy fulfilled person.

Harry and I spent three months paddling 1,450 miles to accomplish our goal—the circumnavigation of Iceland. For us, this was an event in our lives, a period of our existence that was truly lived and will never be forgotten. If asked what I did the summer of 1986, I could recall with clarity exactly how I had spent my life in that summer, and I would once again be reminded that my time was not wasted. Time to me is the most precious commodity in this life, far surpassing the quest for money and power that so many people in this day and age seem to live for.

In addition to his circumnavigation of Iceland, JOHN BAUMAN has paddled nine hundred miles along the east coast of the Baja Peninsula to Cabo San Lucas and a thousand miles in the Aleutian Islands and Aleutian Peninsula. His canoe expeditions include several long-distance trips through Manitoba.

Apart from sea kayaking, Bauman divides his spare time among skiing, mountaineering, rock climbing, and canoeing.

He finances his extended outdoor trips by working as a finish carpenter in Anchorage, Alaska.

WILL NORDBY

Glacier Bay Discoveries

Sssh, whoosh, ssssh. Cold spray whipped back from my plunging bow. Whoooosh. Then flared across my rising deck . . . sssssh . . . leaving a shimmering trail of water beads. Whooosh.

"Hey, Cheechako [greenhorn]," Icy Strait seemed to be saying, "pay attention."

Believe me, I was. This was my first kayak journey in Alaska's panhandle, and while crossing treacherous windswept Icy Strait to Glacier Bay, I felt a need to be more wary than on previous trips along the coast of British Columbia. Alaska seemed huge, unpredictable, and unforgiving by comparison. Fortunately, I was not alone.

To my left, wiry Bob Hultman paddled his self-crafted yellow kayak in strong, measured strokes. Bob, wearing an orange watch cap and muffled in a salt-and-pepper beard glistening with sea spray, was enjoying himself. Slightly behind us was LeRoy, my brother and our trip leader. He had an enduring curiosity and a spirit of adventure for new places to kayak. In past summers he had led extended saltwater tours along the coast of British Columbia. It was on such a trip to Alert Bay, that I was introduced to sea kayaking. Although inexperienced, I came away intrigued with the idea of exploring wilderness areas by kayak.

Sssssh, whoooosssh, sssssh. Now I faced an expanse of menacing whitecaps, which snarled like a pack of wild dogs before

me. The long prow of my kayak pitched and yawed in four-foot
waves as I tried to paddle a straight course to Pleasant Island,
five miles ahead.

We were outward bound six hours from the small Tlingit
village of Hoonah, having launched at 6:00 A.M. under dark
clouds and a light rain. Our immediate destination was the
campground at Bartlett Cove in Glacier Bay National Monument. For the coming week, we planned to explore northward
until we reached Muir Glacier, then return to Hoonah for the
connecting ferry ride home to Seattle. We hoped the fickle
weather would cooperate.

Halfway across the tossing strait I looked back at Chicha-
gof Island. Its diminishing profile was a peaked and valleyed
line whose green contours were changing as tree-hugging
clouds drifted over the island in serpentine masses.

"Looks like a good time to put up my kite," LeRoy shouted
over the wind. Bob and I paused to watch him unfold a multi-
colored parafoil kite.

"No use paddling when you can use wind power," LeRoy
chuckled while lofting his kite into the strong southeast wind.
Bob and I would just have to content ourselves with good old
muscle power.

Paddle, recover, paddle, recover, paddle, recover. The
rhythm seemed endless as the foam-flecked sea sprayed over my
bow dowsing me in cold salt water.

I was concentrating on reaching Pleasant Island to such a
degree that I was oblivious of my surroundings except for Bob
to my left. Nearing shore, it struck me that I had not seen
LeRoy for some time. Surely he must have reached shore already, but no, he was not there.

"Where's LeRoy?" I shouted across to Bob. He quickly
took out his binoculars and glassed the area.

"Don't see him," came the concerned reply.

My pulse quickened. Questions flashed through my mind:
What should be done? Paddle back? Wait here? Notify someone? With frightening suddenness, the trip hung in the balance.

Now, instead of an invitation for exploration, the environment became a place of danger, of hostility. This ominous feeling was enhanced by a charcoal curtain of low-lying clouds

blowing across Icy Strait. Bob and I drifted in silence intently surveying the area where we last saw LeRoy.

My senses were attuned to the slightest movement. Waves lapping on the shore became the predominate sound, accompanied by a vast drone of restless water. Slowly the minutes passed . . . five, ten, fifteen, twenty. I began to expect the worse: an accident, a drowning? I wanted to believe otherwise. But reality was staring me in the face. Damn, if only I could reverse time to have prevented this from happening. I felt empty, numb, afraid of the truth. No matter, I would have to go back and look.

Heartsick, I turned to paddle back across the strait. In doing so I idly glanced at the southwest sky. What was that black speck? A seabird? I squinted against the wind. That's no seabird, that's a kite!

"He's way to the south of us," I yelled excitedly to Bob. Bob directed his binoculars to where I pointed.

"Yeah, that's him all right. But what the hell is he doing over there?"

"Good question," I mumbled. "Damn, what a scare."

A half hour later LeRoy landed and joined us on the beach. He explained that the wind shifted and started pushing him to the west, and he had not been able to untie his kite line or locate a knife to cut it. He tried yelling to us but his voice was lost to the noisy waves. So he simply had to paddle against the wind and the strong pull of the kite. The effort left him exhausted. He certainly welcomed the chance to rest and eat lunch.

For my part, the experience reinforced the need for constant vigilance in monitoring my companions. Trouble could arise suddenly in this vast and unpredictable environment. It was sobering to realize that the nearest outside help could be hours away.

High overhead the sun peeked through bald spots in the shifting cloud cover and teased us with warmth. The scattered rays danced over Icy Strait's scalloped surface creating a flickering sheen of burnished gray. And though the strait seemed calmer now, we were grateful to have that capricious stretch of water behind us.

Others who had passed this way undoubtedly felt the

same. In October 1879, almost 101 years before our arrival on
Pleasant Island, explorer-naturalist John Muir and Presbyte-
rian minister S. Hall Young, with four native guides, stopped
along this western shore one afternoon. One of the natives,
Sitka Charley, having been to Glacier Bay as a boy with his
father, had warned Muir that he would not find any wood
there. Although Muir and the others were skeptical, they
heeded Sitka. Upon landing, they warmed themselves with coffee and loaded firewood aboard their thirty-five-foot canoe for
use at campsites in Glacier Bay. Young, mindful of the threatening skies and surrounding windblown waters, named the
place Pleasant Island because, " . . . it gave us such an impression of welcome and comfort."

Our lunch break ended when the peeking sun disappeared
behind drifting gray clouds. Soon we were bucking west toward
Point Gustavus and the entrance to Glacier Bay, estimated to
be the terminus of the area's great ice sheet around 1750. Evidence has proven that the ice sheet did not originate at Point
Gustavus but, like an erratic tide, advanced and retreated over
the millenia before 1750 effected by the whims of the climatic
conditions. But from that time until the present, the ice sheet
has retreated steadily northward with only minor advances.

The first white men given credit for sighting the entrance
to Glacier Bay were those in the longboat commanded by Lt.
Joseph Whidbey on July 12, 1794. Whidbey was sent by Capt.
George Vancouver from the HMS *Discovery*, which was anchored at Port Althorp, to chart nearby waters. As Vancouver
noted in his journal:

> To the north and east of this point [Point Carolus,
> opposite Point Gustavus] the shores of the continent
> form two large open bays, which were terminated by
> compact solid mountains of ice, rising perpendicularly
> from the water's edge, and bounded to the north by a
> continuation of the united lofty frozen mountains that
> extend eastward from Mount Fairweather

The two bays sighted by Lt. Whidbey and his men indented the coastline about ten miles. Eventually the bays
would join to form the main trunk of Glacier Bay.

Will Nordby

Sixteen years earlier on May 3, 1778, Captain James Cook, while sailing on the HMS *Resolution* off the coast, spotted a range of mountains. He named the highest peak Mount Fair Weather (15,300 feet). Aboard Cook's ship were midshipman George Vancouver and master William Bligh.

Aided by the waves and a slack tide, we arrived off Point Gustavus in an hour and ten minutes. The tide, still near the high water mark, was ebbing but we did not notice a current. A flat sandy beach surrounded Point Gustavus and extended about two hundred feet offshore. As we paddled along the edge of the point, we could clearly see the sandy bottom three to four feet below. It seemed like we were flying instead of paddling.

Long patches of kelp hugged the shore. Instead of going around them, our shallow-drafted kayaks allowed us to paddle over them. Occasionally, we had to turn quickly to avoid large granitic boulders lying just below the surface. These boulders, deposited by the ice sheet that covered the area 130 years ago, were difficult to see because the late afternoon light reflected on the water ahead of us.

Once past sandy Point Gustavus, the character of the environment changed as the noise of the wind-driven waves gradually subsided. It was as if we had crossed a windy prairie to enter an enchanted valley. Glass-calm water stretched as far as we could see.

The air was delicately tinged with a blueness that radiated from the nearby Fairweather Range snowfields. To our right, a thick stand of shadowy blue hemlock and spruce bordered the shoreline and spread over the land like a bumpy carpet. Quiet prevailed, punctuated by seabirds calling in the distance or flying overhead. Like pilgrims before a deity, our conversation ceased. Only the rhythmic sound of moving paddles bespoke our presence. Purled water gurgled softly in our wake, then vanished like footsteps erased. Mountains, sea, and forest; our spirits soared in this ecological splendor. No wonder Muir felt such an affinity for this area.

Despite the beautiful surroundings, my body was feeling the effects of having paddled for twelve hours. My sore and tired muscles began to hurt with each paddle stroke. I keenly felt the blisters on my hands. It became a great effort to keep moving forward.

Two hours later we rounded a bend near the mainland shore and sighted the dock at Bartlett Cove where several boats were tied. Most prominent among them was the white-hulled tour boat, *Glacier Bay Explorer.*

As we landed on the gummy clay beach near the dock, a young man, who resembled the singer John Denver, granny glasses and all, was preparing to launch his blue and gray foldboat.

"Hi," we called out. "How's the weather been?"

"Overcast and rainy. Pretty much like it is now. All you can expect around here is maybe three or four sunny days a month."

"Where is the campground from here?" Bob asked.

"You have to go down the beach a quarter mile." Pulling his kayak to the water he nodded across the cove. "I've been camping over on Lester Island. Too crowded for me on this side."

"Well, I'm going down and set up camp," Bob replied, turning to LeRoy. "I'm hungry."

Pushing away from shore, the foldboater called back,

"Maybe I'll see you up the way somewhere."

"Yeah. We'll look for you."

LeRoy and I carried our kayaks up the clay beach. We wanted to visit the park lodge. Both Bob and the foldboater were well on their respective ways as we climbed a small bank near the dock.

We had not bothered to remove our life jackets or spray-skirts upon entering the lodge. We also wore our usual kayak footwear: thongs and sandals. Water dripped from our spray-skirts leaving telltale drops if we stood in one spot too long. Our trouser legs and shirt sleeves were rolled up. In the company of conventionally dressed people, and aware of some double takes, I felt like a bedraggled stork among peacocks.

To our left was a large gift shop. Next to it, separated by a partition, was the kitchen enclosed in dark brown paneling. Opposite the kitchen was the dining room. Here, a small group of elderly people sat eating. Dressed in colorful outdoor clothes, well groomed, in radiant health, and enjoying their food, they happily chatted about the day's events. I mused over the difference and style of our travel. They were warm, comfortable, and eating a luxurious meal; I was wet, tired, and hungry. But as they talked of seeing Riggs Glacier, one of the tidewater glaciers I had come to see, I was momentarily buoyed by their animated descriptions.

Still feeling the movement of the kayak, I quickly relived the day's experiences: the anticipation of starting the trip; the apprehension of crossing Icy Strait; our concern for LeRoy's whereabouts; the trip's rhythm; my acclimation to the magnificient environment; and now, my response to the amenities of the lodge. The changes in mood and feeling were profound— particularly when compressed into one day. The rigors of the raw sea and weather were finely tuning my perceptions. In contrast, the scene at the lodge was alien. It reminded me of the urban routine I wanted to forget. Civilization and a pure experience of the wilderness just did not mix.

Back at the campground, we located Bob as he was finishing supper. Eating stew from his cooking pot, he sauntered over to where LeRoy and I were setting up camp.

"Think I'll eat near your tent so the bears won't bother me," he laughed.

I did not appreciate his humor at all. There was no doubt

that bears were in the vicinity. A sign nearby stated in bold letters, "This is Bear Country." Below that was a drawing of a black bear and a message to keep food away from tents and stored in a campground cache.

Instinctively I looked around to see if anything resembling a bear was lurking in the bushes. I had never encountered a bear while camping and was uncertain how I might react if I did. I knew I would never totally relax in Glacier Bay because of their presence. And knowing that there were brown bears where we were going in Muir Inlet did not help matters either. I would just have to cope with my fears and hope my imagination behaved when hearing strange sounds at night.

After a quick meal and storage of our food in the cache, it was time, at long last, to climb into our sleeping bags.

Oh what bliss for my tired muscles. As I lay thinking about the day's events, LeRoy checked his map and calculated that we had paddled thirty-two miles. I recounted every one of those miles as I nestled within the comforting folds of my sleeping bag. Lying horizontal never felt so good.

Noisy crows woke me the next morning. I rose slowly and stiffly, using muscles that still protested the previous day's effort. For a fleeting moment, I relished the thought of plopping back in my warm sleeping bag. But no, the vacation clock was ticking, and there was much paddling ahead.

LeRoy found that his left wrist had swollen and was very painful from having paddled against the pull of his kite. With a week of travel ahead, he would have to tough it out. He gulped down a couple of aspirin to ease the pain.

Shivering in the moist, cold air, I grabbed my "Short John" wet suit and wriggled into it. My reward was instant warmth and a positive frame of mind as the black neoprene rubber hugged my body. Let it rain, I was eager to go.

Emerging from the red orange confines of the tent, I observed the sky. Through gaps in the mossy branches I could see marbled gray clouds. The view was reminiscent of an abstract painting where dark linear forms screen colored spaces. But this real-life painting was apt to produce a downpour at any moment. LeRoy and I moved to a log shelter and prepared breakfast. Bob, being an early riser, had already eaten and was taking a stroll around the campground.

After breakfast we repacked our gear, and LeRoy went to the lodge to get information from the park rangers regarding possible campsites and to inform them of our proposed itinerary. (Local rangers strongly recommended that visitors participate in nonmandatory registration for their own safety.) While awaiting LeRoy's return, Bob paddled next to the *Glacier Bay Explorer* and began jigging for bottom fish. He had brought a minimum of dried food and intended to supplement it with fish.

About five minutes later Bob pulled in one of the ugliest fish I have seen, a sculpin. It looked like a small codfish except it was a mottled purple gray. As it flopped sluggishly against Bob's kayak, I noticed its distended white belly. The change in air pressure had expanded its air bladder. Bob promptly dispatched it and tied it to his deck. In a short time he caught two more, enough for his supper. I felt uneasy thinking about him frying them in bear country. Park brochures warned that food with strong odors attracts bears and should not be used when camping. Of all food, fish is one of the most odorous.

"I'm going to head up the channel to clean my fish," Bob remarked impatiently when LeRoy still had not returned. "I'll meet you up there."

About the time Bob disappeared around the bend in the narrow channel, LeRoy returned and launched his kayak. While informing him of Bob's actions, I complained about the delay. LeRoy was unsympathetic, being more concerned with the freshly caught fish attracting bears. It was pointless to argue since I shared his concern.

Resolutely, we dug our paddles into the calm water. With each stroke, a sense of commitment settled in as we headed for the narrow channel ahead. Sibling intuition told me LeRoy had something on his mind as he glanced in my direction a couple of times.

As I paddled close to him, he turned and said, "The rangers were telling me about this backpacker hiking along White Thunder Ridge in Muir Inlet three years ago. He encountered a brown bear. It killed him."

I looked at LeRoy to see if he was kidding. He wasn't. My concern about bears certainly was magnified now. Talk about gallows conversation—now I did have something to think

Glacier Bay

about. We paddled in thoughtful silence. Finally, curiosity got the better of me.

"How did they know it was a brown bear that killed him?"

"They recovered his camera. The last pictures were of the brown bear. Apparently he was taking pictures of it just before it attacked him."

We caught sight of Bob cleaning his fish on a rocky beach to our right. Upon seeing us he quickly launched and joined us in midchannel.

As if to underscore my gloomy thoughts, the overcast had become noticeably darker and rain seemed imminent. We were entering the narrow channel that connected Bartlett Cove with the cluster of Beardslee Islands to the north. Like a curtain, trees on both sides of the channel closed off the small spot of civilization we left. Ahead was a silent, mysterious environment reclaimed from a heavy ice sheet.

The rangers told LeRoy that at low tide the channel went dry and passage was possible only at or near high tide. Otherwise, it was necessary to detour several miles around the western side of Lester Island to return to Bartlett Cove.

Maps of the channel area needed constant updating, because the nearby islands were rising at a rate of one foot every eight years. The earth's crust was like a flexible sponge. As the weight from the ice sheet receded, the crust slowly rose—known as glacial rebound. So, what might appear to be a narrow waterway on a ten-year-old map would, more than likely, be dry land now. That was one reason why the rangers strongly recommended that boaters check with them before venturing out.

As we paddled along, the channel alternately deepened and became shallow. Many large boulders lay just below the surface. At low tide the channel would be dry. In a few years, because of the rising land, there would be no waterborne passage.

"There's a bear," LeRoy suddenly exclaimed pointing to the left.

Bob and I looked and saw a large ball of black fur loping noiselessly along the shoreline. The juvenile black bear did not seem to notice us as it continued its rhythmic gait along a narrow game trail. It conveyed an impression of cuddliness rather than threat. We watched until it disappeared around a curve in the trail.

The impassive landscape acquired character with the bear's presence. Yet, its momentary appearance left me with the feeling that I had just seen a clip from a Walt Disney movie. I was surprised at my indifference. Had the bear been bigger and stopped to take notice of us, I may have felt differently.

Rounding a bend in the channel, we noticed that the crowding trees seemed to fall away revealing open water and distant island groups to the north. It was like passing through a long dark hallway from the anteroom of Bartlett Cove to reach a large backyard. The spacial change also brought on a change in outlook. Our field of vision increased significantly, and it was necessary to get our bearings. Haze and wisps of fog obscured the most distant points, further contributing to a sense of mystery and intrigue. Digging into his kayak, LeRoy took out his navigation map and compass to check our heading. The vastness of Glacier Bay lay before us.

The land mass of Glacier Bay Monument roughly resembles an inverted U on the map. Glacier Bay sits within this inverted U and is shaped like a Y. The main trunk of the Y is wider than either of the upper limbs. At the bottom of the trunk is the invisible boundary between Icy Strait and the entrance to Glacier Bay. The trunk of the bay extends twenty-five miles north where it forks into the northwestern (Tarr Inlet) and northern (Muir Inlet) limbs.

Two hours later we reached the northern edge of the Beardslees and took a break. A freshening breeze shaped the surface of the water into sharp flat waves. Like the babble of a thousand sibilant tongues, the drone of whispering water began to emerge. Tendrils of clouds and mist swirled along the mountainous mainland contours. Nature was creating a dramatic afternoon show. But it was a show not to enjoy as a spectator, but to cope with as a wilderness kayaker.

The onset of heavy rain terminated our break. We swung our paddles into action like horsemen spurring their steeds and directed our kayaks northward into the teeth of a rising cold wind. Visibility decreased in the pelting rain. Ahead lay five miles of open water and the dim profile of the Leland Islands breaking the surface, wraithlike. Nothing to do but paddle, recover, paddle, recover, paddle, recover.

Finally, after battling the combined forces of rain, wind, waves, and tide, we gained the southern tip of the semicolon-shaped Lelands at 7:00 P.M. In the failing light of the wet gloomy day we found a campsite above the twenty-foot tideline of a steeply sloping gravel beach.

We carried our kayaks up the steep beach in record time, and set up our tent. With consideration for us, Bob located his tent a hundred feet east to separate us from his fish odors.

Waves crashed on the beach urged on by a persistent wind. Rain pattered on our taut rain fly like a drumhead. Gray clouds still tumbled across the sky and teased the mainland. In the cold moist air I caught the faint odor of fish and, glancing at the dark stand of spruce nearby, hoped I was the only one. With these impressions in mind, I crawled into the tent and the world of dreams.

Morning dawned in muted light under a dome of gray. Puffs of wind still played with our tent, now sagging from an overnight buffeting. At 8:00 A.M. we reluctantly rose and braced ourselves to meet the dreary day. Our clothes lay damp and cold in the tent; unable to dry in the moisture-laden air. Once into my wet suit, however, I did not feel the clamminess.

We were concerned about the weather, and LeRoy consulted his barometer. It read 29.9 and was holding steady, an encouraging sign. The temperature was fifty-one degrees, which, according to the rangers, was typical for this area.

By 10:30 A.M. we were packed and ready to go. It would be another long carry down the sloping gravel beach to reach the water; it was almost low tide.

Good visibility had returned, and the water was calm. The crests of small mountains along the eastern shore of Glacier Bay were fringed with thick, gray clouds masking the entire horizon. In scattered patches, low-lying fog moved on cat's feet to drift among shoreline trees and fill inlets and coves. In a few places strands of fog climbed the fjordlike mainland and lingered momentarily before dissipating in capricious air currents.

Three miles north, a low bank of fog spread across the water and filtered in among the islands of the Sandy Cove area. The fog, mixed with a few clouds, completely blocked any view up Muir Inlet. The eastern shoreline extended like a huge rampart culminating in three main peaks—the highest being 5,139-foot Mount Wright. The northwestern side of the mountain beveled sharply to sea level terminating in Muir Point. It was here that John Muir built a cabin in 1890 as a base for his exploration in Glacier Bay.

In 1845 the ice sheet terminal of Glacier Bay was somewhere near our present position, fifteen miles north of Bartlett Cove. From descriptions I had read, I could easily picture it. Curving thirteen miles across the bay from east to west, the ice cliff rose perhaps 250 feet above sea level. All along its face house-size chunks of ice crashed thunderously into the water. The sound created by this broad wall of falling ice can only be imagined. The Tlingit people were probably the only witnesses and undoubtedly regarded the experience with humbling reverence.

We reached Garforth Island amidst rain squalls and a dark cloud cover. A distinct chill pervaded the moisture-laden air. Garforth lay a half mile from the steep mainland face that leapt majestically skyward. Several streams plunged from Mount Wright's precipitous western slope in a turbulent cascade of spray. A throaty liquid roar resounded in the gloom. It was as if the mountain, now hidden in clouds, was exulting its existence. In the gauzy light, vegetation, clinging to the mountainside, appeared as coarse-textured green patches against a barren background of purple-gray crags and talus.

A cabin we hoped to stay in on Garforth belonged to fisherman George Dalton Sr., of Hoonah, a Tlingit then in his 80s. Dalton had built the cabin before 1925, when Glacier Bay was designated as a national monument. Although we saw small white boat floats midway along Garforth's eastern shore, we never spotted the cabin from our kayaks. Tall shoreline saw grass, laden with rainwater, discouraged us from going ashore. However, the gentle, shelving beach on the island's north end made an excellent campsite. Here, opposite the ethereal backdrop of Mount Wright, we cooked our supper. It is amazing how hot food on a cold, miserably wet day can brighten one's spirits and outlook.

Despite our optimism, the morning light revealed a continuing heavy overcast. We wondered if we would ever see the sun again. But what we missed in good weather, we subconsciously gained in solitude and harmony with nature. This was dramatically felt when the morning stillness was shattered by the noise of the tour boat *Thunder Bay* as it motored past on its way up Muir Inlet. A spell had been broken.

Soon the noise from a second boat speeding toward us compounded the feeling of intrusion. Not until it was near did we recognize it as a park patrol boat. I used my VHF radio to talk to the ranger on board about the weather.

The laconic reply, "More rain and wind is expected."

For me, that reply triggered a dual psychological reaction. On the one hand, it was easy to project myself aboard the *Thunder Bay*, imagining the tourists being toasty warm while drinking steaming-hot coffee. That thought was an escape from the cold and the wet reality facing me. But, on the other hand, I welcomed the challenge of the environment—despite its unpleasant conditions—because it was a test of my commitment to the trip and my own self-discovery. Philosophically, the message seemed to be: appreciate things for what they are and not for what you wish them to be. I was here and had to adapt to the circumstances for better or worse. Nature, after all, cannot be controlled.

After the park patrol boat passed, I helped Bob launch his kayak. He was eager to fish in Muir Inlet so we arranged to meet him later.

Like a well-orchestrated drama, cloud patterns shifted to highlight portions of the surrounding sea and landscape. These grand visual previews enticed our exploring instinct and drew us northward to satisfy a growing curiosity.

Our entrance into Muir Inlet marked the appearance of floating ice, which signaled a new phase of the monument's environment.

Across the inlet, on the left, sloping tree-covered land lay like a rumpled shag rug below tabletop mountains and, passing close to the cloudy flank of Mount Wright, we noticed small-sized trees growing thickly over Muir Point, which was barren during John Muir's time.

We observed further proof of the changing landscape after crossing the broad entrance to Adams Inlet off our starboard side. Above the shore, a new forest of alder, willow, and cotton-wood was taking root. And unexpectedly, a delightful woodland fragrance permeated the air.

Paddling on, we came to more and more ice in the inlet. Few pieces of ice would drift farther south than this; they had already traveled long distances from the glacier faces farther up the inlet. Most had melted. Fascinated by the ice in the water, we forgot the weather. We could see small icebergs floating in midinlet and dotting the shoreline. The character of Glacier Bay changed dramatically as shoreline vegetation diminished.

Paddling past a headland, we came upon an eye-catching scene. Stretching before us, on our right, was a vast alluvial outwash a mile across, veined with streams flowing to the inlet. Scattered over this broad expanse of gray-blue gravel and detritus were several stranded icebergs of various sizes. Never had I seen this type of landscape. It was as if Salvador Dali had created huge, distorted, icecubes and placed them haphazardly on a starkly barren rocky surface stretching to a distant shelf of scrubby vegetation and small trees. This vast Daliesque outwash came from Casement Glacier located five miles inland.

In 1907 Casement Glacier was at the shoreline of Muir Inlet. And, over the years, the outwash extended farther inland. Now, Casement's broad gravel beach linked another smaller outwash to the north. More icebergs lay there like beached whales on the barren gravel of the stream-braided delta. Offshore icebergs, glowing luminescent green within their white ice bodies, had grounded in shallow water.

After a lunch break, we moved beyond the northern peninsula of Goose Cove. We could see up rock-walled Muir Inlet. The overcast had lowered considerably and swirled along steep mountain sides. A mass of icebergs floated in midinlet. Between Sealers Island, lying outside the entrance to Goose Cove, and the eastern shoreline, a huge iceberg had grounded. Approaching it with caution, we could see and hear waterdrops falling from its sculptured form. Counterpointing this melodious plopping sound was a wall of popping, like Rice Krispies. Thousands of pressurized air bubbles, released upon melting, were causing a noise referred to as "ice sizzle" or "bergy seltzer."

Farther north, beyond the boundaries of the emerging forest, an ebbing tide moved ice floes quickly through upper Muir Inlet, which narrowed between towering rocky land masses. Thick mist filled the air, and the temperature became noticeably colder. Time reversed itself by millennia. Our world became a gray and white monochrome.

Against this isolation and timelessness, a yacht was anchored in Nunatak Cove to the starboard. It seemed out of place in this Pleistocene environment. Yet it was reassuring to have people nearby. Should we need it, help was at hand. At the same time the yacht's presence ruined the purity of our experience.

Two gray figures lowered a kicker from the yacht and noisily motored up the center of the inlet, dodging ice. The mood-shattering noise of the kicker was soon lost in the distance, and silence enveloped us once more.

Looming off to our right was the half-light form of McBride Glacier. Its high fractured face stretched about a half mile across. Dirt heavily covered its lower, southern side and a lighter coating dusted its remaining surface. Distinct rumbling and cracking sounds emanated from its face. Long fingers of gray silt discolored the pale green tidewater at its base and spread outward like a fan.

We felt a sense of foreboding and confinement as we continued north. Patchy fog snaked through the inlet eerily illuminated by a bright auralike glow in the distance. Midinlet, fast-moving water hissed a warning as it carried its cargo of ice. Instinctively, we followed the eastern shoreline in single file. The current was not as swift here, and there were fewer minibergs to dodge. Glacial ice is a hazard; being more compressed than nonglacial ice, it is heavier and acts like a fixed object with sharp edges and points. If we were not careful, a miniberg could puncture the fiberglass hull of our kayaks. Consequently, we literally felt our way up the shoreline. Every so often one of us would collide with a piece of ice and hold our breath fearing damage. But the flexibility of the fiberglass met each test.

Mist hung heavily in the cold air. Our main concern was locating a suitable campsite. If any one of us was worried about finding a campsite, however, the thought was kept quiet. There had to be a campsite ahead; none of us wanted to backtrack. The austere surroundings were unsettling; perfect for imagining odd creatures emerging from the mist and clouds.

One Tlingit legend warns of hazardous inlets and passages that contain evil spirits. Among the feared creatures of the Hoonah Kwan people, ancestral residents of Glacier Bay, were: a giant devil fish with tree-long arms; an aggressive killer whale; and a beast having an arm with a thousand suckers. But most feared of all was Kooshta-kah, the land otter man, who lay in wait for unsuspecting boatmen. He had the reputation of capturing paddlers and taking them to live among the land otters. None so captured ever returned. A muffled rumbling sounded ahead . . . could it be Kooshta-kah?

In the diffused light of late afternoon, we passed a small point and came face to face with Riggs Glacier, grandly dominating a mountainside. It was impressive and otherworldly—a huge contorted cliff of snow and ice gleaming white and luminous turquoise in the drifting mist and low gray clouds. Between us and the glacier, a ponderous ridge of boulders and gravel sloped diagonally upward toward the east. This moraine marked the previous location of the retreating glacier. But the most welcome sight was the flat beach area jutting from the base of the moraine; it would be our campsite.

Imagine our surprise and shock when we stepped into the water upon landing. The water was near freezing. Our feet were numb by the time we finished carrying the kayaks above the high-tide mark. And worse, it started raining to add to the already chilling glacial air. We raced and leapt about to erect our tents and to stow our gear. Then we heard it, a faint cheep, cheep, cheep. A small yellow warbler appeared from nowhere and hopped under a nearby rock. We were so dumbfounded to see another living creature in this gloomy rock and ice-strewn environment that we could only stare at this tiny puff of feathers. The warbler stood forlornly alone and shivered. Its misery made ours seem insignificant. We burst out laughing. In a wink, the warbler flitted from under the rock to stand between LeRoy's feet. After a couple of minutes, our little friend hopped into a shelter in the moraine. The psychological boost we got from that delightful visit was tantamount to being whisked before a blazing fire.

Our lullaby during the frigid coal black night was the rumbling and thundering of Riggs Glacier offset by the intermittent patter of rain on the tent fly. The chilling and moisture-laden air was so pervasive that the simple act of turning over in my sleeping bag brought cold air rushing in. I had to keep the sleeping bag tightly wrapped around me to keep in my body heat. Even then, I was still cold.

In 1890 John Muir had crossed Muir Glacier near Nunatak Cove, just south of where I lay shivering. (The cove at that time was covered by the glacier.) While crossing, Muir fell into a water-filled crevasse, thoroughly soaking himself. Night was near so he had no choice but to camp on the ice. And, as he recounted, "Then I pulled my sled over close to Nunatak cliff, made haste to strip off my clothing, threw it in a sloppy heap and crept into my sleeping-bag to shiver away the night as best I could."

The new day brought a slight improvement in the weather. Thin clouds overhead allowed the sun and blue sky to show through occasionally. Extending to the west, a frosty fog layer hovered over the berg-filled inlet.

Early riser Bob, eager to view Muir Glacier, decided to paddle ahead while LeRoy and I attended to camp chores. Not long afterward the tourist boat, *Thunder Bay,* arrived and motored slowly up to Riggs. It carried four double kayaks on its roof. These were quickly off-loaded and four couples paddled to the beach opposite us on the other side of the moraine. The isolation we felt last night certainly was dissipated by our neighbors.

Around noon, we broke camp and paddled to the face of Riggs. Shafts of sunlight beamed down to highlight various sections of the glacier. All the while, rumblings and cracking resonated through the glacier like distant thunder. Every so often huge ice slabs crashed into tidewater sending resounding plumes of spray skyward.

Even though I wanted to get closer, there was an invisible barrier beyond which I was not willing to go. I favored a position a quarter mile away where I could see the entire glacier. From this distance I avoided the intimidation of a looming glacier and falling ice.

Riggs Glacier extends a mile across its terminus and rises about two hundred feet. It is like a giant ocean breaker that froze at the moment of impact against huge boulders. A thin coating of dirt discolors the irregular surface. A multitude of stress lines jumble together to create an angular profusion of shapes and spaces in the glowing pale blue wall of ice and snow. The ice is compressed at the base of Riggs to such a degree that no air is trapped inside to discolor it. The hue of this ice is a vivid incandescent blue. At the eastern edge of the glacier, a turbulent milky brown outflow runs forcefully into the pale green tidewater.

As we sat in our kayaks viewing and photographing the spectacle of Riggs, Bob paddled up and joined us. He said he had approached Muir Glacier within a mile but had not gone farther because of thick floating ice. Having now seen the upper inlet, he wanted to venture on by himself to poke along the shore and fish. After carefully checking navigation charts and expressing our concern for his safety, we agreed to meet at Bartlett Cove in three days. Bob turned his kayak southward and in a few minutes was lost to sight along the precipitous shoreline. LeRoy and I shifted our attention westward to where the inlet was bordered by three thousand-foot ice-scarred escarpments. With crisp paddle strokes we glided forward, our goal firmly in mind. Arctic terns circled overhead searching for food. Their white undersides appeared lime green as they flew close to the smooth glacial tidewater.

I was captivated by the confusion of perspective. Whenever LeRoy paddled close to the starboard escarpment, he would become a mere dot even though he was only a short distance from me. This was caused by a lack of familiar objects, such as other kayakers, between LeRoy and me to help gauge the distance separating us. That unscaled expanse of water, intersected by the massive background escarpment, confused my brain's spatial-coordinate system.

Ice jammed the inlet at the point it doglegged north around a low, rocky point. From our water-level view the inlet seemed impassable. As we came abreast of the point, however, we saw a pathway could be woven through the ice.

A little beyond the rocky point and to our right, we passed a huge sloping outwash left by a long receded glacier. A steeply inclined canyon twisted between two mud brown mountains marking the path of the glacier's retreat. Now, a large stream carried rocks and boulders down from the mountainside. The noise echoed against the walls of the canyon, sounding like a giant rock tumbler. Over the years, rock and dirt had built up to the extent that a broad cone-shaped outwash covered the shoreline. The normally light green glacial tidewater was discolored reddish brown a quarter mile around the area.

In the distance, to our left front quarter, ice floes spread like a field of white clouds beneath a massive gray palisade. Small brown logs seemed to be scattered on the ice. Paddling closer, we realized the logs were harbor seals as numerous bodies turned, heads raised. Then . . . splash, splash, splash. Seal after seal plopped into the water. Seconds later, heads all along our left rear quarter regarded us with great curiosity. A few followed in our wake like jumping jacks, alternately diving and surfacing. Dozens of pairs of dark liquid eyes behind whiskered faces observed our departing profiles. Earlier, during the spring, this area served as the seals' maternity ward. As such, any human disturbance could easily have caused a mother seal to abandon her pups.

At long last our goal was before us. Cloud-wreathed Muir Glacier crouched at the head of the inlet like an ill-tempered lion growling and rumbling, warning us to keep our distance. Resembling a frozen river, the glacier separated to flow around a small mountain before joining and extending to its terminus. Tall, jagged pillars of ice were being shaped and reshaped as softened snow and ice fell away. With startling randomness, the glacier calved explosively into tidewater. Because the high-walled inlet compressed the booming glacial sound, Muir Glacier was more intimidating than Riggs.

It is estimated that Muir's glacial terminus recedes about a quarter mile each year but, on occasion, it has retreated as much as five miles in seven years. And, in the long course of its retreat, the glacier has quarried a U-shaped valley approximately 4,000 feet deep through bedrock, 1,700 of which is below tidewater.

Cautiously nosing our kayaks closer to the berg-choked glacier terminus, we became aware of heavy currents pouring from its base caused by melting ice. In turn, gray mud whirlpooled from the inlet bottom to mix with the green tidewater in an everchanging arabesque. An inexorable flow of ice was borne along on this current. If I paused to take a picture or just look, I soon found myself being carried into the moving ice. If I paddled away from the ice, I was carried to the vertical rocky escarpment forming the eastern wall of the inlet. To maintain a given position, constant paddling was necessary.

The environment was a paradox, alien, hostile, devoid of life, and yet dynamic—the raw beginning of life in this glacial terminus. The mother glacier gives birth to icebergs. The icebergs give birth to water. And finally, through precipitation, the water gives birth to snow. The cycle repeats generation after generation. I was witnessing this cycle just as humans centuries before me had and centuries after me will. Time, perspective, and scale—fascinating to contemplate from the seat of a kayak in this booming, crashing, swirling world of snow, ice, water, and clouds. This was indeed a special moment to witness the magnificent forces of nature, removed as I was from the trappings of civilization. To fully appreciate the glacier, one has to be alone with one's thoughts. It is easy to understand how the Tlingit people regarded such wonders of nature in a religious context. A person's ego disappears when confronted on a one-to-one basis with the glacier. Its size, sound, power, color, and beauty are uniquely overwhelming.

But it was too good to last; a motor overhead shattered my reverie. An airplane emerged from the low cloud cover and flew close to the top of the glacier terminus from right to left. The scale was astonishing: the plane looked like a miniature toy. From my angle, it appeared to be flying through the ice. As the plane reached the left side of the glacier, where the wall of ice joined the steep mountainside, the pilot deftly executed a tight left turn and banked into the cloud cover for another pass. Soon, a second plane dropped from the clouds and headed northward over the glacier until it looked like the pilot would crash into the mountain behind the glacier terminus. I watched, spellbound, as each pilot maneuvered perilously close, giving the passengers a spectacular view of Muir Glacier. Then a third plane appeared and repeated the precision flying of the other two pilots. Between the daredevil flying of the pilots, the swift ice-choked outflow, the rumbling glacier, and the picture taking, I was captivated, awed, and enchanted. An unusual combination of history, perspective, and scale coincided in a relatively small space. Technological and Pleistocene entities existed in the same time frame. It would take me awhile to absorb what I was seeing. No doubt about it, physically and mentally this was the high point of the trip.

It was late in the afternoon when LeRoy and I reluctantly turned away from the spellbinding face of Muir Glacier and began our return trip down the inlet. My senses were overloaded from the visual poetry of Muir Glacier—the sight, sound, spectacle—the pure drama of nature. I felt a strong empathy with John Muir who, a century earlier, expressed a similar feeling after viewing the glacier:

> We turned and sailed away, joining the outgoing bergs, while *"Gloria in excelsis"* still seemed to be sounding over all the white landscape, and our burning hearts were ready for any fate, feeling that, whatever the future might have in store, the treasures we had gained this glorius [sic] morning would enrich our lives forever.

Ahead, as before, ice floes thickly covered the inlet. There was not a clear path so it was necessary to weave back and forth to a greater degree than when we had approached the glacier. Occasionally I banged into a chunk of ice and held my breath hoping no damage had been done. One of the reasons I was bumping into the ice was the fascination I had for its fantasy—myriad shapes and forms in endless variety. I could imagine birds, planes, faces, boats, houses, flowers, trees—almost anything—rendered in clear or white ice. And all in a state of constant change as they melted and moved in the ebbing current. When thin ice bits collided they tinkled like wind chimes.

The few shreds of blue sky were soon lost in the gathering cloud cover. Mist crept toward the lower elevations and contributed to a diminishing afternoon light. A veil of fog obscured the inlet to the south and dark rain clouds drifted threateningly overhead. It would be another gloomy wet evening.

As we neared the point where Muir Inlet turned south around White Thunder Ridge, we saw the bow of a huge white cruise ship creeping along near the base of the towering gray escarpment. Scale and perspective came into play again. The ship appeared huge to us in our kayaks, but small against the land mass. It was the television "Love Boat," *Pacific Princess*. We were meeting at a point where ice floes thickened before the tide moved them south. Our course would take us through these ice floes and directly across the path of the *Pacific Princess*. The ship was moving slowly as it prepared to execute a tight starboard turn to give the passengers a close view of Riggs Glacier. Within the narrow confines of the inlet it took great skill to guide the ship, and more so with our presence.

We could see passengers lining the rails along three decks and peering through cabin windows. I felt I was in a fishbowl; arms, binoculars, and cameras pointed toward me and LeRoy. We were in line with Riggs Glacier and undoubtedly, we were among the spectacles to see.

I imagined the passengers: warm, comfortable, free to move around, perhaps wondering how it might be to travel by kayak, maybe even romanticizing about the adventure of doing it. That is easy to do when you have food and liquor nearby in a warm protected environment. But here I was, cold and looking ahead to another wet night in cramped quarters.

Within fifteen minutes the ship completed its turn and headed south. Its public address voice trailed like an invisible wreath of smoke advising passengers of the possibility of sighting whales feeding. The ship vanished into the distance with its disembodied voice echoing off the inlet walls. I smiled thinking about the ludicrous differences between a cruise ship and a kayak. But at the same time I was somewhat saddened, remembering the implications when the first steamboat, *Favorite*, entered Glacier Bay on August 19, 1880. As Dave Bohn noted in his book, *Glacier Bay—The Land and the Silence*, "Steam power had been substituted for the cedar canoe and as a result the Bay ceased to be Indian country at that moment in time. Those who understand wilderness know of the transition, which is irreversible."

It would be three years later in July 1883, when the first tourist steamer, the side-wheeler *Idaho*, would come into the bay. Captain James Carroll took the ship to within an eighth of a mile of an imposing glacier near Mount Wright and dropped anchor. In recording the event in the ship's log, Carroll gave both the inlet and the glacier the name "Muir."

We worked our way through ice floes in the canyonlike inlet and, four hours later, camped on a shale-covered point of Sealers Island near the entrance to Goose Cove.

The familiar patter of rain on the tent greeted us at 7:00 A.M. Because this was the first morning that Bob was not camped with us, we missed his early morning movement; it acted as an alarm clock. We decided to sleep until the rain quit. Three hours later it did, and we got moving.

A cover of leaden stratus clouds layered the sky. The continuing grayness was making us irritable. LeRoy and I argued over petty matters as if they were important. This new day of continued overcast made us believe the entire trip would be sunless. Our spirits were at a low ebb.

After a late breakfast, we packed our gear and set off at noon under sporadic showers. A moderate breeze rippled the water surface as we glumly paddled along the western shore of Sealers Island and continued eleven miles south to Garforth Island. Paddle, recover, paddle, recover, paddle, recover—mile after mile.

Nearing Garforth Island we saw two dark figures sitting beneath a tarp. A small campfire, located adjacent to the tarp, sent up a wispy column of blue smoke. Nearby on the gravel beach was an orange and white kayak of unusual design. As we drew closer we saw a tripod-mounted camera and telescope pointed up Muir Inlet. A teapot steamed over a nearby camp-fire.

We were glad to stop and talk to the two kayakers as a welcome change in our monotonous paddling routine. They were dressed identically in dark green rain pants, parkas, and black felt hats. One had a blond beard, the other, a full black beard. They were from Norway and had traveled from Ketchi-kan by kayak—over 400 miles.

"When did you leave," LeRoy asked.

"June 28th."

It was now August third—thirty-seven days of kayaking.

"How's the campsite?" I inquired.

"It's okay."

"When we were here two days ago," I continued, "there was another person with us who was cooking fish for his din-ner. We thought he would attract bears."

The black-bearded camper smiled.

"I was walking along the beach this morning," he said pointing to the east, "when I rounded that point and came face to face with a black bear."

LeRoy and I exchanged knowing glances.

"We both stood looking at each other for a moment then retraced our steps."

I felt sure the bear had been attracted to the beach by the fish odor Bob left. My earlier concern was justified. The half-mile gap of water between Garforth Island and the eastern mainland certainly did not deter bears in search of food.

We bid them good luck, then LeRoy and I paddled along the western side of Garforth Island. Ahead lay Sturgess Island, five miles distant.

As we neared the beach we were greeted by the harsh cry of an oystercatcher. Soon it was joined by four other oystercat-chers. They formed a flying picket line to protest our arrival at "their" beach. Only after we landed and began to unpack did they settle down.

Oystercatchers are comical birds, the same size and color of crows but distinguished by a long red bill and yellow eyes. When they walk along the shoreline, seemingly their favorite pastime, they bob up and down as if hiccupping and move forward in a slow motion ice-skating step. It appears they are carefully counting all the rocks on the beach.

To our utter delight, there was enough driftwood on the beach for a bonfire even though most of it was soaked by the rains. After a few trys I got a fire started, and it began to warm us. The cheery pop and crackle was music to our ears. As we huddled by the fire, the oppressive cloud cover began to break up. We were delighted to see the sun shine through. Magically the snowy peaks of the Fairweather Range emerged as the clouds thinned. Soon, the setting sun's soft golden glow transformed Glacier Bay from a dungeon of gray to a garden of lights. Visibility increased a thousandfold as did the liveliness of our spirits.

We sat and drank deep draughts of the evening vista not really believing our eyes. The weather transformation was as dramatic and stunning as the spectacle of Muir Glacier. Now light replaced sound as the element of wonder. Crisp silhouettes of trees, rocks, and mountains gradually softened in the sun's fading amber. Water lapped gently along the shore as a broad pathway of afterglow shimmered across the bay to the base of the Fairweather Range, still wreathed in slope-hugging clouds.

It was 10:00 P.M. when I went to bed, drowsy from the warmth of the fire and intoxicated by the beautiful evening. In falling asleep I recalled the words of John Muir on the magical beauty of nature:

> These beautiful days must enrich all my life. They do not exist as mere pictures—maps hung upon the walls of memory to brighten at times when touched by association or will, only to sink again like a landscape in the dark; but they saturate themselves into every part of the body and live as always.

The next morning, as we prepared to leave, Bob was paddling south of Garforth Island near the mainland shore. He could see our tent and planned to stop. Unaware of his plans, we broke camp. Forty minutes later we were headed south again. Bob, drawing near, did not see our tent and figured we had left, so he continued paddling along the mainland near Sandy Cove.

Upon rounding a point, he spotted a black bear rummaging near an unattended foldboat on the beach. The sight caused him great concern, and he feared for the kayaker. As he approached, he began shouting and whistling in an attempt to scare the bear away. However, the bear merely looked at him and continued pawing through the camping gear scattered near the blue and gray foldboat.

"Hello. Do you need help?" Bob shouted again and again toward the shoreline trees.

Ominously, there was no answer. Bob then reached into his kayak for his 8mm movie camera to document the event. As he filmed, the bear continued nosing through the gear until, fifteen minutes later, it wandered into the trees above the beach. Cautiously Bob landed and investigated the boat. Among the scattered camping gear he saw a library book from Juneau and a mandolin wrapped in plastic. Warily looking around, Bob called and whistled once more . . . silence . . . dead silence. Securing the boat to a rock, he returned to his kayak. It would be another day before he could reach Bartlett Cove and inform the rangers.

Oblivious of Bob's findings, LeRoy and I continued our journey southward. In the lower bay we noticed an increasing variety of seabirds. Loons, puffins, gulls, murres, kittiwakes, pigeon guillemots, and northern phalaropes busied themselves gathering food. The haunting cry of the loon resonated across the silky water, symbolizing pure wilderness. Colorful puffins remained at a distance, not wishing to get too close. But the petite phalaropes treated us as fellow phalaropes. We paddled so close that we almost touched them with our kayaks before they moved. High overhead, a V formation of Canada geese flew south honking. An entirely different facet of Glacier Bay revealed itself with the good weather. Undoubtedly, the seabirds favored the milder lower bay to the austere upper inlets.

For our campsite we chose the eastern tip of Strawberry Island. The island, located near the Beardslees, was once the site of a fox farm in the 1930s.

Bob, as we learned later, changed his mind about camping on the mainland shore and spent the night at our earlier campsite on upper Leland Island. Nine miles separated us.

The next day the sun awakened us with its brilliance and eventually warmed us out of our tent. The sky was clear, the water calm, the air brisk. Birds sang in nearby trees. Beads of dew sparkled in the intense sunlight and bejeweled magenta fireweed blossoms. To the west, dazzling white snow freshly mantled the mountainous Fairweather Range. Everything seemed newly laundered in the morning light.

Life, full and genuine, was without a worry or a care. Experiencing nature's beauty on such a morning was an end in itself. No need for a before or after, just a now. To walk and bask in the sun was a luxury. We were free from cringing and cowering in the rain. Perhaps it was predestined this way so we could appreciate the contrast between dreary clouds and this effulgent sunlight. It was tempting to shout in celebration of this grand environment and the enjoyment of life.

Around noon, bathed in sun lotion and high spirits, we launched our kayaks and paddled southeast across the chrome blue water toward Bartlett Cove six miles distant.

As we neared the dock, I happened to look at the pilings and spotted Bob, fishing. We were a group once more. Paddling up we saw he had two sculpins tied to his kayak. We joked about his fish and bears and told him about our conversation with the Norwegians on Garforth Island. It was then he told us about Sandy Cove, and why the rangers wanted him to stay around until the incident was investigated. As a result, our plans for leaving the next day became uncertain.

At 6:00 A.M., while we were still sleeping, seasonal rangers left for Sandy Cove in the up bay patrol boat to investigate Bob's sighting of the bear and the foldboat. Two hours later they arrived at the scene and began their investigation.

At 9:00 A.M. we awoke to the feisty chattering of crows and ravens—some territorial dispute no doubt. Cheery sunlight filtered through the campground's mossy hemlocks heralding another beautiful day. After breakfast we were visited by the chief-of-operations, the ranger Bob had contacted. The former had just received information from the rangers at the site. He told Bob it would be necessary for him to stay for more questions later in the afternoon.

Although we had not heard any results of the investigation, there seemed to be a growing seriousness about it. Word of the incident had spread; helped in part by Bob telling others what he had seen.

The sound of an engine overhead directed our attention to a yellow and white seaplane. Banking into a tight right turn, it landed on the north side of the dock and taxied to a halt. Aboard was a state trooper from Juneau who was going to assist with the investigation. Thinking I might overhear their conversation, I walked onto the dock. But only cursory greetings were exchanged as the two left to fly to Sandy Cove immediately. With a roar, the seaplane took off.

Nearby, a patrol boat was readied by four young rangers. They talked in hushed tones as they huddled in the rear of the boat. It was when they moved apart that I noticed they were carrying weapons—a 30–06, .357 magnum pistol, and 12-gauge shotgun. Obviously something serious had happened.

After our trip, I obtained a report of the Sandy Cove incident (case 1; incident number 800,060) from the National Park Service that detailed the investigation.

Upon arriving at the scene, the rangers saw the folding kayak. Shortly, a black bear appeared at the edge of the trees. After looking at the kayak, and keeping the bear in sight, the two rangers continued into the dense spruce and found a campsite thirty-six yards from the kayak. It consisted of assorted camping gear and a collapsed tent. While they were carefully checking these items, the bear moved toward them. When attempts to scare it off failed, one ranger killed the bear at close range by shooting it with two 12-gauge rifled slugs. A further search of the area revealed, according to the report: "scattered human skeletal remains located about 30 yards from the camp . . . consisting of an intact skull, shoulder blade, long bones, and 4-inch section of spinal cord."

When the chief-of-operations was informed of these findings, he contacted the Alaskan State Troopers in Juneau. A state trooper, acting as deputy coroner, photographed the scene and then flew the remains to Juneau.

The dead bear was retrieved by the four rangers in the patrol boat and returned to Bartlett Cove where a necropsy was performed the next day. A National Park Service biologist and an Alaska Department of Fish and Game biologist did the examination and determined the bear was a four- to six-year-old female. Its stomach and intestinal tract contained human remains.

The victim was a twenty-seven-year-old resident of Juneau. He had left Juneau on July 10 and paddled north to Haines, then back again, and proceeded west to Gustavus with stops along the way. He called his roommate in Juneau from Gustavus on July 27. From there, he continued into Glacier Bay apparently stopping at the lodge at Bartlett Cove. He did not talk to any National Park Service personnel, nor did he participate in the recommended, but nonmandatory, registration system. It was estimated that his encounter with the bear occurred sometime between July 31 and August 3. Could it have been the young man we had met at Bartlett Cove seven days earlier? We did not know. I am sure none of us wanted to know. But the evidence left little doubt.

The day of that awful discovery, for the first time in our Glacier Bay trip, a humpback whale was seen feeding in the cove opposite the campground. Almost immediately, a crowd of people gathered on the beach to observe the whale as he surfaced and rolled his broad back out of the water. Occasionally he would raise his flukes high into the air before sliding underwater. Bystanders stood looking in fascination as the leviathan continued to surface in roughly a square mile area near shore.

Watching the whale brought a satisfying conclusion to our trip after the shocking bear incident. Bob had received word that he would not be needed any longer, and we were free to go.

Before leaving on the return trip across Icy Strait to Hoonah, I felt a need to be by myself to sort out the events of the past week. As a Cheechako I was apprehensive of the unknown wilderness of Glacier Bay, especially from the viewpoint of a kayaker. There were potential dangers from weather, glaciers, sea conditions, and wild animals. Yet to be close to this wilderness and experience the grandeur of the scenery was an enrichment of life beyond measure. Underlying the willingness to participate was the need to be aware of my surroundings, to take the necessary precautions, and to learn the lessons nature has to teach. A common-sense approach but one dramatically reinforced by the trip. Traveling by kayak made me feel intimately a part of Glacier Bay's unique environment and a part of its history—a discovery and a defining of existence, truth, identity. I was still a Cheechako but a wiser one now that I had absorbed a tiny facet of Alaska's awesome reality.

WILL NORDBY grew up in the Puget Sound area of Washington State. Introduced to salmon fishing at an early age by his father, Will immediately developed an affinity for the sea.

In 1971, he began sea kayaking. His paddling experiences along the British Columbia coast and islands of southeast Alaska so captivated him that he began to write about them for magazines such as *Oceans, Explore, Canoe, Sea Kayaker, River Runner, Small Boat Journal,* and *Ocean Sports International.*

Originator of the Sea Trek Paddle Float, a sea kayaking self-rescue device, Will works for KRON-TV in San Francisco as a videotape editor and cameraman. He also serves as the safety chairman for the Bay Area Sea Kayakers Club (BASK).

The Canoe

It was three years before I went back. The beauty of the country still outweighed the hazards and was more important than the bruises. What could I learn to help me make an easier trip on Moloka'i? What equipment could I devise?

Most of the experienced divers and boatmen I knew had seen so many sharks around the islands that they could not share my lack of concern about *mano*. They urged me to use some kind of raft that I could climb on or into.

In fifteen years of skin and scuba diving in the Islands I'd only had one shark encounter, but the lack of such episodes was probably because I rarely used a spear. Certainly I was edible and very vulnerable, but without a string of bleeding fish or the unnatural movements nearby of a speared and dying one, I simply wasn't attractive to sharks. But there might always be that hungry or unpredictable one.

The clan and I often set lobster nets in front of the house—nets here in Hawai'i instead of the traps I'd used for commercial fishing in California. To haul the nets in and out through the surf and rocks, we used an inflated inner tube with a lashed-in center floor of plywood. Would it be more durable than the foam box, and could I climb up on it in case of emergency? I would still need the pack frame though, to carry the rig from Waikolu Valley to the Kalaupapa airstrip at the end of the trip. Also I'd need a pump to inflate it, or else carry the awkward thing all pumped up while hitchhiking from the Moloka'i topside airport out to Halawa at the start of the trip, looking like a giant walking doughnut.

I learned that there were alternate access routes into Wailau and Pelekunu, up and over the top from the south shore. There were no trails then, but some of the route was tagged with small nylon tapes tied to trees. The visibility there is fifty feet through the rain, and it usually rains. In many places the ridges are only two feet wide, but the *uluhe* fern might catch me as I slid off. I could take a machete and chop a route for ten hours a day. It has been done, by Lorin Gill, an Island mountaineer, by Hajime Matsuura of the Geological Survey, and a few other strong competent ones—far stronger than I. Behind a machete I don't have much weight and power, though I float and swim well enough.

Besides, if I walk into one valley with no swim gear, then I must perforce walk out, seeing only one valley and no coastline, and there is no way to walk into the sliced cleft of Papalaua, my mystic valley of rain and *mo'o* and the high waterfall. So it has to be a sea voyage.

Then in the spring of 1967, in the catalog of the Smilie Company of San Francisco, an outfit that specializes in mailorder equipment for backpackers and mule packers, I found a listing and a picture of a small, French-made inflatable kayak. They called it a kayak, but it looked more like a canoe. The bow and stern were only partially covered, and the width-to-length proportions were more like a Hawaiian canoe than a kayak. Besides, canoe or *wa'a* were terms familiar to the Islands. Kayak was part of a foreign culture. Would this tiny thing work for me? I studied the specifications.

It was six feet long with separate compartments of air on each side, tapering to pointed bow and stern, and was inflated by means of a lightweight, squashable rubber foot pump. An air mattress shaped the bottom and could be removed at night to sleep on. The double-bladed wooden paddle separated into three parts for carrying. The whole rig, deflated, rolled into a bag twelve by eighteen inches and weighed fourteen pounds.

I ordered it and hoped it would arrive in time for the trip. I had carefully planned a leave from my job, and had scheduled my summer session university classes to allow for a week on Moloka'i. I could do it that week or not at all that year.

As so often happens, time ran out before I had thoroughly tested the canoe. Chichester and Slocum had the same problem with their boats before going around the world, as did Byrd and Fletcher with their gear before Antarctica and Grand Canyon. Although the twenty-mile route along north Moloka'i was a small jaunt compared to their expeditions, I had problems enough.

Accustomed to inflatable objects, which collapsed—tires, air mattresses, balloons, myself—I was wary of the new rig, so I brought along the foam box that had endured so well. It was the combination of the bulky box inside the tiny boat that was nearly disastrous on this third trip.

Bill Lacy, who lived up the road from me at home in Hale'iwa and has flown into every remote area of the Islands in a variety of aircraft, offered to drop me off by helicopter at Puahaunui, the first peninsula, on his way to a job survey on the Big Island of Hawai'i.

How small the chopper looked at the airport in Honolulu; but I'd heard that Bill was one of the most competent pilots in the Islands, and I figured he was just as interested in staying alive as I was.

We flew low to the western point of Moloka'i, then lifted to 900 feet along the cliff edge and across the settlement of Kalaupapa. The cliffs were three times higher than we were flying now, and the rain blew in rivulets across the bubble shield. It was familiar country to me, yet new each time, and even more vivid so close in and at this height. I saw most of it through the camera's viewfinder, shooting the torrential waterfalls, the blue gray cliffs, and the dark misted Papalaua.

We landed at Puahaunui beside the walled-open area of the *heiau*. Bill lifted off, and when the noise of his motor faded away in the distance there were only the sounds of the wind and the sea. I did not own a waterproof watch, so had brought none. It was sun and belly time from now on.

There was no joy that night. Was I tired or older or lonely, or was the transition simply too fast, from crowded Honolulu to this isolation? A case of culture shock, I decided. But for the first time on these journeys, I wished for company.

The night wind and the rain came as always, but I was warm and dry in my lean-to, and almost comfortable now with the new air mattress from the boat. As I slept, one hand strayed out on the ground and unconsciously flicked in response to the hundred footfalls of the centipede that crawled across my finger. He sank his double claws into the tip; there was no mistaking that pincer bite and the pain, an occupational hazard to those who sleep on the ground in Hawai'i.

The pain subsided sooner than expected. I remembered the first time I'd been bitten. Then, a newcomer to Hawai'i, I'd stepped square on the center of an eight-inch centipede with my rubber *zori*, trying to mash him, but uncertain of which end did the damage. Was it the tail, like a scorpion? No. I learned instantly that it was the head as he twisted and sank his claws into my toe.

I was awake now and listening to the surf, apprehensive about the wind and rough seas. I wanted to read myself back to sleep, but my library had only three choices: a pamphlet on Hawaiian birds, a series of oceanographic articles, and a paperback of the lyric poetry of Edna St. Vincent Millay. It was too dark for bird watching, I was too wary to concentrate on science, and too emotionally vulnerable for Millay.

What I needed was a super anthology for seagoing backpackers that would include philosophy, humor, travel, fishing, and hiker's gourmet cooking, with Hawaiian history, fish, animal, and plant information. That would mean collaboration by Bertrand Russell, Farley Mowat, Sheila Burnford, Ballard Hadman, and Trixie Ichinose, plus Gavan Daws, Vernon Brock, Alan Ziegler, and Heather Fortner all in one book—a four-ounce waterproof paperback, dehydrated.

I fell asleep planning a dinner party for them all here at Puahaunui, along the line of Hendrik Willem Van Loon's book, *Lives*, where he invited compatible people from the past and present. The invitations for Vernon Brock and Bertrand Russell would be carefully placed under that strange wooden deity over there under the *hala* tree . . . a potluck menu, freeze-dried . . .

In the morning I found a quiet place to launch in the lee of Puahaunui peninsula. I pumped up the boat and tried to pack in the gear. The foam box would scarcely fit with me inside the boat, so I towed it along behind. I paddled around the ledge of Haka'a'abim then in toward shore at Papalaua, looking up

. . . the wave lifted, curled with a hiss. . . .

toward the deep-set waterfall of the *mo'o*. On the calmer side of the arch of Keanapuka, I stowed the paddle under the bow and stern and put on the fins and mask, which had been lashed to the boat, then rolled over the side and into the water. I tied a line from my waist to the canoe and swam for shore, giggling under water. Did we look like a line of decoy ducks—me, the boat, and the box—all bobbing along? Or perhaps the humps of the Loch Ness sea serpent? I landed on the rocks with only a few bumps and reeled in the other parts of my monster. No wonder a shark would not attack.

I yelled up the valley to whatever inanimate friends were still in residence. "Hey, hello. I'm home." Some of the driftwood lean-to boards of three years before were still there, carefully scattered in the jungle as I'd left them so as not to leave any obvious traces in the wilderness.

I set to work and cleared away the scratchy *hala* fronds, replacing them with fragrant ginger leaves, rebuilt the shelter, and bathed in the cold stream, clothes and all, to wash out the salt. I wrung out the clothes and hung them to dry by the fire.

Dinner was pork chops, fried potatoes, and applesauce, one of the pre-fab dinners now being packaged for backpackers; tasty, but infernally complicated by steps one through five of taking this and adding that in numerous pots and cups.

After dinner I lay on the matted grass below the jungle, arms crossed behind my head, looking out to the north and watching the stars come out. The high black sides of the valley hid the view to east and west. I lay there thinking of the early Polynesian navigators and the contrast between shore-hugging forays and their months of voyaging into the unknown.

Yet they were quite certain that there was land here. Birds came each year from the north, and left in the same direction. Land birds, not sea birds. Driftwood that had been shaped by man washed ashore, some of it with metal parts intact. Land and people were there in the north somewhere.

Polynesians had seen the Southern Cross revolving around a black void below the horizon. They had seen the Big Dipper swing around an opposite northern pit, which they could aim for. There was no fixed Polaris to guide them in the sixth century. The earth's axis was tilted at a different angle to its orbit, and *Hoku pa'a*, our stuck star, then revolved around true north.

But there were many ways to stay on course. At night they could keep the rising stars of Orion always at the same place on their starboard side. They knew the way back home by the series of known stars rising behind them, and knew how to compensate for winds and currents. They knew the zenith stars of each island. When Arcturus was directly overhead at its zenith, then they were in the latitude of Hawai'i.

I sagged into the ground, my relaxed knee falling sideward, then roused myself and went back up to the shelter. By my rationed candlelight, I pulled the Millay book from the plastic bag. It fell open to "Exiled." She was "weary of words and people," "caught beneath great buildings," and wanted to "fear once again the rising freshet." Yes. That is the way I had been, but now I was here, wary as always, but ready for this place.

The candle was burning faster than the last trip, a different brand. It would not last the week. "It will not last the night." Millay kept fitting in. Next time I must bring extra batteries for the new four-ounce Mallory flashlight. What a strange blend of her lyrical tender yearning and my abrupt pragmatism.

Next morning I went up to the head of the valley again, to the falls and the dark pool, but now the sun was glistening on the *ti* leaves and sparkling on the water. In the warmth of noon I shampooed, using the soap of old Hawai'i, the fragrant and gelatinous red ginger blossom, then rinsed off at the edge of the pool. Usually I swim under waterfalls, exhilarated, battling into the foam, trying to cling to the rocks behind the pounding white curtain, but I was still wary of this pool. The mythical *mo'o* were only sleeping, deep beneath the sunlit surface.

Back again in camp I decided to rig and push on to Wailau. The wind was fresh, but I could not hope for the relatively calm seas to continue. There were whitecaps but no big swells.

I tried to launch from the calmest place along the rocks, but with the pack in tow, even the three-foot shore break was too much. With just the pack it would be okay, or with just the boat. I tried lashing the pack on top of the bow, but it was top-heavy and appeared likely to capsize, so I paddled back toward shore, then swam and towed the boat in. We all took a beating on the rocks. I reached down in the water in the midst of the scramble, and with a quick finger twist, bent a perpendicular big toenail back to a flat parallel.

So I came back, set up camp again, and pondered all the possible methods of taking off. I was worried, and I knew it. The next morning I allowed myself the use of real toilet paper instead of leaves, figuring that every small bit of moral building was going to be needed during the day. I decided to put all the gear in the boat, swim-tow it out through the breakers, then put the box overboard on a towline and climb into the boat myself.

As always, there were the many details to remember: put adhesive tape around the base of the thumbs to prevent paddling blisters; keep the gloves, camera, light meter, fruit bar, jacket, and knife accessible. I was thinking of wind shifts and the 2,000 miles between here and Alaska. If I were blown out to sea, how long could I survive? How long would the boat last? I lashed the fins and mask to the boat.

We launched all right, and got the pack floating fine along behind, but it was a drag, a sea anchor. Two days before, coming down before the wind, it hadn't mattered, but here the wind was blowing toward the west shore of the bay, and the seas had a six-foot chop already. To get out of the bay and around Kikipua Point I had to paddle with the wind on my starboard bow. There was no keel or centerboard on the canoe to prevent sideways drift except for my own bottom curving down through the flexible hull. If I stopped paddling, we'd blow onto a lee shore, the terror of every yachtsman.

Paddle?

Over my shoulder I saw a sail approaching.

"Want a lift?" they shouted.

"Yes!"

"Try to get out to sea a bit farther."

As they tacked the catamaran around I paddled harder, then was scooped up by strong arms—boat box, and all—onto the deck. They scarcely slackened their fifteen-knot speed. The maneuver was elementary to this gang, Carter and Emily Pyle of Hahaina, and two crew members of the winning yacht of that year's Trans Pacific Yacht Race. They didn't even say "what the hell"; paddling this treacherous coast in a six-foot boat was no more unreasonable than sailing it in a light racing catamaran.

We skimmed on down to Wailau, anchored, then swam ashore for lunch. While they sliced a freshly caught bonito into sashimi and opened a chilled bottle of German wine, I pried *'opihi*, the small limpet, off the rocks, and we shared potluck internationale.

Then they headed back the way they had come, up the coast for Maui, upwind and tacking, but with skill and man-power in a boat Carter had designed. Alone again, I launched next morning in the opposite direction with the foam box laid flat inside the boat. There was little space left; I was scrunched into the stern with my legs up on the gunwales around the box, a half-sitting, half-lying position hard on the belly muscles. I was figuring my systems as I went along. In all my reading about the sea, there wasn't any guideline for this kind of expedition. It was all trial and error, mostly error.

The boat was down by the stern, and there was no way to trim. It was raining, the dark clouds lying heavily on the sea. I stroked around the first point, Waiehu, with the wind becoming stronger and the seas steeper. Then the tops of the waves began breaking off. One lifted, curled with a hiss, and broke over my head, half filling the boat. I tried to bail and keep the waves in back of my right shoulder. I dared not look back at them after the first glance, when a twelve-foot sea, twice the length of my boat, came looming up overhead. I was half a mile out from shore, but there was no shore now, only three thousand-foot cliffs dropping into the sea.

I paddled for two hours. Paddle and bail and paddle. It rained harder. When I was in the water, swimming, looking down at the rocks and coral below as I was lifted in the waves, then I wasn't afraid—I was part of it all. Boats were a different matter.

There was a mile to go to round the point into Pelekunu. A tern screamed down, its harsh cry shattering through the sounds of sea and rain and wind. Another wave broke over my head, nearly filling the boat, but it was still floating, responding to my paddle. I could not stop to bail and still steer to keep the waves in back of me. If we turned sideways, the boat would broach and roll over. With my weight forced back by the bulk of the box, the stern was almost awash. The next wave would swamp and capsize us. Turned over, could I cut the fins and mask clear of their lashing, put them on while holding the boat and pack, then tie the boat and pack together and lash the towline from me onto the boat? Perhaps I could. I didn't think so.

Tired, it is hard to get your breath in a strong choppy sea. A few mouthfuls of water, and you gag. Exhausted, breathless, you quickly lose consciousness. I knew at last that I was paddling for my life, gasping and terrified. This was the worst.

Paddle! A whimpering, desperate grunt with each stroke.

The terror filled me to overflowing; it could intensify no further. Dig, stroke, steer, paddle for an eternal hour. Salt tears mixed with salt spray, but I could only keep paddling.

We came around the point, and the seas lessened. I shipped the paddle and bailed out twenty pounds of water, then started the long steady pull to the shore, difficult against the currents of the bay, but no longer dangerous. I paddled on, toward the tiny black sand beach in the sheltered corner. All else around the half-mile bay was rough lava and rolling rocks. I dragged the boat up the sand with the wave surge, then lifted the pack up onto the higher rocks. Paddle, wet gear bag, fins, mask and snorkel, shoes—each item I lifted up to higher ground, then the boat, then I lay on the rocks, limp and trembling. After half an hour I could move again.

I put some rocks on top of the boat to keep it from blowing away, and stowed the paddle and fins inside. I tied the rest of the gear to the pack frame, and started across the boulders toward the trail on the far side, which led to the shack. Along the shore I broke up driftwood and carried it in my hands for a cooking fire for supper.

Coming to a curve on the trail, I stopped short. The hairy black pig stopped too, ten feet away and waist high. I yelled, half in fright, half to frighten him away, and clutched my jagged sticks tightly. He came toward me a few paces, uncertain, weaving his head to get my scent, his tusks curving upward. I grabbed for the camera, but he had turned and run back through the brush. "Camera first, idiot. Yell later!"

The trail was washed out under the *hala* leaves and between the roots. One hole dropped a hundred feet to the rocks below. I had mental images of the pack catching on the roots while my legs waved frantically below.

The shack was in even worse shape than three years before. With tools and equipment I could do a lot toward repairing it. I put a layer of rusting metal scraps on the rotten floor, four rocks to hold my grate, and made a tiny fire to boil a cup of water for soup, then sipped it while hunkered in a dry corner, my back against the wall. At least I had a wall to put my back against. I wasn't assailed from all sides.

It was getting dark, and the heavy rain came through the roof in thirty places. One bunk was a little less wet than the others. I put my plastic sheet on the top bunk to catch the rain, laid my boat's air mattress on the lower bunk, and in damp jacket, damp jeans, and dry socks, lay down to sleep, not quite warm enough and not at all dry.

It rained all night, hard, then eased, then came pounding again, hammering against the walls and pouring through the roof. When I slept I had intensely clear, dramatic dreams. When I woke every hour or so I was terrified. The sea roared, and then the rain drummed louder than the sea, and things went bump and screech in the dark.

Finally the sky lightened. I threw my plastic sheet and some boards up onto the roof, climbed up the cliffs behind the shack, and hoisted over to the eaves. With the boards to hold the sheet down, I made one end of the shack somewhat rainproof.

A cloudburst with lightning and thunder came tearing across the bay in a dark wall. The lightning was nine seconds away, six seconds, three. I tensed, waiting for the blasting shaft, but it passed on. I could not see the beach, and three torrents between here and the shore made the trail impassable. *Maninini*, "the pouring-off place," is what the Hawaiians called this cliff to my right. Had the boat washed away?

Of one thing I was certain. I would not leave here for a while. I would not go on my own unless the seas became very calm. Even the ignominy of being rescued was preferable to another four miles like yesterday's.

I tied my pink bra upside down to the top of a bamboo pole stuck in the ledge outside above the catwalk. It was the only bright color in all my gear and perhaps would serve as an international distress signal. Should a boat come close enough to see what it was, they might be curious to investigate further. Below it I lashed my jacket. Both flew in the wind, but the only planes were high and far away, and no boats passed at all. A wry grimace. "You got yourself here, Aud. Now get out."

I rested and wrung out my clothes in the one dry end of the shack. How could I best prepare for the night? The sun was out only five minutes all morning and even then it rained steadily. The whole bay was brown with mud from the streams. I rationed my food, now knowing how long I'd be here, but was not really hungry.

The one creative satisfaction all day was making a stove candle. I found a jug of kerosene in the sagging toolshed and put some in a jar, then punched a slot in the lid and inserted a folded wick of old gunnysack. It worked fine, shed a bit more light than a candle, and slowly brought water to a boil.

At sunset, after four hours of lighter rains, the bay was almost blue again. I squished along the path to the shore and brought back the boat. The rain had filled it to the brim, and the weight of the water and the rocks had kept it from washing away. For dinner I ate an excellent Lipton beef stroganoff. My morale improved.

I repacked, figuring how to arrange the gear for the morning departure. What could be left behind to lighten the load? A small voice stood off and said, "But promise, Aud, that you'll try it only if the seas and wind are reasonably calm. You know you have no heart or courage for this."

A wave hit the ledge below and threw spray up thirty feet to the level of the shack. I held a pair of green nylon bikini underpants on a stick over the kerosene wick to dry them out to wear under the jeans as another layer for warmth that night.

In years to come what would I remember of all this? The terror, or the splendor of the mountain across the bay this evening? At sunset the top of the mountain reflected a shining bronze from its wet leaves and rocks, while the shadow of the ridge and peak behind me made a silhouette of gray gold halfway up. A rainbow arched over it all, brilliant against the darkening clouds, and out beyond a mile of heaving sea a second, lower, rainbow outlined the black rock of Mokohola Island.

I was not sure that I would go, but I woke before daylight and went outside. The wind had been blowing hard all night; half-awake I had heard it screaming and felt the shack quiver, but now it was almost quiet. There were stars between the clouds. I hurried to be ready by dawn. By 9:00 A.M. the wind would rise and the seas would be choppy again.

By the light of my homemade smoky lamp, I carried out my own terse orders of preparation. Leave a note to greet the next user of the shack, or to someone who looks for me in case I do not make it today. Climb up to the roof to retrieve the plastic sheet to use for shelter if needed that night. Take only two meals. Leave the rest so as to lighten the load.

Lower the pack by a nylon line from the catwalk in front of the shack. Drop down the unbreakables. Carefully let down my very breakable self. Inflate the boat and shove the packsack in under the bow. Turn the foam box on its side, so as to push it farther forward than before, making more room for me and a better trimmed balance. Lash everything in tightly so that if the boat capsizes I can just right it and tow it along, even full of water.

Daylight now and gold in the east. Wear jeans and a shirt for warmth in the water and for a little protection when I land on the rocks. Put on the socks to pad the ankles, and then the fins. Don't tie the fins and mask to the boat; have them on, ready to swim. Spit in the mask and smear the saliva around, then rinse it in a tide pool so that it won't fog up on my face from breath. Check the fastening of snorkel to mask. Put the mask on my forehead and tie a line from its buckle to my shoulder strap. Put bandages on my thumbs, pull on the gloves; my hands are not calloused enough to withstand the constant friction of the paddle. Lash a line from the paddle to the boat, and another from the boat around my waist. Should we capsize, the wind could carry an untethered boat away faster than I can swim after it. I'm learning.

Now. Pull the mask down over eyes and nose and clamp the snorkel in my teeth. Hold the boat and all on one thigh. Step down from the ledge to a jutting rock, awash a foot below. Ten feet to the right the surge crashes up into a crevasse. Surge and backwash. Surge and smash and spray twenty feet high. I threw a piece of wood in here last night and watched it float back and forth. It was not sucked in, but I have had bad experiences with ledges and am wary.

Look to the left. The waves swell across the bay and wash around my knees. Wait for the lull. What lull? I drop the boat into the water and jump into it. The boat tips and I roll out the far side. It's not time to be funny, Aud. I grab the stern, and power kicking with the fins, push it out away from the ledge. Then floating up to parallel the surface, I grasp the far and near gunwales in each hand and slide across and in. Pull the double paddle out from beside the foam box. One detail forgotten. The pull apart paddle is together, but the blades are neither parallel nor at right angles. The joints are cold and corroded. I cannot twist them. The boat rolls and pitches. The waves crash into the crevasse. I push one blade forward and wedge it with my fin against the pack and twist the other blade. It creaks into place.

Now paddle for the first point. The sun is up.

Paddle!

It is only a quarter of a mile. Halfway there already. I do not look back. From somewhere comes a sudden mosquitolike high whine. Air is leaking from the boat. I reach under the hull to the valve but all is in place. The side does not seem to be losing much air. Just paddle. Planes fly with one engine gone. If it loses all the air on one side I can tow it on half a boat and the inflated bottom if necessary.

Round the first point, *Pau'eono*, literally, "the death of six." Don't make it *ehiku*, seven. The two rock stacks thrust upward. I want photos but didn't loop the camera around my neck this time, nothing extra to hang and tangle. Go between the rocks. The one on the right rises sheer a hundred feet above the white froth. Steer around behind it, hoping the lee will cut the chop. The wind builds. Paddle for the next point, Pahu, the drum, another half mile. I wedge my outstretched legs up and over the round sides trying to keep out the slop. The green swim fins stick upright on the gunwales.

Round Pahu Point into quieter water. Pass the ledge of last trip's disastrous attempt at landing where I lost my mask. Keep paddling. Head in toward the waterfall of Haupu Bay. The water near shore is murky from the heavy rains. It is not a sand beach by the waterfall as it looked from a distance, but only a boulder shore. I land easily, find the tiny leaking hole, open the pack, and apply a drop of fast-drying glue. Get out the camera and take delayed-action shots of a grinning voyageur sooty from the kerosene lamp last night and this morning. The most dreaded part is past.

I head out to sea again, past Kapailoa, the long lift, and look into the lava tube tunnel. I've heard of boats motoring from one end to the other, and I would like to try paddling through, but the water is boiling around the entrance, and the rise and fall seem to suck into the gaping mouth.

At the next point, Kukaʻiwaʻa, there is a thirty-foot gap between the rocks. I surf through it on the leading slope of a breaker. Below my left paddle, the lifting wave sucks out, baring the gleaming yellow seaweed on the rocks. Past the two hundred-foot Huelo—black, phallic. Head for the last point, Leina o Papio, a mile to go. Tiring now.

I think I can—the children's story of the little engine. Count one hundred strokes. Count again. Every fifth stroke is a correction to bring the boat back on course. Sometimes the chop is so high that held momentarily on a crest, I cannot reach the water on either side.

Hoe aku i ka waʻa. Paddle ahead the canoe. Lift the paddle, reach, dig, pull, and finally you will get home. A tricky stunt won't do it, a sudden burst of speed won't help—just lift, reach, dig, pull. Each word is grunted with a stroke of the paddle.

Hoe-aku-i ka-waʻa. Over and over.

The blisters break. It does not matter. *Hoe! Hoe!* I come around the last point to Waikolu and start yelling. *Hoe.* Yaaaay! *Hoe.* Yaaaay! A shout of triumph all the way to the shore. I land, haul up the gear, laugh, yell. I made it. I made it. By myself.

I gather ʻopihi to take to friends, then carry the forty pounds of pack a mile along shore and get a ride with some of the kind people of Kalaupapa across the peninsula. The small plane arrives, and we fly to Honolulu International Airport. A telephone call brings my daughter. Waiting for her, I drink a quart of milk straight down. Cars honk, tour buses blast out their black exhaust, the canned voice reiterates, "This is a three-minute passenger loading and unloading zone, please do not leave your car. This is a three-minute . . ." but we head out toward the North Shore and soon leave Honolulu behind. Through pineapple fields and sugarcane acres and small towns I come home again to the long old house by a quiet sea.

AUDREY SUTHERLAND has lived in Hawaii for thirty-five years, and has paddled most of its coasts, as well as parts of Scotland, Norway, Ireland, the Greek Islands, Samoa, and Palau. Since 1980 she has soloed 4,500 miles in Southeast Alaska and British Columbia in an inflatable kayak.

She is the author of two books, *Paddling My Own Canoe*, and *Paddling Hawaii, A Guide to Kayaking in the Islands*.

CHRIS DUFF

The Lucky One

A biting cold wind from the north funneled down the Hudson River, bringing with it the chill of the early spring. The wind kicked up whitecaps near the middle of the mile-wide river and, closer to shore, the first hint of a current swirl around the green channel buoy indicated ebb tide had begun. A week earlier the river had been a grinding flow of broken and jagged pack ice drifting slowly southward with this same ebbing tide. I had followed the progress of the ice for two weeks, watching and waiting for this north wind, which I knew would sweep the river clean. Now, two days after the winds had arrived, the river flowed free once again after three months of drifting snows and ice.

A small crowd of people stood patiently, their backs to the wind, as my boat was loaded with an array of color-coded nylon bags. Each bag had its assigned place in one of the sealed compartments, one forward and one aft of the cockpit.

I had carried my boat alone, dozens of times, across this windswept beach during the prewinter weeks of training. Today, unlike those days, my father and I struggled with 150 pounds of camping and survival gear packed within the two sealed compartments of the boat. A more important difference was that I wasn't going out for a day of training, I was headed south on the first leg of an extended journey.

On the faces of the people waiting for the final send-off, I saw all the questions I had asked myself during the months of preparation. There were looks of concern for my safety, long searching looks at the fifteen feet of fiberglass sitting with its stem cradled in the sandy beach, and quiet thoughtful gazes that I interpreted as acceptance for what I was setting out to do, yet could not fully explain.

As I eased into the cockpit, I became lost in last-minute adjustments: seat, foot braces, water bottle, and spraydeck. The questions that ran through my mind were all familiar and, in the final moments, I found them not as unsettling as they had been just hours earlier. It wasn't that I had any of the answers, but rather the comfort of knowing I was now finally setting off to find those answers.

I came to sea kayaking from a point of need rather than recreational desire, which I see now as a very positive influence on my learning. A strong urge deep within told me that I was no longer challenged and satisfied; my spirit was being smothered with confusion and bureaucracy. It was time for a change. I decided to leave a promising and successful military career full of stress and conflicting ideals to search for a life of deeper meaning and value. By way of a simple magazine article, I was introduced to sea kayaking, and now I was beginning an eight thousand-mile, solo journey based on little else but a need to get away and rekindle my life.

I realized that the possibility of failure loomed large, but admitting this was going to be the key to success in everything related to the trip. Because I had never kayaked before in my life, the odds were stacked high against me but I took that as a blessing, not a curse. To succeed I would have to discipline myself to become better than average, to be aware of everything around me and open to every opportunity for learning. I would have to be very critical in my judgments and in every move I made, because my safety was solely my own responsibility.

I guarded my ego and confidence from success. I knew "ego" had no place on my lengthy journey of discovery, and overconfidence could be deadlier than any wave or rocky headland. To fail after having given my best would not be failure, but to fail because of lack of discipline *would be*.

It was late March of 1983 when I directed my kayak down the Hudson River to link up with the intercoastal waterway in

New Jersey. The waterway, my route to Florida and the first leg of my trip, would be a testing ground.

My first open-water crossing was from the Verazzano Bridge in New York City to Sandy Hook, New Jersey, seven miles to the south. The feelings of apprehension I had looking around and not seeing the other side were enough to make me weak-kneed and jittery. The dreary gray sky made the waters look dangerous and cold and the ten mile-per-hour northeast wind chilled me in the brisk March air.

Once out in the open water, and away from the protection of the land, the wind increased to twenty miles per hour, driving steep waves before it. Sea spray froze on my yellow life-jacket and turned my fingertips into stiff, frozen extensions of my numb hands. Each black wave, with its hissing white top, looked larger and more deadlier than the last. I wondered which one would be responsible for drowning me before continuing to shore as though nothing had happened out on the howling seas. My heart pounded in my chest, my breathing was rapid and shallow, and my body reacted to the surges of adrenaline with tense rigid movements. The paddles flew. First a low brace on one side, then a fast series of strokes between breaking waves, followed by another brace.

After half an hour of being thrown and pitched from side to side like a half-filled bottle, I realized that what was driving me into this state of half panic was not the waves and the winds, but my mind. I forced myself to calm down and concentrate on a circle fifty yards around the boat rather than watching the thin line of shore four miles away. I worked hard to slow my breathing. Once in control of my body, I began working on my mind.

I thought about the words "calm" and "relax" and, except when the waves broke on the boat, I mentally repeated them over and over. Gradually my upper body began flowing with the elements rather than stabbing at the water. I calmly watched each approaching wave and knew how I would react when it reached me. I knew I would never make it across the remaining few miles by sheer power. The only way to survive the chaotic heaving of the sea was to grind along at a slow, determined pace. The fear of dying, with no one even knowing where I was, was forced from my mind.

Slowly, by the hour, the shoreline took form, and I could hear the sound of surf breaking on the beach. I was close to being hypothermic and bone weary from my three-hour ordeal but I had survived! Physically, I could not have launched the boat again through the surf if I had had to, but somehow I felt stronger. I had learned more in those seven miles than I had in years. All crossings, all fears, all searches for control of the mind and body would be gauged against that day, and already I felt a core of confidence beginning to form within me.

It was only a matter of two or three weeks before my new life took on an even flow of events throughout the day. Equipment was rearranged within the boat so that I knew exactly where each item lay for the transition from water to shore. The awkward movements between shore and sea in the cool mornings, and sea to shore in the fading light of evenings, were now very systematic and enjoyable. I began to realize the beauty and simplicity of establishing a home within twenty minutes of landing on some remote island or beach. All that I needed to survive came from the confines of this slender boat, which with care could take me anywhere I wanted to go.

I ate simple high-carbohydrate meals and drank only pure, cold water; a diet that saw me through twelve months of paddling in every kind of weather imaginable. Like a second person removed from the actual work of each day, I constantly watched and listened to my body, critically looking for any adverse effects the trip might be having on me. What I saw after the first month of sore muscles and learning the ways of this new life was positive and encouraging. The deep restful sleep, which overtook me the minute I crawled inside the sleeping bag, was a time of magical rejuvenation that charged my body and mind for the next morning's light.

My body amazed me with its ability to withstand day after day of cold winds, the bounce and the strain against the pull of the paddle, and a diet most people would say was enormously inadequate. I looked at this first leg of the journey as a time of testing and rejoicing with the fitness that I felt from within.

Out on the water, I was conscious of a different kind of growth that was just as satisfying as my physical growth. For the first time in years I had the time to appreciate the tender moments of nature that I had known as a child growing up in the country. I saw from the seaward side of a crashing surfline the first hint of green buds high up on the overlooking bluffs of Chesapeake Bay.

The tangle of branches built into a crook of one of the trees showed the silhouette of an osprey, whose mate, moments before, had plunged into the bitter cold water for the morning's catch. I had watched him struggle back into the air after missing his prey, his feathers carrying the weight of the clinging water. Twenty feet higher he shook his body, sending a shower of sparkling diamonds down on the bay. These moments and those of a peaceful rising or setting sun soaked into me and awakened a quiet youthful joy.

I began to treasure what my senses told me, and wondered where I had been for so many years. I heard beauty and excitement in the heavy rumble from miles of surf or the almost indecipherable tingle of waters that ever so gently touched the shore. The comfort from the sun's warmth on my face was as welcome as the firmness of the earth beneath the tent at night, and I thanked God for the gift of both. My eyes, ears, skin, and even my sense of taste, reminded me of how precious everything was, and how I should cherish every minute of every new experience.

The thought that I was so fortunate to be a part of all that was happening seemed overpowering and almost dreamlike. Other than surviving, I didn't have a care in the world, and surviving meant living a rewarding, disciplined life enhanced by the rigors of a life exposed to the elements. The water and weather patterns I had traveled through had molded my mind and body into a being that was toned, healthy, and spontaneous. There were no rules or regulations, hence no surprises in my wilderness life, and I learned to live and react with, and not against, what I found.

Without any preconception of what I should find, I freely accepted every new experience at immediate face value. I was the visitor briefly encountering events—natural and wild—that had been there before me and would continue there long after I had quietly slipped away. These new experiences were not surprises. They were, and still are, treasures of the mind and spirit.

In North Carolina I had sat five miles from shore in the middle of Albamarle Sound and was held spellbound by a sunrise that could best be described as a grand culmination of the changes that had taken place within me during the first month of my travels. I sat riveted by the beauty of an orange crescent of fire rising from the sea with a backdrop of radiant pinks and blues. A spectrum of colors ranging from a pale pink to a brilliant gold reached outward from the sun and flooded across the water, engulfing me in its warmth. I sang to the gulls quietly soaring overhead and to the sun beginning its walk across the sky and to the spirit within and above that had made it all possible.

A week later, on another deserted stretch of the waterway, I waited patiently for a black line of rain-filled clouds to overtake me. A mile away I could see the sheet of rain falling, being driven toward me by stiff, gusty winds. Slowly the storm drew closer, the air filled with the sounds of the pelting rains and darkness engulfed the bay. I felt my body, my muscles, and my mind building with the storm, and I held the paddle low on the deck for the first wild gusts of wind.

When the storm finally cut loose with all its force and beauty I began to sing for all I was worth. I don't know why I sang; it seemed like an answer to the force that surrounded me. I couldn't just sit there and watch the storm, I had to be a part of it. I felt the rain peppering my sun-darkened skin and tasted the salt being washed from my hair. I laughed loud and free and raised my paddle high overhead, risking a capsize, in a salute to the power that was greater than me.

The spirit within me, smothered for so long in the past, was now bursting in my chest trying to expand beyond the mere human form containing it. My reawakened spirit wanted to fly, to swim, to run across this new world and see everything there was to see.

My awareness of nature's overflowing energy led to another discovery: a realization of the unbounded joy of living so closely to a world that I had missed for so long. This was another unforeseen blessing of the trip.

The East Coast Intercoastal Waterway and the Gulf of Mexico trained me physically and mentally for surviving and loving my new existence. Looking back now, it seems the next leg of my journey tested that love and, in the end, though near my limits, I would have to say it again strengthened me.

Because of a brief meeting with a complete stranger, I began this portion of my journey with strong conviction and optimism despite the uncertainties that lay before me.

The bright red deckhouse and gleaming brass water cannon of the New Orleans fireboat glistened in the noonday sun. A half mile away, across the swirling muddy brown water, the city of New Orleans looked out at the barges slowly churning upriver. The paddle-wheelers, *Natchez* and *President*, rode easily at their mooring as the barges' wakes rolled beneath them.

Back on my side of the river a slightly built man with short, dark hair and deeply tanned skin appeared on the deck of the fireboat. The flash of my wet paddles in the sun caught his eye and with a friendly wave he called out, "Hello, where are you going?" His voice carried a pleasant Spanish accent.

I allowed the river current to quickly sweep me against the hull of the freshly painted boat and came to rest immediately below the smiling stranger. I explained that I was headed upriver to St. Louis.

The conversation that followed gave me a much needed break from the strain of fighting the river. In answer to his questions, I told him of my travels and how I had come to arrive in New Orleans. He listened quietly, occasionally shaking his head but smiling in a way that said he understood.

His name was Danny Aguilar and as we sat in the ninety-degree heat, he told me how he had traveled around the world as a merchant sailor before settling in New Orleans. His words were spoken gently but with a quiet confidence that was soothing. I liked the man immediately although I knew very little about him. During a comfortable lull in the conversation, I asked him if he thought it was possible to paddle northward against the strong river currents. His reply was almost immediate.

"Yes, yes it is possible. It will be hard but you will make it. I am sure you will."

With that he disappeared into the deckhouse and moments later reappeared with a white envelope in his outstretched hand.

"I want you to have this," he said, "to help you with your travels."

I knew what was in the envelope. I also knew what I would say because along my route the offer had been made before. I hoped he would understand the gentle independence I believed in and would not be offended by my refusal of his gift of money.

As I briefly explained my philosophy, our eyes met and I knew he understood.

With a knowing smile, he quietly replied, "I don't want you to feel bad that you've refused this. Do you understand?"

"Yes sir," I replied. "I understand very well. Thank you."

His strong but gentle manner was the greatest gift he offered. I would remember his confidence in me in the weeks that followed and lean heavily upon it when I doubted my own ability.

The Mississippi River was one thousand miles and five weeks of the hottest days and nights I have ever lived through. Temperatures that hovered at the 101-degree mark matched the persistence of the river's currents to either harden me or break me. Dehydrated from the lack of sufficient fresh water, I once resorted to drinking small amounts of the tepid gritty river— enough to deliver me weak and on the verge of collapse to the next town.

On two occasions, due to the sheer exhaustion, I tipped my boat over trying to fend off the branches of a fallen tree, which the river's current washed me into. Massive tugboats, with their fleets of twenty to forty barges before them, churned northward while I hugged the muddy, crumbling banks inching my way behind them. I spent the nights collapsed in a comalike sleep filled with wild dreams of having to get off the river and find a camp before nightfall in order to rest from the day of sun and paddling.

The river had become an obsession, a monster of sorts that was trying to make me quit—trying to force me southward— trying to push me back to the gulf on its five-mile-per-hour currents.

Now and then I would see paddlers in canoes flying downriver out in the middle of the channel. Hoping to get information about upriver conditions, I waved to get their attention.

Chris Duff

But no one stopped. Apparently I was invisible against the foliage of the river's banks.

I had been making thirty miles a day as I had on the intercoastal waterway. And though, at the end of each day here on the river, I was too numb physically and mentally to set up my tent, I could still smile because I was thirty miles from the previous night's camp. What I had known of the Mississippi River before was nothing to what I knew and felt for this river now.

Any number of books written about the powerful river could not have showed me its strength and character. I would not have battled the wakes of the monstrous tugs, pulled my scarred boat over rock and timber wing dams, or tasted fried catfish at the home of a plantation owner. Had I not taken a right at the Port of New Orleans, neither would I have camped beside a bubbling stream of crystal-clear water and watched as it poured into the mile-wide, muddy Old Man River.

All the memories from the five weeks of fighting the river come back in a collage of towns, grain elevators, emotions, heat, exhausted sleep, and finally, the 630-foot stainless steel Jefferson Memorial arch and St. Louis. Now when I hear stories of the Mississippi, I know what the river is all about. Now when I hear the word "impossible," I know what the human spirit and the strength of hidden resources are all about.

I traveled from the Mississippi into the Illinois River and then into the Great Lakes where I headed northeastward into the mystical and silent world of the "voyageurs." The time of year was early spring, May 1984, and the hidden pockets of ice and snow hinted at what the winter must have been like. I wanted to paddle these northern waters of Lake Huron before the summer's warmth filled the waters with sail- and power-boats. The cold ice blue waters, bordered by stretches of pink granite scarred heavily from the retreating glaciers, had a mysterious feeling that could only be captured in their silence.

I tried to imagine the Native Americans, the fur traders, the early missionaries, and trappers paddling by the very islands I was paddling by, squinting into the fragmented sun for a landmark familiar to them from previous passages. The rocky island that I hid behind, seeking refuge from the piercing cold wind, had most likely protected those explorers; the Canadian winds, which had carried the Frenchmen's songs over the blue water, now carried mine; the gulls and terns were undoubtedly there; and the same sun and stars that I watched had watched them.

There, in the North Channel of Lake Huron, I felt a strong presence of yesteryear. The few towns along the route were hidden from view and easily avoidable so as not to mar the illusion of timelessness. Perhaps it was only in my mind, but the chill of the air seemed pure, the sun's warmth healing to the soul, and the clarity and taste of the water wonderfully medicinal.

Many times, for no reason, I sat quietly—afraid to break the silence. I did not know what I was looking for or straining to hear, but I knew there was something there. Where were all the spirits of those trappers and explorers? Could spirits as strong as theirs simply vanish as the world marched on to another time? Didn't anyone remember what had happened here and how adventurous and thrilling that life must have been? These waters, these winds, these islands, and the mountains farther off to the east were special and held a vision of a time not so very long ago. I felt a kinship with that time because I had arrived here upon a craft paddled, upon a spirit soaring.

What was it about those stormy, ice-cold waters that ignited a spark that fanned into a roaring flame? The feeling of complete wild and mystical freedom was everywhere, and it pervaded my soul like the sun's warmth.

I rode a whitecapped sea in wonderful communion: a singing paddler and a roaring sea and wind. The higher the winds built, the louder I sang, and the faster I surfed from wave to wave. My bow was often buried under the water foaming over the foredeck. Terns chattered overhead and dove in aerial acrobats while my heart pounded with sheer joy of being a part of it all. I was caught up in the power of the moment and racing crazily with the wind and waves. The freedom and the purity of everything around me was exhilarating. The thought of being so lucky and so alive was overwhelming.

I talked to the hissing wave behind me and told it to give me a fast ride but not to roll me. I talked to the winds and asked them to stay at my back. I talked to God and thanked Him for both. I thanked Him for the sun, my strength, for my learning, and most of all, for my life.

Where are the spirits of those trappers, those Native Americans, those early voyageurs? They are still here for those who search. They are in the wind, the sound of the waves, the warmth of a sun-soaked granite island. They are in the wolf that watched me from a point twenty yards away—eye to eye. The spirits of those people came from all that I saw and felt. Their songs and their urge to explore were fueled by a love—a love for the wilds and the intangibles.

The Saint Lawrence River and the open Atlantic pulled me from the solitude of the peaceful North Channel and Georgian Bay. Ahead lay some three thousand miles of unknown water and adventure. It was time to move on. My passage through those silent waters would stay with me and become a part of me—a part of me that I could call upon in a time of need for peace. I promised to return.

Every leg of the journey was different than the last but just as exciting and revealing. Now where I paddled the water was swift and smooth and, for once, at my stern and carrying me effortlessly. I shared the river with ocean freighters from the world over and rode gently through their rocking wakes.

In my fifteen-foot sea kayak, I passed alone through the dripping confines of the 1,000-foot-long locks that made the river navigable for those giant freighters. A drop of forty feet was completed in minutes and when the massive steel gates cracked open, I was off and running once again toward the sea.

Downriver of Quebec the ebb tide raced me farther along my journey—sometimes in the dark of night with stars overhead, a black towering shadow of a mountain at my side, and the lights of a freighter silently passing offshore.

In the early morning hours, a three-masted tall ship appeared from the horizon downriver and drew closer with the morning's light. Quebec City, one hundred miles behind me, was celebrating its 450th anniversary and, one by one, the tall ships were arriving to be part of the festivities. Square riggers from every corner of the world struggled upriver with the same determination that carried the ships of the Old World to Quebec years ago. In the predawn light, the ships presented a scene that sent my imagination sailing off with them. The white sails billowing against the blue sky and surrounding rugged mountains were a picture from the past. What century was this?

The restless sea water of the Gaspe Peninsula was now beneath my boat, and my companions were seals, beluga whales, and curious black guillemots. There were few places to land along the rocky shorelines. Often, I had to paddle through a surfline to make an uncertain landing among rocks and steep gravel beaches.

Winds, born somewhere to the north, blew endlessly and did not care about the days I spent watching the cold, raging waters from the beach. The winds did not have to worry about the coming of fall and cold weather only three months away. My travels were still young with many miles yet to paddle. However, these exposed waters were dangerous—far too dangerous for impatience. I watched and waited and, in the corridors of marginal weather, I paddled.

The Gaspe Peninsula fell behind me during July. Ahead lay the long sandy beaches of New Brunswick and the rocky coastline of Nova Scotia. The sun crept out of the sea at 5:00 A.M., but long after I had settled into my night's camp, the summer sky was still bright. I was in the long warm days of the north, and the memories of cold numb hands and freezing spray were forgotten. Now I listened to the huge Atlantic swells breaking with a thunderous roar on the rocky shore, and I smiled. The clear blue water showed me the depth of each stroke before the swells rolled on and ended their wanderings on the coast they had been destined to find. I was in a dreamland of wild beauty and peace.

Questions flooded my mind. Why had my boat, which I had christened the "Lucky One," survived the violent surfs, the congested harbors and ports, the tugs that had barely missed it in South Carolina and in St. Louis? Why had I known all the challenges and, finally, the rewards for those challenges? Why me? Why had I been privileged to see all I had seen? If it was because I had searched, then why had I begun the quest? Was it because I had listened to that voice within me that had told me to break loose and run? The voice had been so small and sometimes muffled by so many outside voices. What if I had not listened? I realized what a terrible loss it would have been to have never known the potential for achievement that we all have within us.

I had, in the course of the trip, experienced perhaps every emotion that a person could feel. I had met some unbelievable challenges and had known a satisfaction so intense I could almost hold it in my hands. I had known fear, cold, hunger, contentment, and ineffable joy. And, through many strangers along my route, I gained faith in mankind's compassion.

I remember a young boy along the Delaware Bay who helped me keep my journey in perspective. I never knew his name but we had shared a couple of makeshift sandwiches sitting on the rocky beach during a brief rest stop. His eyes lit up when I said I had to catch the tide, and he asked if he could help push me off into the still waters.

With as much enthusiasm as one might expect at the launching of a grand ocean liner, he gave a mighty shove, and the kayak slid gracefully backward, afloat once again. He stood and waved for a minute, then turned and raced home to tell his friends of our meeting.

The boy was understandably excited by his encounter with me and my odd-looking boat. I empathized with his excitement and knew, except for our difference in age, I was very much like him—caught up in the energy of discovery.

My journey was not an expedition. I never wanted, and strongly denied, the label of "expert" or similar descriptions of my abilities. The trip was as fascinating to me as it was to anyone else, and every day was a new learning experience. The mileage and months on the water were almost incomprehensible when I thought about it, because I had always looked at the trip as a series of thirty-mile days. I never worried or even planned for what lay five hundred or a thousand miles in front of me. My concerns were for the next day's paddle and perhaps the village seventy or a hundred miles down the coast where I could restock my food supply.

I passed through the Straits of Canso and moved slowly down the exposed and ruggedly beautiful southeast shore of Nova Scotia. The rusted hull of a freighter sat crippled on the rocks, waves washing in and out of a ragged hole in her sides. I slipped through the port side and sat rolling in the rebounding waves as I looked around the cargo hold. Out again in the sunlight I tried to envision her death in a winter's storm. Signs of wreckage from dozens of boats were scattered along the three-hundred-mile exposed shoreline. The islands and the water were beautiful to see in the warmth of the summer sun but I would not have wanted to be out there in the icy cold winds of winter.

It was late August when I started up the Bay of Fundy, a foggy, dead-calm run of four days. I was staring at my map of the bay and trying desperately, like so many times before, to squeeze answers from its pages. The bay, I was told, had thirty-foot tides and currents in many places that left veteran fishermen white with fear. Countless tales of sudden storms and ensuing tragedies had given it a reputation not to be taken lightly. If I was going to paddle around the entire bay, it would have to be done in harmony with its force and not against it.

I stopped at a scallop-processing plant in Digby at the beginning of the bay and sought the owner. A half hour later I walked out with a new tide table and more information about the bay than I could have hoped for. From all the owner had told me, one comment appeared to be the key to paddling these waters, "The fishermen here waste time to make time. Ride the flood on this side and if you make it to New Brunswick, ride the ebb." It was short, no nonsense advice from a man who made his living from the sea. I liked that kind of approach.

Heavy wet fogs, with visibility often less than fifty yards, hid the shoreline during my three-day paddle to Halls Harbour. Riding a smooth flow of water, I slid through the mist in silence, completely oblivious to the shoreline a hundred yards to my right. To catch my bearings, I would lay the paddle gently on the cockpit and strain to hear the faint wash of the waters against the rocky shore. I was lucky. The bay was like a pond, and the sounds of this dripping world carried far.

I almost bumped into the timber dock of Halls Harbour in the soupy fog. Through the mist I saw a young boy climbing about the rocks. Like most boys of ten or eleven years, he had the energy of youth—something I had rediscovered during my journey, and I related well to his hundred and one questions.

In the tiny village, it did not take long for Brian Crosbie to spread the word that "some guy in a little boat was down at the wharf." As typical of the Nova Scotians, I was welcomed into their homes and lives, where for five days we sat watching the fog and then the winds before planning a crossing of the bay.

Retired fishermen, whose fathers and uncles had lived on the sea, appeared and gave advice carefully, almost hesitantly, because a sea kayak was something they had never seen before. How a boat so small and fragile could have come so far, and was now going to attempt a crossing of the bay, was almost inconceivable to them.

Fred Parker, a retired lobster fisherman and current owner of the small general store, unfolded his charts on the glass counter beside the cash register. In front of us lay the waters of the Bay of Fundy and, on the far right end of the chart, the waters that I would attempt to cross. Fred ran his hand generally across the chart to Cap 'Dor, eight miles away, and said, "I've fished these waters for twenty-five years, and I know how bad it can be. You get a wind against a strong tide, and it'll sink the best boat out there. If you're going to try the crossing, you gotta do it two hours before slack low water."

He then reached down below one of the shelves and pulled out a dusty and dented brass compass. The needle swung freely within its protective brass dome and finally settled out as he placed it gently on the counter. He explained that when he sold his last boat and retired to the store, the compass came ashore with him as a reminder of his fishing days.

"In those days we didn't have radar or even a radio. We just had a pocket watch and a good compass to navigate with. That's all you've got, right?"

I smiled and nodded, appreciating the understanding he had for simple dead reckoning. Having the challenge of the bay as common ground, we sat and became friends in discussing tidal rips, winds, and the ever-present threat of fog.

On the morning of my departure half the village gathered on the rocky beach for a moving send off. They were genuinely concerned for a stranger in a small boat who, for a short while, had shared their lives and his stories. Now they stood and watched. Each time I looked back at the increasingly distant shoreline, the figures on the beach stood where I had left them.

I remembered the same caring, the same look of youthful dreams in the eyes of people I had met throughout my route. There was the couple on the Chesapeake Bay who watched in the bitter cold as I shoved off across open water. There were

friends in Florida who snapped pictures while the *Lucky One*
floated away on the mirror finish of the St. Luce Canal. There
were people on the Mississippi, the Illinois, the Great Lakes,
and of course my family at home who were all part of the trip.
Their caring, their prayers, their words of encouragement
boosted me when I was down and kept me going. Without
these people and hundreds more along my route, the trip would
not have been possible. It was very reassuring to find so many
good people in a world that seldom sees their kind.

Mist-shrouded cliffs, with looming towers of eroded rock,
greeted me after an uneventful crossing of the bay. A sincere
regard for the powers of the water and local weather patterns,
in addition to the sound advice I had received, had been the
key to the crossing. Patience, listening, and watching had prevailed once again.

The final weeks of the trip were beautiful euphoric days of
unusually still winds and warm sunny days. I threaded my way
between the islands and towns of Maine and the long expanses
of beaches in New Hampshire. I paddled three miles offshore
cutting across bays and camping on points of land or islands
jutting into the open sea. I wanted to remember each day's
passage and keep it alive and vivid in my mind.

The trip had begun a year and a half earlier on a bitter
cold blustery March day. The changes in me, and the experiences I had encountered were too awesome to comprehend. I
was very different from the individual who had left that promising military career not so very long ago. I spent many hours
wondering what I would do now that the "real" world was
again confronting me. I had tasted the fruits of unbound freedom and I did not know if I could settle back into a life so
demanding and restrictive as a "normal" life. I did have the
comfort of knowing that whatever I set my mind to accomplish
I was capable of achieving. That thought encouraged me to
look ahead. Whatever the future had in store for me I would
face it with the qualities of life I had found in my search. It
would not matter what, where, or how difficult the challenge
might be. I would take one small step at a time, and I would
succeed because of the discipline, the will to learn, and the
persistence I had come to rely upon in the past eight thousand
waterborne miles of my life.

Massachusetts, Rhode Island, Connecticut, and finally

New York passed beneath the sun-bleached and patched hull of the *Lucky One.* Down the length of Long Island Sound and up the Hudson River, with its autumn colors and protective highlands escorting me, I finished a segment of my life with such happiness and appreciation that it bubbled out of me. I knew I would never be the same. For this I gave a prayer of thanks.

Like life, my journey alone needed guidance. I had to be willing to learn, to ask questions, to be silent in watching. I had to listen to the voice that did not always speak, but which was often felt—a silent guidance system that proved always to be right.

What did life lived as a lone paddling experience mean to me? It meant rejoicing in the beauty of love, sun, wind, and awareness of all that there is; passing through quietly and leaving no trace other than the memory of a caring individual, attuned to the existence of a greater presence and ever searching for it. Furthermore, it meant having known the wonder, the awe, the purity and strength of the unbounded natural world; having laughed and sung with open-hearted joy and thanks for each moment lived; having appreciated the importance of a spiritual being and standing before it asking, rather than demanding; listening rather than acting; admitting limited strength and power in the face of unmeasurable depths of both.

The spiritual values I found as a solo sea kayaker are as powerful and as satisfying as any I have experienced. And those values will forever remain an integral part of my being.

CHRIS DUFF began his life of travel and adventure at age eighteen as a deep-sea diver for the U.S. Navy. The demanding and rewarding work as a diver taught him the great respect he has today for the beauty and the power of the sea.

He recently completed a solo paddle around England, Wales, and Scotland. Between travels, Chris makes his living renovating old houses and enjoys "breathing life back into abandoned buildings."

CHRISTOPHER CUNNINGHAM

Voyage of the Paper Canoe

My canoe was dissolving. The scratches that crosshatched the hull oozed a milky solution of glue and water. In the deepest cuts the water of the St. Lawrence River had softened the laminate of paper that formed the hull and decks. Blisters of soggy kraft paper tore and peeled off like sunburned skin.

A century ago the toughest, lightest, and fastest boats were made of paper. In 1867 a young George Waters, inspired by the construction of a paper-mache mask, built the first paper boat by laminating glue-saturated paper over the mold of a thirty-foot racing shell. From that first experience grew the Waters Paper Boat Company of Troy, New York. While their paper racing shells won nearly every rowing championship in the country, the best-known boat built by the Waters Company was the paper canoe, *Maria Theresa,* built for Nathaniel H. Bishop.

In 1874 Bishop and his companion David Bodfish set out from the city of Quebec in a wooden canoe. After four hundred miles of paddling and sailing they reached Troy on the Hudson River, where Bishop met George Waters and commissioned him to build a Rob Roy canoe. When the *Maria Theresa* was finished, Bishop continued his voyage alone to Cedar Key, Florida.

One hundred and nine years later, in August of 1983, my partner Courtney Bell and I set out to follow the route from Quebec to Cedar Key, Florida, described in Bishop's book *Voy-*

age of the Paper Canoe. Courtney paddled a sleek fiberglass kayak, I paddled a paper canoe.

The fall of the tide on the St. Lawrence revealed a line of rocks, gray and rounded like the backs of elephants, that dotted the edges of the shipping lanes. By nightfall the stones had become a barrier between us and the shore. Twelve miles up-river from Quebec, the only light on the river was the silver blue streak of reflections from a paper mill near Donnaconda. We steered into the light and watched the lens-shaped shadows of rocks drift across our course as the tide carried us sideways into rocks we could not see. I winced at the sound of every gritty collision.

Once we were through the rocks our paddles scraped bottom. In the half mile that remained between us and the banks of the river there was a plane of stone as flat as a concrete pavement. We sat in the boats until the turn of the tide. As the water began to rise we walked with our boats in tow behind the flood's slow slide toward shore.

As we continued up the St. Lawrence the next day I stared into the cockpit at the varnished skin of paper. Between the ribs and stringers of the yellow cedar frame I noticed dark blisters of waterlogged paper.

In the lee of a point that pressed into a bend of the river we put ashore on a beach shingled with flakes of black slate. We set up the tent to keep out of the wind while we waited out the seaward rush of the ebb tide. I crawled into the tent and lay down, resting my head on my forearm. I thought of the months of work that I had put into the boat. Courtney rolled out her foam pad and lay down beside me. "It's not going to make it."

I had ignored my doubts about the canoe. The information I found about building paper boats was incomplete. Though descriptions of the laminating process developed by Waters was quite thorough, there was no reference to the composition of the glue he used. I went ahead with the project, using the only glue that was neither too brittle, too toxic, nor too expensive—aliphatic resin, a common carpenter's glue. It was tough and worked well with paper. Yet, even before we launched from Quebec, I had made two repairs where rainwater had softened the seam between the deck and hull. While aliphatic resin is labelled as water resistant, its resistance to

water is no more than a brief hesitation before melting into a
worthless solution.

The sun made it hot and stuffy in the tent. I went to the
canoe, emptied it, and turned it upside-down to dry the scarred
bottom. With my pocketknife I scraped away wet paper and
applied patches of fiberglass and epoxy. When the glue had set
we packed our gear in the boats and headed upriver.

Above the tidal reaches of the St. Lawrence, head winds
made the river uncomfortably rough. We paddled along the
shore where the waves rolled flat and smooth under thick green
mats of grass and algae. At Nicolette, a yachtsman offered us
the comfort of his sloop, fed us, and put us up for the night in
the forward cabin.

When we woke in the morning I felt well rested for the
first time in a week. As we paddled across Lac St. Pierre, a
bulge in the river twenty miles long and eight miles wide, I told
Courtney, "Boy, I sure slept well last night. I think it's the first
night I've slept straight through."

I felt invigorated that morning. I was not bothered by the
strangeness of the first awkward days of our voyage—I knew
from previous experience that we would soon be comfortable in
the routine of travel. Nor was I disturbed by the diseased condition of my boat—I had built it; I knew I could fix it. But there
was tension. It grew from the difference I saw between me and
my traveling companion. To the difficulties that began to surface between us I knew of no solution.

In the fifteen years since I had taken to the outdoors I had
walked, pedaled, and rowed a few thousand miles. Most of that
ground I had covered alone. My solo experience grew out of a
nagging curiosity about what sort of company I would be to
myself lacking the distractions of civilized society. It turned out
I was no kinder to myself than anyone else. I could sit and visit
for only an hour or so before I got restless. So I kept moving.

In western culture covering ground has an aura of pur-
posefulness. Go west young man! Or east, or north, or around
in circles. I once hiked myself into an episode of cardiac arrhy-
thmia. Years later, I rowed until the skin began to peel from my
palms. I occasionally listened to the dialogue of my own
thoughts. But more often I chased myself through the country-
side. Though people admired my independence and endur-

ance, I had become a tyrant to myself. I had also fallen into a confusion about the merits of aloneness. If a tree falls in the woods, and you are the only one that hears it, is the experience significant?

Time erased the memories of pain and boredom and polished those of adventure. Then, in 1980, as I rowed seven hundred miles north along the Inside Passage of British Columbia, I took careful notes of the cost of traveling. I photographed myself when I was bored or scared. When I returned, I was and remained disillusioned about my solo experience.

In Courtney I saw an uninhibited enthusiasm for adventure that I thought could rekindle my own. Two weeks before I was ready to head to Quebec, Courtney dropped everything and bought a kayak. Suddenly I had a traveling companion. (Courtney was as strong as she was pretty. At one time she had worked as a model. Before photography sessions she would hold her arms above her head to shrink the veins that ran like cords along her forearms and across the backs of her hands.) I would not have to go alone. All too soon, however, it became apparent that I had not tested and proven our partnership any more than I had tested my canoe.

Even as we drove from our homes in Seattle to the Banks of the St. Lawrence in Quebec it became apparent that our expectations of each other and of our voyage would not find harmony. The bond that had brought us together had grown out of loneliness. Like the glue in my canoe, it would not hold. It was simply the wrong stuff. The hardships of cruising would not be responsible for the disintegration of the relationship any more than they were responsible for the weakness of the glue; they would only speed up the dissolution.

At the west end of Lac St. Pierre we turned south at Sorel into the Richelieu River. At nightfall we were still within the riparian suburbs of Sorel.

At the south end of the Richelieu the riverbanks flared away from each other opening up to Lake Champlain. To the west we saw a swath cut through the woods, part of the great kerf across the continent dividing Canada and the United States. After checking in with U.S. Customs we paddled into the glitter of sunshine scattered across the lake. The wind was fresh at our backs and hurried us along the shore of Wool Point.

Before crossing the wide mouth of Monty Bay, we peered into the northern end of the bay like children craning their necks up the street before entering a crosswalk. In the shadow of a tower of cumulus clouds the water glowed white under a sudden lash of wind.

"Turn around," I shouted to Courtney. "Head for the beach!" We were only thirty yards from land, but by the time we had dragged the boats up on the gray bouldered beach, branches torn from the shoreside trees were dropping all around us. We looped the painters around long, heavy rocks and ran into the lee of a beach house.

The surface of the bay was lifted into a thick layer of spray that skidded across the lake. The wind then dropped as quickly as it had risen—a meteorological sneeze. In ten minutes the water had settled enough for our crossing.

At the south end of Lake Champlain we entered a lock chamber that lifted us into the quiet rural water of the Champlain Canal. The angled evening light skimmed across the foredeck and revealed a pattern of small gray shadows. I ran and slid my fingers over the deck and felt dimples in the skin where staples attached it to the wooden framework. The entire shell of the canoe had swelled with the water it was absorbing. The epoxy and glass patches and duct tape repairs were not keeping up with water seeping into the laminate. I decided we would have to stop for repairs at Troy, the southern terminus of the canal. The former home of the Waters Paper Boat Company seemed the most appropriate place to do the work.

At dusk a cloud of swallows skimmed along the canal with the broad sweeping turns of an ice skater. The flock stretched and condensed itself as if it were a single organism moving within a mass of transparent protoplasm. If we sat still the flock would wrap about our boats like an amoeba, and the swallows would veer narrowly around our heads as if slipping past sleek canopies of unfeathered air. The flexing of hundreds of quick, tiny wings rustled like crinoline skirts. The last light of the evening mulled the western sky and cut a sharp-edged silhouette of the trees, rooftops, and steeples of Schuylerville.

We paddled on into the dark and groped along the marshy shore for a place to camp. Near a two-story apartment building we pulled our boats onto the muddy fringe of a lawn.

We set up our tent on a distant corner of the lawn. Several times during the night I awoke with a start and listened through the walls of the tent while my heart pounded. We rose to our alarm clock while morning was still dark, packed quickly, and left unnoticed.

That afternoon we arrived in Troy. We met Irving Moore, the city's historian emeritus, who was well versed in the story of the Waters Company. Mr. Moore gave us the use of his garage for our repair work and aided us in our search for materials to rebuild my paper hull.

We peeled eighteen layers of damp paper from the bottom of my canoe, leaving only a thin four-layer membrane over the framework to keep the shape of the boat. Limited by the selection of materials available in Troy, we purchased polyester resin, rolls of brown paper towels and paper wipes for the lamination of the new bottom. After thirteen days I had a new hull that was strong and waterproof. I felt confident it would last the remaining two thousand miles.

It was in Troy that Bishop parted company with David Bodfish, writing, "Experience had taught me that I could travel more conveniently and economically without a companion." After two weeks of paddling, I, too, could compare that experience with traveling solo.

Many of the practical difficulties were easily solved as we went along. We equalized our speed by transferring cargo from Courtney's kayak to my canoe until we felt an equal measure of fatigue at the end of the day. We split the responsibilities at our campsites to quicken our settling in for the night and our departures in the morning.

But while our experiences were, as I had hoped, validated by the sharing of them and sustained by our common remembrance, I felt I had lost the sharp focus and immediacy of my solo experience. The entries in my journal had become like tourist snapshots, where the wonders of nature and civilization become fuzzy backdrops for portraits of my fellow vacationer peering patiently into the round, black eye of my camera.

In Troy, two weeks into the voyage, Courtney and I discovered that we couldn't really talk to each other. The things we had hoped to find in one another were things that we would have to find within ourselves. Under different circumstances

we might have said good-bye then. All we found we shared was
a commitment to paddle to Cedar Key. Neither of us would
give up the voyage, and I insisted that it would be unsafe to go
on separately.

As we approached New York City on the first of October, I
was wary of Bishop's warning, "A great city offers no induce-
ment for a canoeist to land as a stranger at its wharves." Bishop
had dodged tugs and ferries until he was safely beyond New
York's heavily traveled harbor. We paddled the western shore of
the Hudson River along the ragged edge of Jersey City. There
seemed to be no end of abandoned wharves of dark, splintered
wood and rusted corrugated metal. On one of the piers, three
boys had ignited a red distress flare and were throwing it above
the pier and running under its parabola of white smoke.

A cluster of black and silver balloons overtook us, sailing
before the wind like a great Portuguese man-of-war and trailing tentacles of curled ribbon through the water. Courtney
raced after it. When she caught up with it she tied it to her
foredeck and started paddling back toward me. The balloons
swallowed her so that I could see only the waving of her paddle
blades. The balloons broke free, darted through a pier and
drifted deep into the wharves. As Courtney's lark turned into a
rescue operation, I grew more anxious about finding a place to
get off the water before dark. The balloons could fend for
themselves. I shouted for her to turn back.

"We have to figure out what we're going to do for the
night."

"Whatever you think is fine," she said curtly, a bit miffed
at me for having spoiled her fun. I showed her our map of the
area.

"We can keep going this side and hope we find a safe
place, or we can cross to the other side of the river where our
only chance is the 79th Street Marina."

"OK," she said, "Which way are we going?"

"I'm asking you."

"It doesn't matter to me," she shrugged.

"Dammit, it does matter!" I shouted, "Look, I don't know
what we should do. I only know that we are running out of
daylight."

Courtney snapped back, echoing the harsh tone of anger

and frustration in my own voice. "Well, if it were up to me I'd head for the marina."

"Fine." We set our jaws and our bows in the direction of the heart of New York City and paddled with an extra margin of water between us.

It was the first time in a month of paddling that I had asked for Courtney's opinion about our course. I carried the charts in my boat, and I kept track of our position and course. The computations of speed, current, and wind were a buzz that occupied my thoughts as steadily as paddling busied my arms. Yet I rarely spoke to Courtney of the considerations by which we traveled and camped. I was still traveling solo, only this time I had someone with me. It was, without giving it much thought, the simplest thing to do. Yet for Courtney, changes in our course came suddenly and arbitrarily, and it was impossible for her to set her pace to match the changing demands of the day. And when the decisions were no longer simple I was, by the pattern we had established, still stuck with the burden of them. Our society of two had become undemocratic and discontent.

Courtney's decision to go to the 79th Street Marina was the right one. The first man we met there, John, was a live-aboard and a paddler, who had both enthusiasm and room for us. He was relentless in offering us anything we needed.

"Well, Courtney's boat needs a rudder." I mentioned, "We were hoping we could find the hardware to make one while we are in town."

"What do you need?" John asked. I recited a long list of parts: cables, fasteners, aluminum.

With a smile John pulled up a floor panel and revealed a hold full of tools and materials. Everything we needed was beneath his deck. We stayed with John two days while we worked on the rudder for Courtney's kayak. In town we toured Broadway, Times Square, the "Met," and the Museum of Modern Art.

Upon leaving New York, we paddled into the waterways behind Staten Island. Where Bishop wrote of endless plains of marsh there were now chemical plants and oil refineries. The waters of Arthur Kill and Kill Van Kull ran black with their effluent.

"Fall into that stuff," shouted a deckhand from the stern of a tug, "and you won't last twenty-four hours!"

At Perth Amboy we turned up the mouth of the Raritan River. Along the banks of the river were mountains of garbage a hundred feet high. New hills, reeling with clouds of gulls, were growing under the roar and squeak of bulldozers. The older hills were cloaked in soil and grass, but the erosion at their bases revealed the strata of rust, glass, and tattered plastic trash bags.

After a few hours of paddling, we portaged from the river into an old canal, which formerly connected the commerce of the Raritan and Delaware rivers. Once a busy avenue of mule-drawn barges, tugs, and schooners, the canal is now a forty-mile-long park. Trees arch up from the banks and weave a canopy of leaves above the water. Their roots grip the cut stone riprap along the old towpath like gnarled fingers. The locks and wing bridges are no longer operative and a number of portages around them are required.

The canal once went through Trenton. It now ends there. Our map of the Delaware and Raritan canal park showed a dotted line along the old route of the canal. The legend read "canal in culvert." At the edge of the city we entered the culvert, a pair of concrete tunnels four feet tall and fifteen feet wide. The ceiling was not high enough for Courtney to use her double-bladed paddle. She separated the two halves of the paddle and continued paddling canoe style. Several hundred yards in, a turn to the right eclipsed the light of the entrance. Lighting our way with flashlights, we paddled a long straight stretch before the tunnel turned to the left. The map showed we were a mile and a half into the tunnel, somewhere near Junior High School No. 5. When we turned off the flashlights, we could see a dim glow of light ahead of us. We noticed too that the ceiling was getting lower. When it was too low for us to use our paddles, we walked our hands along the ceiling. The ceiling sloped lower. Courtney stopped. I laid back on the afterdeck and pushed forward until my chest squeezed against the wet brown slime above me. "That's it." I shouted and a chain of echoes rang from the darkness behind us.

We backed to a widening in the culvert where we could turn our boats around. On our way out, we stopped beneath a

Christopher Cunningham

tall shaft that poured a pale gray light into the culvert. I climbed out of my boat and ascended a ladder of wet, rust-covered rungs to the top to get our bearings. From a pair of iron grates on either side of the narrow tube I peeked across wide slabs of oil-patinaed concrete and through blurs of speeding tires and flashes of chrome. The shock waves of air pushed by cars and trucks buffeted against my head, and the whine of tires and engines drove into my ears like ice picks. We were beneath the express lanes of the Trenton freeway.

By the time we had returned to the entrance of the culvert it was late in the afternoon. A few blocks from the canal we spotted a lumberyard and a truck large enough to carry our boats. Two of the workers there agreed to pick us up at the canal and carry us to the banks of the Delaware on the other side of Trenton. As they drove us through town along the Trenton Expressway, I watched for the storm drains at the edge of the left-hand lane. I was looking for eyes.

On our way down the Delaware I paddled alongside Courtney and slipped the chart of the river under the shock cords on her foredeck.

"We are here," I pointed out, "just coming up on Florence. After a while you'll get the hang of how fast we are moving on paper."

Her head sagged over the chart, and her hair closed like drapes around her face. When she looked up she was not looking for landmarks, but at me. Tears had drawn twin plumb lines down her cheeks.

I had thought then that she was upset by her unfamiliarity with map reading, and it did not occur to me that her sadness might have been over how unfamiliar we continued to be to each other. We were not travelling to Cedar Key for the sake of being together. Rather, we were together for the sake of paddling to Cedar Key. We had made our relationship part of our baggage. And though we often discarded extra equipment and sent our accumulation of momentos home in order to keep our load light, we carried this burden of disappointment and sadness with us and could not travel far without feeling its weight.

Along the densely populated Delaware we made our evening stops at yacht clubs. The clubs at Bordentown and Camden were having their last weekend social at the close of the boating season. We were scooped from the water and treated to the best food and accommodations the clubs had to offer.

It was Monday when we reached the yacht basin at Chester, Pennsylvania. Three yachtsmen sat at the bar of an otherwise empty clubhouse, rattling the ice cubes in their drinks with nautical swizzle sticks. A television hung high on the wall at the end of the bar was turned to the evening news. During the commercials the bartender asked us where we'd come from, and where we were headed.

"Damn," he said, "that's something. Where you going tonight?"

"We were hoping it would be OK to camp on your lawn," I answered.

"I don't think anybody around here'd mind. But it's kind of a rough neighborhood. Stay close to the clubhouse when it gets dark, and you oughta be all right." With that we went out to break the gear out of the boat.

There was a tall cyclone fence around the backside of the club. The buildings beyond it were in various states of decay. In the parking lot a tank truck was spraying the weeds that grew from the cracks in the asphalt. Our boats, sitting at the edge of the lot had been doused with herbicide. I was furious. I looked at the two guys with their high-pressure sprayers and decided it would be better for my health not to pursue the matter. I rinsed the decks and threw away all of the food that had been spoiled by the poison that dripped through the spraydeck. I dropped the food into a garbage can at the edge of the lot. A rat streaked across the sidewalk, levitating on a blur of legs.

"I think you'd be better off spending the night in my boat," came a voice from the clubhouse. A man in a black suit walked across the lawn to us and shook our hands. "My name's Gerry. I understand you've come quite a distance."

Gerry helped us carry our boats down the dock next to his small powerboat and unlocked the cabin. "It's not much but you'll be safer here. Make yourselves at home and button 'er up when you go. I wish I could talk with you but I have to rush off to a meeting."

Late that evening, just after we had turned out the lights for the night we heard a voice on the dock. "Did you have anything to eat?" It was Gerry. He had come this time with his wife. They stepped into the cockpit and handed a flat box through the companion way. "Here's a pizza. The speaker at the meeting was so boring. We were just dying of curiosity about you two."

Courtney and I sat up in our sleeping bags and set the box between us on our knees. As we ate we told them about our last five weeks of traveling.

"I wish I had your guts." Gerry said when we had swallowed the last bites. Neither Courtney nor I thought what we were doing took extraordinary courage. As we gained experience, we were less daunted by the hazards of the waterways we traveled.

If we had guts, it was in leaving the security and comfortable predictability of home. Though we occasionally went without things we wanted—cookies, dry socks, comfy chairs—we never were denied what we really needed. Our voyage into unfamiliar waters had become so regularly serendipitous as to become a compelling argument for divine Providence. Perhaps that's what it was.

When Gerry and his wife left, Courtney and I smiled at each other. "I guess we'll have to brush our teeth again," she laughed. There was a knock on the cabin wall. Courtney opened the port. It was Gerry again.

"Just one more thing," he said. "Would you be insulted if I gave you some money?" He handed a twenty-dollar bill through the port. There was between Courtney and me the same wide-eyed look of bewilderment that I remembered in the penultimate scenes of "The Lone Ranger" episodes. Like hapless homesteaders, we had been stunned by the sudden and anonymous philanthropy of a masked stranger. We stared at the twenty as if it were a silver bullet, and the clatter of footsteps on the dock faded into the night.

We did well with the tides the day we left the Delaware River. An ebb pulled us by Wilmington to the entrance of the Delaware and Chesapeake Canal, and the following flood shot us through the cut into the northern reaches of Chesapeake Bay. When we landed at Elk Neck we had covered a surprising thirty-seven miles.

The Chesapeake was mottled by geese in flocks so large that there was no way to avoid disturbing them. At our approach the geese closest to us curled up into the air and looped over to the far end of the flock. When they landed, the flock had become a loop of raucous geese that rolled ahead of us like a giant flat tire.

At the mouth of the Chester River we paddled east to Kent Island. At the north end of the island, the waves lapped at the base of a line of sandy cliffs. Crisp-edged blocks of sand at the base of the cliffs had broken along the lines of alluvial strata, revealing the ripples of sand deposited at the end of the Ice Age. I pulled the stern up onto a narrow bar of sand at the water's edge, and stepped out of the canoe with my camera. While I was looking through the viewfinder I heard a sound like a pillow thrown against a wall. I looked toward the noise and saw a fifteen-foot-high wall of sand collapse and bury the stern of my canoe.

Courtney paddled in to take my camera and to stand by with an eye on the cliff above me while I dug like a dog for my buried boat. When I was able to pull the boat free, I found the afterdeck split along both gunwales and the rudder bent. I ran my hand along the bottom. It was still intact. As we paddled to safer ground I looked over to Courtney. "Neat!" I liked geological phenomena, more, perhaps, than my canoe did, and I had long since resigned myself to an endless routine of repair work.

We had fair weather until we reached the mouth of the Potomac River. A strong northeasterly held us there for three days. Not far from our camp were the ruins of the prison camp at Point Lookout where Rebel POWs waited for the end of the Civil War.

The first day of our captivity I stepped out of my boat barefoot onto the ragged edge of a broken bottle. My feet were almost numb with cold so I did not think much about the twinge I felt until I saw that I had sprung a considerable leak.

Dale, a young oysterman with arms as big as my legs, drove us thirty-five miles to a hospital. He dropped us off and promised to check on us in an hour.

I got six stitches and a dose of antibiotics for $90. The doctor told me to keep my foot dry for a week. I imposed upon Dale for a ride to a department store, and I filled my prescription for shin-high boots.

Two days later the wind was still pushing sizable waves up

the Potomac. We wandered through the woods and came across a family cemetery. A young man of twenty-two was the last to be buried there, in 1863, "cut down in all his bloom." Nearer the shore, in the rubble of a fallen brick chimney I watched a praying mantis eating a cricket as if it were an ice cream cone. We grew restless and decided to cross the river.

The waves were tall enough to hide Courtney and me from each other when they popped up between us, but they were not uncomfortably steep. I had studied the Virginia shore carefully before we had started, for the only charts we had were in a cruising guide. It showed us the harbors but not much else. I thought the bands of light and shadow that streaked the woods on the far bank of the Potomac were a sign of a shoreline as irregular and as protected as the one we had left. I was wrong.

Neither of us made graceful landings on the surf-swept Virginia riverbank. Courtney, in a kayak that fit like a pair of panty hose, surfed in on a wave that carried her halfway up the beach. Before she could slither out of the cockpit a second wave rolled her into the froth. I had the advantage of a cockpit I could unzip and step out of. The foot that I was to keep dry, though, was at the wrong end of my body to be carried safely ashore. When my bow grounded I jumped out and hopped twice on my good foot before plowing my face into the sand. The dry boot at the top of my uplifted leg was the flag that marked our beachhead.

The weather remained somewhat sour during our remaining days on the Chesapeake. When we got to the bay's southern end we were eager to paddle narrower waterways that would leave us less vulnerable to the wind. When we rounded Old Point Comfort at the entrance to Hampton Roads, we were suddenly faced with waves that sprang up ahead of us as tall and as steep as living room walls. We had been paddling in a lee and were caught off guard by the southwesterly running free across the Roads. At the bottleneck between the Roads and the Chesapeake, a strong flood tide worked against the wind and squeezed the waves together like the pleats of an accordian. The paper canoe, with its twenty-eight-inch beam and its heavy load settled comfortably into the waves. But Courtney's kayak teetered at the crests and lurched into the troughs. She was visibly frightened.

"How are you doing?" I shouted to her.

"Not so good."

"Keep paddling forward. We'll wait for a lull in the waves. When I yell, push full right rudder and paddle as hard as you can to the right."

As soon as there was a leveling in the wild mound of water I shouted, "Now!" We both snapped our rudders over and paddled fiercely to starboard. I was grateful for the quick turning our rudders allowed. No sooner had we turned tail to the wind than the waves rose behind us. The wake of a tanker heading out into the bay rose beneath Courtney as she was at the crest of a wave. Green water flooded over her decks, and the ends of her kayak stuck out from the wave like horns. The collapse of the crest slapped the paddle out of her right hand. I saw her hand drop to the edge of her cockpit.

In that expansion of time that prolongs the moment of a sudden accident, I saw that we should have made our turn away from shore, for if she were to capsize I would have very little time to get her before the waves pounded her against the stone bulkhead along the shore. I heard in my thoughts my own voice, quiet and sad, saying, "No, no this should not happen to her." I could see the weight of her hand settling on the gunwale of her narrow kayak and her spine bend as the kayak began to roll.

In that moment I felt my greatest admiration for her. Her hand upon the gunwale marked her as a novice paddler. She had never learned to roll because of the fear that seized her when her head was submerged. Yet for two months, in spite of her inexperience, she had endured the risks and discomforts of paddling. She had bound herself to her decision to finish this trip in spite of the failure of the relationship that had drawn her into it.

"Get that hand back on the paddle!" I screamed. Her hand shot forward and latched onto the paddle shaft. As her kayak accelerated into the trough, Courtney pushed against the wave with her paddle and regained her balance.

We paddled back into the lee of the point and pulled our boats up on the beach. I did not tell her how moved I was by her struggle to stay upright. Very little we had said to each other since Troy served any purpose other than to move us closer to Cedar Key. Instead I drew in the sand diagrams of waves and explained to her the techniques of paddle braces while she stood shivering.

In the evening, when the wind was down, we set out again from Point Comfort and crossed to Norfolk.

A string of rivers and canals led us through the thick cypress and gum swamps of Virginia and North Carolina. There was no land along the water to speak of, only a barrier of trees and the tangle of their roots. We spent long days in the boat, paddling six or seven hours at a stretch between patches of solid ground.

Along the Pasquotank River we came ashore at the edge of a small clearing. At the top of the rise that sloped gently up from the water was a two-tone car with a police car's tiara of chrome and flashers. Hank, a county sheriff, took a long look at our boats. "I wish I'd a done what you're doin' when I was younger," he sighed. When he looked out toward the short arc of the river that tucked its ends into the swamp there was pain in his eyes. "I grew up by this river. I always wanted to build me a raft or a punt and see where it went." Hank was about forty-five or fifty. He still had his boyhood dream, but he had never built that punt.

I am only beginning to see the quickness with which my time slips by. Traveling slowly and deliberately under the power of my arms and legs has made it possible to keep pace with time. From Quebec to the curdled water trailing from our sterns, we had knit time to geography with paddle strokes. We could, and often did as we paddled, double back in memory to Quebec, and name the towns we passed, the people we met, their dogs, and remember the direction of the wind or the color of the water. Our time was not lost but carefully spent and accounted for.

In Charleston, South Carolina, we were interviewed by a television news team. The cameraman hired a skiff and a driver and taped our departure. We were eager to see how we looked on the tube. That evening's dinner hour found us in the backwaters of the Edisto River. We nestled the boats in the marsh, and I waded to the lawn of a large house shaded by live oaks. A silver-haired woman with sharp green eyes came to the door. She listened quietly while I introduced myself, explained our voyage and expressed our wish to watch the evening news. When I finished she peered around me toward the boats.

"Honey, you don't get your thugs or rapers of old women coming in canoes. Besides, I consider myself a good judge of character, and I like the cut of your jib. Get your friend and come in," she said, and paused. "You might slit my throat and steal my jewelry, but at least I will have died a trusting soul."

Mrs. Wyatt heated up a pot of chili and set dinner for the three of us around the television. The boats looked good on television. I sounded like a damn fool. Courtney, for the sake of a conservative Charleston audience, was an anonymous partner edited into the background. She was stung by the slight.

In the morning, Mrs. Wyatt showed us around her property. Hidden in her woods were the soft contours of earthworks that were fortifications during the Revolutionary and Civil wars. After getting a late start we paddled only fifteen miles before coming ashore in the afternoon. Courtney had not been feeling well since our quick lunch of cheese, soda pop, and potato chips. The symptoms seemed to indicate food poisoning.

While Courtney rested in the tent, I walked along the river to where a black man in his fifties was fishing. After admiring his catch, I asked him about the Aiken Plantation on Jehosee Island. Bishop had spent an evening there as a guest of a William Aiken, then a former governor of South Carolina.

"Oh yeah, my great-grandparents used to work there," he said, pointing across the river to an island of oak and pine in the middle of a plain of marsh grass. "And my aunt, she come from there, too. She's ninety years old."

Jehosee was not a large island. His grandparents, I was certain, had seen Nathaniel Bishop.

Bishop's voyage was big news in 1875. As he rowed south, people on the shore shouted out to him. He wrote, " 'Is dat de little boat?' they asked, viewing my craft with curious eyes. 'And is dat de boat made of paper?' they continued, showing that negro runners had posted the people, even in these solitary regions, of the approach of the paper canoe."

That night Courtney left the tent several times to empty her aching stomach. It was hot and muggy and gnats poured into the tent as she left. Each time Courtney returned, I zipped the door closed behind her. I thumbed the gnats against the wall of the tent, staining the nylon red with our stolen blood.

As with our Bishop, news of our voyage traveled ahead of us. While we paddled south from Beaufort, South Carolina, the marines at Parris Island, a Marine Corps Recruit Depot, had us under telescope surveillance. Military police were waiting for us as we landed. They escorted us to an interview with the depot newspaper, *The Boot*, and then to our quarters. We were billeted in a guest suite in the well-appointed home of the base commander and his wife.

We left Parris Island and faced a three-mile crossing of Port Royal Sound to reach Hilton Head Island. The water was only slightly corrugated by a westerly as we headed out from shore. Courtney was not paddling up to our usual pace so I moved ahead of her hoping to draw her up to speed. She did not take the bait. I drifted to a stop and waited for her to come alongside. Her eyes were fixed on the bow as she paddled. When she drew abeam she did not look across to me. With rigid, outstretched arms she rested her paddle on the crown of the foredeck.

"Are you OK?"

"Yeah," she answered flatly.

I started paddling again. She kept up with me for a hundred yards before she began to lag behind again. By the time we reached the middle of the crossing the wind had raised an uncomfortable chop and spotted the water to the west with whitecaps. I stopped and waited for her again.

"The wind is beginning to pick up. We can't afford to stay out here very long." She slashed into the water with her paddle and shot ahead of me.

In my solo experience I had discovered that the prolonged stress of travel wore my patience thin and revealed elements of my personality that I had thought I had outgrown. The process is like peeling an onion. The first few layers come off easily, the rest get progressively messier and more difficult to endure.

The most trying circumstances—usually a combination of foul weather and exhaustion—revealed in me a willful, petulant child whining, "I just want to go home" or "I just want to go to sleep. Is that asking too much?" It was always asking too much under the circumstances. In the middle of a rough, open water crossing there is no alternative to hard, often painful, work.

Visitations by my petulant child came often in my early travel, and I was always surprised by them, "What? Are you *still* here?" I now try to avoid his unpleasant company by keeping out of situations that call for more strength and patience than I have on hand at the time.

It was inevitable, I think, that the hardships of our voyage occasionally pushed Courtney into that raw state that made her ill at ease with herself and strained the relationship between us.

I followed Courtney as she bolted across the sound. I didn't know what anger drove her paddle. I could only wait until she expressed it or came to terms with it. At the moment it served to get us out of the wind's way, and that was all that mattered.

The wind was up again when we paddled through the backwaters of Savannah toward Ossabaw Sound. A fisherman passed us coming off the sound, caught my eye and traced a wavy line with his finger and shook his head—too rough. We headed for the closest high ground, a small hummock bearing four or five small palmettos.

Crowded on the high ground were an aluminum skiff, upside down with tarps and squares of plywood on and around it, a bicycle, at least a dozen five-gallon paint buckets, and a smoldering campfire. The man who called this place home was headed toward us across the marsh with an armload of firewood. He wore white dungarees held up by suspenders and over them a pair of large, brown corduroy pants hung from a necktie sash, and at least three shirts. He dropped his load of firewood twenty yards shy of his camp. We could begin to make out his narrative as he drew near us. "When I get tired of hauling I jus' let her drop, don't matter where. Firewood ain't goin' nowhere. When I feel like haulin' again I'll go git it. You like fish?" He dumped a dozen fifteen-inch sea trout out from one of the buckets, and they slithered across the grass. "I only need a couple of these small ones, these two 'ere. You kin have the rest."

We interrupted him to introduce ourselves, a formality I think he considered unnecessary. As he spoke his voice glided over a range of almost two octaves, hitting falsetto highs when he mentioned something that was either perfectly obvious or completely baffling to him. Arthur, we learned, was raised in a Savannah orphan home and had spent most of his sixty-one years on the water and the marsh. We accepted his offer of fish and asked if we might join him for dinner and share his camp for the night. He answered, "Got a shovel here you can knock the brush back with. Y'all like beans?" Another bucket went bottom up and cans rolled out alongside the fish. "No sense digging around to find what you want. Git it out where you kin see it. Thought I had me a can of beans in here."

Before dinner Arthur walked us around across the marsh to see the ruins of an old moonshine still, pointing out the signs of marsh wildlife as we went. No park ranger could have told us more. Courtney and I were spellbound by his vitality, sensitivity, and humor.

In the evening, after we had eaten our fill of fish, we stared into the fire. Arthur poked at the coals with a straightened-out coat hanger. He talked of his loneliness, of his lost ambition, and of learning to play the harmonica backwards, with the scale rising from right to left. "Now how do you explain that I wonder?" he squeaked. He showed us cast nets he made and fished with. Their diamond mesh was small and even. The thousands of knots fell into flawlessly straight rows. "They got machines now that can tie one of these up faster'n you can sneeze. Takes me a week." He flicked a coal into the fire and a trail of orange sparks floated above the fire. "I ain't a *has been*," he complained, "I'm a *never was.*"

I quickly came to admire him as a man of the marsh with a perception of its natural order as clear and as penetrating as his sky blue eyes. And if a man's wealth were measured by what he would give away, he would be among the richest, for there was nothing he valued so much that he would not share it with a friend or a stranger.

When we parted company with Arthur the next morning, he pushed our sterns from the muddy sand at the edge of his hummock, all the while telling us which turns we should make in the backwaters of the marsh to paddle a shortcut to Ossabaw Island. The chart in Arthur's head was as accurate as the one I had in my lap. Even when we were out of earshot we could see the wild dance of his gestures pointing our way through the waters of his home. Courtney and I paddled in silence for a long time, staring over our bows, for we knew that if we looked at each other we would weep at leaving such a man to his loneliness.

We hopped from one island to the next along Georgia's chain of barrier islands known as the Golden Isles. Each island was a world apart from the next. Ossabaw had been a large plantation. The last family heir, who grew up in the plantation's pink stucco mansion, had turned the island into a retreat for artists and authors. Small black feral pigs were scattered by the hundreds over the entire island.

St. Catherine's Island is an ark to animals from all over the world. The foundation that owns the island has established a research facility to study and breed animals that are being driven to extinction by the destruction of their natural habitats. The supervisor of the island showed us rhinoceros hornbills, Galapagos tortoises, sandhill cranes, and African gazelles. On the south end of the island a team of archaeologists walked us through a dig that revealed the ruins of a Spanish Cathedral built at the beginning of the fifteenth century.

On Doboy Island we found mounds of brown pebbles, unusual since there is no rock indigenous to the sandy Georgia coast. We learned later that the stones were Dover flint, brought from England as ballast aboard sailing ships and dumped before they took on loads of lumber from a sawmill, the ruins of which still stand.

I can't be sure why we were so well treated along the Georgia coast. There, more than anywhere else, we felt like a part of the coastal community. It could have been simple "southern hospitality." It could have been that we were traveling late in the year (December), long after the seasonal migration of countless pleasure craft, and the islanders liked the company of an occasional stranger. Whatever the reason, I'd like to think that they remember us for something other than our appetites.

High ground in the southern marshland is scarce. We depended upon the people that owned it for our camps. In the middle of a twelve-mile stretch of marsh, we stopped at Homestead Bluff. The high ground was occupied by handsome cabins. White paths of crushed shell meandered between the cabins across trimmed lawns.

The caretaker, the only soul on the grounds, was adamant that we could not camp there. When we returned to the boats the sun strained through the trees along the bluff. We were unhappy with the prospect of paddling in the dark to the next high ground, six miles to the south. (The truth is that we were quite miffed. We hadn't practiced humility in weeks, and we were a little rusty at it.) We walked back to our boats over a beach littered with clay pigeons. I took a spiteful count of the vast numbers of untouched targets.

We dropped into our boats and began our paddle to Cumberland Island. Courtney kept her eyes tuned to the dark and called out navigation lights to me as she saw them. In the blinding glare of a flashlight, I kept track of our course on the charts and followed Courtney's lead. Between the two of us, we managed to get to the Greyfield landing without any serious trouble.

We had been running south ahead of winter for three months but when we turned west up the St. Mary's River between Georgia and Florida, it caught up with us. A cold Arctic air mass dropped the temperatures into the teens and rimmed the tannin-stained waters of the St. Mary's with a fringe of ice. On Christmas Eve, Courtney pulled from the forward compartment of her kayak a package of tinsel garlands. She decorated our camp and laced the rest of the tinsel along the tie-downs on her kayak's deck. Christmas Day we were no longer an expedition but a parade.

In the middle of the St. Mary's wild meandering, Courtney asked for the chart. I lifted it from my lap and handed it to her over the water. With it strapped to her foredeck she guided us up the river while I brought up the rear and enjoyed the scenery.

The headwaters of the St. Mary's brought us to the only break in our 2,500-mile-long route. We hitched an eight-mile ride in the back of a pickup to the Okefenokee swamp. We unloaded the boats between a park-managed boat livery and the cypress-tree swamp water.

Before we launched into the swamp, we went to the concessionaire, as the signs at the water's edge had directed us, to obtain the permit required to enter the Okefenokee. The concessionaire directed us to the ranger in a tall cedar-shingle and glass building that housed the interpretive center. The ranger told us that we should have called for a reservation months ago. When I told him where we had been in the last three and a half months and pressed for a chance to cross the swamp to the Suwanee River, he gave us the number of the park manager and directed us to the pay phone outside. The coin slot of the phone was jammed with quarters that had apparently been hammered with a rock. We used the ranger's phone to call the manager. The manager, who was at a loss as to how he should handle people who had parked boats instead of a car next to the swamp, suggested we call the director of the park.

From the director I learned a few things. Though he would gladly issue us a day permit, it was a seventeen-mile paddle across the swamp to the Suwanee River.

"Great!" I said.

"How's that?" the director asked.

"We can do seventeen miles between now and midafternoon. We've been averaging twenty-five to thirty-five miles a day."

"The middle portion of the trail is a bit rough," he countered. "Even experienced canoeists can only make one mile an hour."

When I asked about the length of the rough section, he told me that it was five miles long. I calculated the time it would take to cover the other twelve miles in the daylight available. It still seemed reasonable to cross the swamp in a day.

"Even so," he said, "I can't let you do it. We only allow one party on each trail per day. If you were to cross paths with them you'd spoil their wilderness experience."

I was not one to argue against wilderness experience. Courtney and I walked back to the concessionary and tried to ease our disappointment by eating peanut butter candy bars and drinking soda. I looked over the shoulder of the concessionaire at a calendar on the wall. On it were the names of the canoe parties with permits.

"Who's scheduled to go out this morning?" I asked.

"Nelsons, a party of four, but if they're not here in five minutes they've lost their chance."

I looked at the clock on the opposite wall. It was 9:55 A.M. Below the clock was a hand-lettered placard stating that all parties had to be on the water by 10:00 A.M. The Nelsons, sensible people I'm sure, were at home, indoors. What kind of wilderness experience can you have when it is sixteen degrees below freezing?

We trotted back to the visitor's center and delivered the news of the forfeiture in turn to the ranger, the manager, and the director. The director then spoke to the ranger. And the ranger gave us forms to fill out. As I filled out our registration, our permit, and our liability waiver, we were told we must take two days for the crossing.

"You're to be out of the park at the time specified on the form." The drone of the ranger's voice suggested that I was being read my Miranda rights. "If you do not leave the park at the specified time a search for you will be mounted at your expense. If you leave early you will be subject to a fine." The ranger separated each of the triplicate forms with a snap and handed us the pink copies and a handful of pamphlets. We wasted no time in getting on the water.

Our "wilderness experience," of a sort, began almost immediately. From deep within the swamp came a roar and a whine, then, above the low brush in the distance, we saw a plume of blue vapor. An olive-drab punt turned into the canal and raced toward us. Two bearded men smiled at us as they went by and saluted us with beer cans held high.

Shortly after lunch we reached our assigned campsite, a concrete slab with a roof over it and a picnic table in between.

In the morning the swamp brightened only to a gray half-light beneath a leaden overcast. From the west came the heavy rumbling of a thunderstorm that grew louder as we ate our breakfast. As the first bull's-eyes of rainfall spread across the water, we launched our boats and paddled west toward the storm.

The rough section of our course through the swamp was as difficult as the park director had suggested. I would not have described it, as our brochure did, as a canoe trail. It looked more like a wet footpath. Thirty minutes along the trail, we reached a clearing flanked by tall cypress snags. Beyond the branchless trunks, we saw the heart of the storm moving toward us. The clouds lit up for seconds at a time with an unsettling pink glow. I remembered seeing something about lightning in one of the pamphlets we were given. I huddled over it and read, "Lightening is probably the most dangerous feature of an Okefenokee experience." Period. The words of advice I had hoped to find were conspicuously absent.

Not sure whether we were supposed to be in an open area or next to a tall tree, we split the difference and paddled into a patch of medium-sized brush. The thunder that crashed over our heads made us flinch as if it had thumped us on our skulls. By the time the storm had passed, our heads were slung from our shoulders vulture fashion.

The time we had lost put us in a race to reach our exit deadline. Once we reached the network of open canals, we paddled as fast as we could without losing our trail. We reached the west side of the park on time and dragged our boats up on the earthen dam that separated the swamp and the headwaters of the Suwanee River. On the top of the dam were the two ruts of a roadway, with no evidence in the mud or the grass that it had been traveled in weeks. There were no buildings, no rangers. We slid the boats into the Suwanee and paddled into the current that would carry us to the Gulf of Mexico.

The pine woods at the head of the Suwanee were flooded by six feet of water. Many of the alleys we followed through the trees were dead ends. We often let the boats drift, in search of the strongest current. Several miles from the swamp, we passed knots of high ground and eventually the land began to consolidate into the banks of the river.

We camped on bars of white sand between the woods and the river. Courtney usually took charge of the tent while I combed the woods for firewood. The best fuel was fat lighter, the resinous heart of a pitch pine that remains after the bulk of the tree's wood has rotted away. It looks like amber with annular markings, and it lights with a single match even when wet. As it burns it drips a bubbling black tar. We sat around the fire long after dinner and let the heat of the fire seep through our bodies.

The sphere of light around the fire reduced the size of our evening world. Beyond the fire's yellow mane of flames, we could see only each other. Within that circle, we retreated to our journals and wrote what two people committed to each other would have spoken. The sound of branches combing air into the river whispered in the dark around us. It reminded us that the current would carry us quickly to Cedar Key.

The night before we reached the mouth of the Suwanee, I took out of my duffel the candle lantern that had shone in most of our camps. With the point of my knife I scratched into its brass "Voyage of the Paper Canoe." I held it out to Courtney saying, "I think you should have this."

She took it in both hands and began to cry.

One does not make gifts of things that are to be shared. I think even then we knew what we refused to admit—that there would come a time when we would not share with each other the memories of our voyage. The candle would not always shine between us.

On the Gulf of Mexico, the sun beat down on the water and pressed it as flat as sheet metal. The water tower on Cedar Key rose first in the shimmering distance and stood like a spider on the horizon.

On the south side of the Cedar Key, Courtney and I landed, congratulated each other, shook hands, hugged, and set the camera's timer to take pictures of us by our boats. It was not until that evening, when we paddled toward a cluster of rental cottages between the water and the causeway to the mainland, that I began to understand the change that was about to happen. When there was no more traveling to be done, we would have to face each other over the cargo of broken hope that we had carried and one of us would have to ask: What are we going to do with this?

Courtney hauled her kayak up on the oyster shell beach by the cottages and went to make our arrangements for the night. I realized that whatever occurred in the course of the next day, I would have no cause to remember it. I sat motionless in my canoe, a few yards offshore, staring into the bottom of the boat. Though Courtney and I had paddled 2,500 miles together, the discovery of a person is a voyage of another sort, and the two of us had not traveled far before we had returned to the protection of our own shores.

When I heard Courtney's footsteps return to the beach, I looked up from the boat. I knew I would travel alone again, for

I had discovered that the solution to my loneliness would come not from someone else but from within. The water around the boat was as still as ice. I picked up the paddle and swept it past the flanks of my canoe for the last time.

Epilogue

When Courtney and I left Cedar Key in January of 1984, I left the paper canoe behind. It eventually found a home in the Cedar Key Historical Society Museum. In autumn of that year, I began work on a solo rowing boat. Courtney and I parted company a few months later. In the winter of 1985, I launched the boat at Pittsburgh and rowed, alone, 2,400 miles down the Mississippi and Ohio rivers, and along the Gulf of Mexico to Cedar Key. I followed the route described in Nathaniel Bishop's last book *Four Months in a Sneak Box*.

CHRISTOPHER CUNNINGHAM was born in 1953 and raised in Edmonds, Washington. Lacking a proper sandbox, Cunningham and his sisters played in the hulk of a four-oared racing shell. He learned to row at age seven.

In 1978 he built a canvas-skinned kayak and a dory skiff, which he later rowed solo up the Inside Passage of British Columbia. In 1980 he began to build boats professionally, specializing in replicas of traditional Eskimo kayaks and wooden rowing and sailing boats of the nineteenth century. In 1987 Chris built a replica of a ninth-century Viking rowing boat and set out with his wife for a thousand-mile-long row north along the Inside Passage.

HANNES LINDEMANN

An Impossible Voyage

From November 1955 to January 1956 I crossed the Atlantic alone in a self-built African canoe, setting out from the Canary Islands and arriving at the Virgin Islands in January 1956. A year later I set out again from the Canaries, this time in a folding boat.

In all of us there is an impulse—though it may be deeply hidden—to leave behind our ordinary lives and go beyond the morning to seek our fortunes. This urge is usually thwarted in our time by the restricting responsibilities of family or society. Yet some continue to climb almost inaccessible mountains or to explore the distances of the sea, dreaming of other coasts. And the curious thing is that when this impulse comes to the fore in some individual and is acted upon, most men are puzzled; so remote and fantastic, perhaps, do their own dreams seem.

Second Voyage: Resolutions and Preparations

I returned to Hamburg in April 1956 already contemplating a second voyage across the ocean. While sailing the dugout canoe, I had often thought back on the years when I had sailed a rubberized canvas folding boat at sea, and I found myself slipping into daydreams of a folding-boat crossing of the Atlantic. But it seemed an impossible dream and nothing more. It would be too difficult, too dangerous, too much would be demanded of me—my experience in the canoe told me that.

It was not until I learned something of voodoo in Haiti
that I began to give really serious consideration to my new
plan. Through voodoo I learned that one can, by deep concentration, a kind of self-hypnosis, change one's fundamental attitude toward a problem, that ultimately through voodoo, one
can rid oneself of fears and doubts. "Impossible is not Haitian,"
runs the motto of the newspaper in Jacmel, owned by my
friend M. Brun, and this motto I took for my own.

Therefore, on my return to Hamburg I read everything
that could teach me how to develop self-mastery and conquer
my anxieties, for I knew that self-doubt and hesitation were my
worst enemies in danger. My first step was prayer, the invisible
weapon of man, which brings him healing power and relaxation, recovery and renewed energy. True prayer penetrates the
unconscious, bringing peace to the individual and thereby
helping him to overcome disturbing traits in his character.
Without self-mastery, achieved through prayer and through
concentration, I knew my voyage would fail.

The problem I had to tackle, first and foremost, was sleep;
my experiences on the first crossing proved to me that lack of
sleep leads to delirium and hallucinations and from there to
deadly danger. If I wanted this second voyage to succeed, I had
to train myself to sleep in short intervals, to exist for a whole
week without regular, long stretches of rest. I remembered the
system—a form of self-hypnosis—advocated by a German psy-
chiatrist, Dr. J. J. Schultz, which he called autogenic training,
whereby one concentrates to such a point of relaxation that the
environment is forgotten, and the self is found. I had made
good use of this method before when I had trained myself to
snatch a few minutes sleep riding home from work. So now I
began to accustom myself to short intervals of sleep, which
would enable me to renew my physical and emotional strength
when at sea.

Of major importance in my preparations was the need to
create within myself the assurance of success. I had to rid myself of all traces of fear and self-doubt, so for three months I
concentrated on the phrases: "I shall succeed" and "I shall
make it." I hoped to make these thoughts second nature. At the
end of the three months my whole being was permeated by a
strong conviction that I would succeed; that, no matter what

happened, I would survive my trip. It was only then that I decided definitely to carry through my plan.

I only told my closest friends of my intentions. I bought a folding boat, planning to make the necessary changes in it myself. The plywood framework of this boat can be folded like the frame of an army cot, its hull is made of strong five-ply rubber and canvas, the deck of clear, royal blue canvas. Air tubes, built into the hull at the gunwales, give the boat added buoyancy. Its length is seventeen feet, one inch, and its width only thirty-six inches. It weighed approximately fifty-nine pounds.

The little harbor town of Las Palmas in the Canary Islands was to be my point of departure again. I chose it because of my many friends there, because of its favorable weather conditions, and to avoid a dangerous and time-consuming coastal trip. When I arrived I found that nothing had changed since my previous trip; the employees of the hotel were happy to see their *navegante solitario* back. I was given the same room and slept on the same lumpy mattress. It was comforting to be in such familiar surrounds; I knew the shoeshine boy in the Santa Catalina Park, I knew where to find the best pastry in town, and the members of the yacht club were my good friends. A newsreel with scenes of my first trip had been shown a month before, so that I was recognized and spoken to in the street more often than in Hamburg.

My boat had not yet arrived, so I spent my time reading the case histories of castaways to gain insight into their psychological problems. I came upon the report of a French ship's doctor, Jean Baptiste Henri Savigny, who with other castaways had spent thirteen days at sea after his ship sank in 1816. What happened during those thirteen days is hardly credible. Desperation and mass hysteria took over; suspicion and panic spread among the survivors, some committing suicide, others jumping overboard in a useless attempt to swim to safety. Murder, even cannibalism, gained the upper hand. Human excrement was eaten. Out of the 150 men who survived the shipwreck only 15 were left. Those who died, died because of a moral breakdown that could have been prevented by disciplined leadership.

The observations of another ship's doctor confirmed the importance of morale; the castaways of his ship, the *Villa de*

Sainte-Nazaire, which went down in 1896, were adrift for seven days in an open boat. By the second day delirium and hysteria had taken hold of every one of the survivors. And one year later, when the *Vaillant* sank, only one quarter of those saved survived the six days in a lifeboat. Here again death was due to a breakdown in discipline, for we know now that castaways can survive for nine days in the temperate zones, without food and water. Why did so many die unnecessarily? It was due, I believe, to their inability to adapt themselves to new conditions; the crumbling of morale and discipline was followed by physical calamity.

One can cite many instances from the last war of castaways who could not survive the trauma of a shipwreck or who, through ignorance, handled their food supply with suicidal stupidity. We see what men can endure as castaways when we consider the voyage of Captain Bligh of the *Bounty;* with eighteen men and a mere handful of food he sailed 3,600 miles in an open lifeboat under the tropical sun. His knowledge and his tremendous discipline brought the boat safely to Timor, after forty-two days sailing across the Pacific.

As I read the histories of castaways and shipwrecks, I became more convinced of the importance of morale, discipline, and calm to the single-handed sailor. Friends who have sailed the Atlantic in yachts have told me of finding encouragement and peace in prayer during moments of danger. I, too, prayed, but I felt I should do more to prepare for my second voyage; I had to drill my whole being—conscious and unconscious—to accept my plan. So I continued what I had begun in Hamburg. I repeated to myself, "I shall make it," and I added new autosuggestions, "Never give up, keep going west," and "Don't take any assistance." Gradually I felt my doubts and fears disappearing, yielding instead to a really positive optimism and confidence.

I congratulated myself on having chosen a folding boat, or foldboat as they are often called, for now I would be able to relive exactly the feelings of a lonely castaway; I would share his suffering, his hope, and his despair. I would know his thoughts during the long nights at sea. I would, in fact, have to contend with even greater discomfort than a person afloat in the life raft of a plane or in a ship's lifeboat. By suffering to the

Hannes Lindemann

utmost from the elements, I could test the durability of the human machine and, in a cockleshell like mine, I would learn much that we need to know about survival at sea.

Experience had already proved to me that in challenging the sea I had picked an implacable adversary. But it is in the nature of man to better his own achievement; it is normal and healthy to strive continually for new records. Each newly established record, after all, makes a positive contribution by setting the limits of human achievement. Thus the athlete who has run the one hundred meters in 10.1 seconds is only satisfied when he has run the distance in 10 seconds. But it is a fact well known to all good athletes that only the man whose past performance justifies it should try to break new ground. What is true for the athlete is also true for the sailor; I was able to challenge the Atlantic in a foldboat because of the experience and knowledge I gained during my first voyage in a dugout canoe.

At last my foldboat arrived in Las Palmas, and I was able to make my physical preparations. I christened her the *Liberia III*. My old friend, the sailmaker, sewed me two square sails, reinforced the stern by sewing canvas over it, and brought the canvas on the starboard side—from which I could expect most of the winds and waves—as far forward as the foremast. The mast was reinforced by two backstays, and I made a mizzenmast by putting a paddle in a wooden socket stick and slicing off one third of the blade.

President Tubman of Liberia stopped in Las Palmas on his way to Europe. He and his fellow countrymen had shown a great deal of interest in the ocean crossing of a canoe of the Kru tribe, and the *Liberia II* is now in the possession of President Tubman in Monrovia. For my second voyage he wrote a message of good luck in my logbook.

During my final preparations I continued my self-hypnosis. The last weeks before departure I fell into a mood of complete self-confidence. I had a feeling of cosmic security and protection and the certainty that my voyage would succeed.

Departure: October 20, 1956

"Hey, Hannes." A friend's voice, hushed so as not to disturb the early morning quiet of Las Palmas, woke me.

"Coming, coming," I answered, as loudly as I dared.

I had spent the last night on the *Tangaroa*, a double canoe owned by friends Jim, Ruth, and Jutta. As I awoke slowly, I heard footsteps from above, and Ruth's voice came down to me questioningly.

"Are you awake, Hannes?"

"Beginning to be," I answered and forced myself out of my bunk and onto the deck.

My friends were already up, waiting for me in the dawn. I expected to sail in about an hour. In the last days I had exuded self-confidence; yet, despite my techniques of self-hypnosis, I felt tension. I could not avoid an inner questioning: "Am I really doing this? Am I really crossing the Atlantic in a small rubber folding boat?" I countered these questions and calmed my nerves by repeating, "I'll make it, I shall make it. Stop worrying."

"You act as though you were about to cross the harbor," my friends teased me; so perhaps my tension did not show.

A few last-minute touches were still required. The underwater spear gun had to be fastened to the starboard side; Jim tied plastic material around the mast to keep it dry; Jutta sewed my spray cover; and Ruth handed me last-minute items from the *Tangaroa*. She also prepared a traveler's breakfast for me, fried eggs swimming in butter to give me a last boost of energy this side of the Atlantic. These three friends, convinced of my success, did everything to help and encourage me. Jim had advised me—as had friends in Germany—to use an outrigger when I was undecided between it and air tubes around the waterline. I finally decided on an outrigger made out of half a car inner tube, sealed at both ends.

Then the sun came up. Everything appeared to be taken care of, although I knew that I could spend another day in the harbor making changes in this and that, altering the trim of the boat in one way or another. But I knew I had to draw the line somewhere. This was it, now. The moment to leave had come. My friends tactfully spared me the painful emotions of a leave-taking; they climbed into their small dinghy and rowed over to the Santa Catalina wharf, a good spot for last good-byes. I paddled the *Liberia* through hundreds of fishing smacks over to a lobster crate on which stood two other friends. "You'll make it," they shouted.

I set the square sail forward and paddled slowly from the fishing harbor, passing the Santa Catalina wharf, where a handful of curious people stood watching me. Jim, Ruth, and Jutta, motionless, were among them. I could well imagine what was going on in their hearts and minds; I was far from cheerful, myself. They had their little dog with them, whom they had saved from drowning, and even he seemed nervous and anxious. Few people knew my exact destination, but many must have had an inkling. They remembered that before my last voyage I had told everyone that I planned to sail down the African coast, and instead I had gone across the Atlantic. This time, when I first arrived at the yacht club, my friends asked, "Hannes, are you sailing down the coast again?"

"Claro," (but, of course) I answered, only to be openly laughed at.

In the harbor basin I hoisted the gaff sail. Trade winds had blown strong for the past few days, but in the protected harbor I could not feel them. The clouds above me sailed northwest. It was now nine in the morning. I could hear cars honking from the shore and the whistle of steamers from the water. To hasten my progress, I took up the paddle again. It is an old rule for motorless craft to sail out of sight of land as quickly as possible. As I left the protected harbor behind me, the first gusts of wind flowed over my rubber and canvas craft, the swell heightened, and the first waves wet the canvas. I passed Las Palmas on the right, in the shadow of the old cathedral spire.

Then from behind me I heard the sound of an approaching engine. In the high swell I made out a white object. "Aha! they are probably looking for me." A moment later I recognized the local pilot boat, and my hope of leaving without official obstruction was dampened. They were definitely heading for me. I left the sail up, but the boat came closer, and the men on it waved me back toward them. I ignored them. They came alongside, the pilot shouting, "The harbor master wants to see you."

"Why?"

"I don't know. All I know is you're supposed to come back."

"I am sailing to Maspalomas, and for that I do not need anyone's permission."

Maspalomas is a beach to the south of the island, and it was true that I had thought of going ashore there to make some necessary changes in the trim of the boat. I sailed on. The pilot boat came up once more, this time on the port side, where I had attached my outrigger with a paddle. They drove right over it, breaking the paddle, and bringing me close to capsizing. I immediately took down the sail, trembling with rage at their carelessness. They threw a line to me. Furiously, I threw it back at them. The paddle blade was broken and would have to be fixed, so in any case I would have to stop somewhere for repairs.

"I'm going to paddle back," I shouted at them, and they left.

I felt limp, tired, and depleted. My paddling was too weak to get me back to the harbor. The pilot boat disappeared while I was still trying to paddle against the wind. I was only about three miles from the harbor, but somehow I didn't have the strength to get there. Perhaps it was the impact of my first disappointment, my first setback, and the sudden realization that I might not be allowed to make my voyage. No! I would not allow that to happen. My plans and preparation wasted because of a harbor master's whim? My savings, my hard-earned money thrown away? A voice inside me repeated, "I'll make it, I'll make it," and on a quick decision I turned around, hoisted the sails and set off again with a fine wind.

The trade winds freshened up, combers sprayed and splashed me. Nearly all the seas swept over the entire length of the boat, so that it became clear that she was too deep in the water. But as yet I had no time to take care of the problem. First I had to get the feel of the sea again and find out how to handle the loaded boat. The pointed bow lacked buoyancy, plowing the water to such a depth that at times the seas came to my foremast, while aft they ran to the mizzenmast.

I felt a little queasy. That morning Jim had reminded me to take pills against seasickness, as I do at the beginning of every voyage. Although the foldboat with its outrigger did not roll much in comparison with the dugout canoe, the motion bothered me, and I was glad I had taken the pills.

As I left the protection of the island, in whose lee lies the harbor of Las Palmas, the winds blew more strongly. Soon I took down the one-and-one-half-square-yard sail from the foremast and sailed with the three-quarter-square-yard sail of the mizzenmast. The aft mast was a paddle that sat on the aft washboard. I had arranged the steering as on the *Liberia II;* cables ran from the rudder to where I sat, and I could control them with my hands or feet. Also, I had arranged the boat so that I could sit relaxed, leaning back against the aft board, with my knees straight out in front of me while I steered with my feet. I could also sit closer to the front with bent knees, still using my feet for steering. It was only later in the voyage, after I had eaten some of the canned food and the boat was roomier, that I could stretch out my legs completely and then only on windless days when I did not have to steer. My friends had overestimated the speed of the *Liberia;* the loaded boat did not make more than three and a half knots. Now the little square sail on the mizzen was taking me south at two miles an hour. But as long as the trade winds blew, I was satisfied.

At twilight I reached the beach of Maspalomas. As the wind blew directly toward the coast, the surf was too high for a landing. I remembered previous expeditions to the beach with my Spanish friends, when we had gone there to picnic and swim. Early that evening I rounded the southeastern tip of Gran Canaria. The sea was calmer, so I took the opportunity to check the outrigger and the paddle, which had been cracked by the pilot boat. I took off the paddle and lashed the inner-tube outrigger to the deck, while I tried sailing for two hours without it. But it was too difficult. The boat rolled and my discomfort was acute. I had been rolled to last a lifetime during my first voyage. Ideally, I should have had an outrigger on both sides, but the boat was not strong enough for that. To keep her afloat in case she capsized, I had stored the inflated other half of the inner tube in the bow and several empty airtight containers in the stern.

October 21

While I worked on the outrigger, the night passed quickly. In the darkness I heard an occasional clap from flying fish. I was worried by the spray cover, which I had made and waterproofed myself in Las Palmas, for water leaked through its two layers of canvas. Water washed continuously over the deck and the spray cover, leaking through to my knees despite my oilskin pants. At nine that morning I wrote in the logbook, "The torture has started." Of course, no one knew better than I what awaited me, but even so I had forgotten that my skin was extremely sensitive to waterproofing ingredients. After these few hours of exposure it hurt badly; when I touched a spot on my body the whole surrounding area burned as though hot tar had been poured on it. It was impossible for me to change clothes in the heavy sea, and the pain became so great that I seriously considered turning back or trying to reach the African coast. But I had to keep on. I reminded myself of the phrases I had continually repeated in Las Palmas: "Keep going west; don't take assistance; never give up." I had hammered these words into my very innermost being back in the hotel when my heart and mind were calm. Now, in this moment of near panic, I needed them. In my first anger at my skin trouble, my weakness came to the fore, but the often-repeated words kept me going.

During the day the wind came from all points of the compass; flat calm alternated with contrary winds and choppy seas until evening, when the old trade winds blew again. Butterflies fluttered over the water. I pulled a locust out of the sea, and wondered if some day someone might not do this to me.

Water continued leaking through the spray cover. With a little rubber syringe, the kind a doctor uses for cleaning ears, I drew it out. Then at last I found time to concentrate on a quiet meal. I had eaten nothing the day before except my hearty breakfast, but I had drunk twice my usual amount of liquid to prevent dehydration. I had deliberately avoided food for thirty-six hours, hoping to dull my senses by fasting and thereby to make the discomforts of the journey easier to bear. Now I drank my ration of unsweetened evaporated milk and ate several oranges. Suddenly I noticed that my leeboard had fallen off and was floating away. It would serve no purpose to worry over the loss; the ship's doctor of the *Liberia* had forbidden worry, for it could only sap my strength. I was better off in this one respect than most single-handed sailors: I had my own physician aboard. I knew myself well and knew that after the problem of thirst would come the problem of morale. I had to keep my sense of humor and a relaxed outlook; I had to remain cheerful, unconcerned, and emotionally stable.

As the second night approached, I tried hard to concentrate on relaxation so that my strength would be renewed for the coming day. I had to learn the art of sleeping while sitting. This is an easily acquired skill, but I was forced to check on the course at the same time. I felt empty, drained of thought, my feet hardly able to control the course. Then, for a fraction of a second, I fell into a dream. A wave awoke me. In the morning I discovered that my head had sunk onto my chest in sleep several times. I realized that I was a simple man with simple needs, a tired creature who needed sleep urgently!

Yesterday I lost sight of land. Now I was really alone. For how long? I counted on seventy days. As I left the protection of the Canary Islands, winds and seas became heavier. In the morning a steamer passed two miles to port, unaware of the little *Liberia*. I sewed a plastic layer over the deck so that less water would come through the spray cover. Because my freeboard was too low, water washed over the boat. The wind was only twenty miles an hour, but even this was too much for the *Liberia*. I had to throw something overboard to lighten her.

First went the quinces, lovely, sweet Canary Island quinces, 22 pounds, quite unspoiled, floated off into the Atlantic Ocean. But the boat was still too heavy, so, very reluctantly, I got rid of another 22 pounds of canned food. The boat sailed better now, and I was less worried. The sea would replace what I had lost, as long as I had the means of catching sea life. I sailed on, carrying 154 pounds of food and drink for the seventy days that might still lie ahead. Despite my previous experience, I might have miscalculated. But it did not matter. What I had read of castaway reports from the last war convinced me that there is enough food in the sea to ensure survival.

I suffered intensely from the oversensitivity of my skin under the sun that day. It was so bad that I began to despair: "Jump overboard. Who cares about you? Who knows where you are? Not even at home do they know of your new voyage." These thoughts ran through my head, taking hold of my senses, until I drove them off by repeating. "Never give up. Keep going west."

My fingertips were swollen, the skin raw from handling wet articles and bailing the boat. In Las Palmas I had painstakingly developed calluses on the palms of my hands and a tan on my nose, but I had overlooked the need to toughen my fingertips.

As the sun set, the first curious birds inspected the foldboat from above. These creatures all seemed bigger than I remembered from the first crossing. Was it perhaps because I felt so minute in my rubber boat?

And then again night came. The mizzen sail was set, demanding constant watchfulness from me to ensure that I stayed on course. Under the most favorable conditions a boat as flat as mine has trouble keeping on course with aft winds. I concentrated on putting myself into a state of dozing in which my feet would still control the rudder, but no actively conscious thought would disturb my rest. On a clear night, when the stars were visible, I had no trouble steering with my feet, but with cloudy skies I had to use the flashlight to light up the compass.

My pulse that night had sunk to the slow rate of forty-two beats a minute; hunger, inactivity, and my physically good condition played a part in keeping my pulse slow. My whole system was influenced, I am sure, by my total concentration on relaxation.

October 23

The weather improved, making it possible to dry out my drenched clothes. Above all, I wanted to expose my skin to the sun. My whole lower body felt as if someone had been sticking pins into it. I could hardly wait for the noonday sun to start my cure. At midday I put a paddle over the washboard, forced myself out of the opening in the spray cover and sat down cautiously on the palm of the paddle. I steered with my hands. Slowly, I peeled off my thin rubber jacket, oilskin pants, shorts, thick sweater, and undershirt. Everything was soaked through. With a few clothespins I fastened my wardrobe to the shrouds of the mizzenmast. How superb to feel the sun warming and drying my skin! From then on the noon hour was devoted to health; it became my "hour of hygiene and preventive medicine." I sat high on my little seat, bailed water from the boat, dried the kapok cushion in the sun and made myself very comfortable. At the end of the hour I dusted my clothing with talcum powder, rubbed my body with a washcloth, and dressed. Then I settled down again in the shadow of the mizzenmast.

The mild wind made a pattern of shingles across the surface; the *Liberia* rocked gently in the swell; and the ocean showed me its friendliest aspect. I felt peaceful.

Again the night put a dark veil over the sea. In small boats, nights at sea are disagreeable and uncomfortable. Fortunately the mizzen sail, which had been up since Las Palmas, protected me from the cold wind. My hope and ambition was to leave it up until I reached St. Thomas. Contrary winds, of course, could force me to take it down. I had chosen St. Thomas as my final destination. I felt an obligation to the yacht club there, of which I was an honorary member, so my bow pointed straight to the Virgin Islands.

I was beginning to feel that dozing and emptying my mind of all conscious thought, that concentrating on nothing, would not, in the end, be a sufficient substitute for sleep.

October 24

I passed an agonizing night, knowing there would be many others like it to follow. It was cold. When the sun finally shone I cut up a large seabag and sewed it aft over the spray cover. I was delighted with this accomplishment. The wind blew favorably from the east, and my skin burned less. But my buttocks were uncomfortable; I could only hope that the condition would not worsen.

I found that I daydreamed a great deal. Girls appeared in my dreams, but I knew that in a few days they would be banished for the rest of the trip. A hungry man generally does not think too much about women.

On land I pray regularly; at sea I prayed for alertness and for comfort. I found that praying, which can be a sort of sinking away, a forgetfulness of the outside world, strengthened my morale. The night was clear; the moon outshone the stars, so that I could barely recognize the planets. Inside the boat everything was soaked. The trade winds, as they had done a few days before, came from all directions—one minute from the north, the next from the east, and a minute later from the northeast. In a small boat wind irregularities are much more noticeable than on a yacht. Crosswaves slapped the foldboat, giving me the feeling that we were running athwart the sea. But the compass showed that it was the waves, not I, that had veered.

October 25

On that morning I was pleasantly surprised to find a bottle of orange juice that Jim had hidden for me. Later on, as I took my noon position, I found a photograph of Jim, Ruth, and Jutta, stuck into my nautical almanac. He had written across the top, "Dear Hannes, keep going west. Your friendship meant a lot to us." And Ruth's message. "Don't worry, you'll succeed," strengthened my determination.

I knew I could rely on the accuracy of my noon position. I measured the longitude only approximately, from the difference between Greenwich and local time, but I had tested my chronometer, and I knew it was trustworthy.

A little later I discovered a locust, clinging to the block on top of the mizzenmast. I christened him Jim in honor of my friend and then worried about how to free him. The butterflies that fluttered by the *Liberia* had never thought of taking refuge on her.

Once that night I fell into deep sleep, to be awakened by the flapping of the mizzen sail. In my sleep I had dreamed that a friend had taken me to the safety of a harbor where I could sleep without fear of capsizing. The dream was nothing but a rationalization of my weakness in falling asleep.

October 26

My first concern that morning was for my locust friend, Jim. He was still alive, and a little later I photographed and took movies of him from every angle. The winds still blew from the east. My luck was holding at the beginning of this voyage. By now I was completely familiar with the outrigger and knew its reactions in all weather conditions. I had fastened it to the port side, the side that is more on the lee during a crossing like mine than the starboard. The Polynesians carried their outrigger on the weather side but mine was not like theirs. I, at least, preferred it on the lee. I had had great difficulty setting the sails on the dugout, but now, with the stability given by the outrigger, it was simple.

In order to lighten the boat, I ate only from my supply of canned food for the first week. My only uncanned food was garlic and some oranges. I took garlic along because it keeps so well under the worst conditions; not even saltwater spoils it. It is also a better aid to digestion than the onion, although it contains fewer vitamins. In the morning I drank a can of evaporated milk, in the evening a can of beer, together with my meal of beans, peas or carrots, and a few slices of garlic. Milk and beer raise the energy level of a hungry man. I have sometimes thought that on steamship routes, where rain can supplement the water supply, lifeboats should also carry milk. It is true that water is the beginning and end of a castaway's existence, but milk is more than a liquid, it is a food. It helps control the factors in a hungry man's body chemistry that make for panic and delirium. The ability to stay calm and in control of a situation is of paramount importance to the castaway. Expressed in simple terms, one can say that hunger creates an imbalance in a man's metabolism, which may cause moments of delirium. The alkali content of milk and beer, as well as their easily absorbed calories, can counteract this condition.

In spite of my knowledge of the dangers of dehydration and the care that I exercised to prevent it, I noticed its symptoms in the cracking and peeling of my skin folds. Because man's thirst does not reflect his need for liquid this is a constant danger.

October 27

Jim disappeared from the top of the mast. I looked everywhere for him, but he was gone. A pity! The wind weakened. The night before I had slept a little. I managed it by changing the sails so that the wind was freer, and I could handle the boat more easily. Then I lay down on my left side, with my knees bent and my feet still controlling the rudder, my head resting on the washboard. It was no luxurious bed, but the sleep strengthened me. I slept for half an hour on one side, sat up and then turned onto the other side. I felt I had found a solution to my sleep problem and was only sorry that it could not be done when the winds were stronger.

Last night Madeira petrels danced around the boat. Mediterranean shearwaters, which regularly accompanied me during the day, were seldom visible at night. I wondered why it was so difficult to catch seabirds in these zones. Castaways from other regions of the sea have told of catching quite a few. The castaways of a Dutch luxury steamer that was torpedoed in 1943 hold the record; they caught twenty-five birds in eighty-three days afloat below the equator. It is possible that seabirds prefer to rest on floating rather than sailing objects.

The sun burned with pitiless intensity on my mizzenmast. I sprinkled the sail with sea water and found its shade cooler after that. I took the noon position, then sat down on the paddle seat for my hygiene hour. I was amused at the thought of a steamer suddenly seeing a man take a sun bath on the edge of a foldboat in midocean.

Before my departure I had developed a method aimed at disciplining the blood vessels of my buttocks. For three months I spent fifteen minutes a day relaxing and repeating to myself, "I am quiet, I am quiet, my body is relaxed, completely relaxed. My thighs and buttocks are warmer, much warmer. Pleasant, warm blood flows through the buttocks." This was no cure-all for my problem, which came from the fact that I had to sit for so long in wet clothes, but perhaps it helped to heal my saltwater sores. I found it difficult at first to do this on the boat; possibly I was disturbed by my new environment, and in heavy seas I did not try it at all.

Now I began to see small fish under the boat. I had painted her underside red, just as I had the dugout canoe. Little fish were attracted by the shadow cast by the boat, hoping it would afford them protection from their enemies. I am not sure as yet whether large fish, like sharks, will avoid the color red. I had brought with me certain other preventive measures against sharks. First in the line of defense was a piece of shark meat to throw at them in case of necessity (after three days it stank so horribly that I had to throw it away). Secondly, having heard that sharks are frightened by metallic sounds, I had tied together some pieces of old iron to throw at them in case of attack. I knew that sharks do not intentionally attack boats. Other big fish follow the same rule. Despite this knowledge, I was still worried. After all, the fish might feel that here was such a cockleshell of a boat, and they had nothing to fear from it.

October 28

That morning, looking for something on the boat, I found two presents from my friends of the *Tangaroa;* a bottle of rum about the size of a finger and a copy of the *Bhagavad-Gita*, one of the world's great religious works.

The trade winds freshened. Far too much spray and far too many combers washed over the spray cover, but in a foldboat these are as impossible to avoid as dust on a motorcycle. I felt myself as safe and sure on the high seas in a foldboat as a bicyclist on the road. In fact, in some respects I was safer; I did not run the risk of being pushed into a ditch. I owed this feeling of assurance to my previous trips in a foldboat and to the knowledge that the air tubes built into the hull of the *Liberia* would keep her afloat if she capsized.

My noon latitude that day was 26 degrees north. As I was returning the sextant to its waterproof bag, a dolphin took the bait I had hung over the starboard side. My first fish of the voyage! I hauled it on board and killed it with a knife. First I drank the blood, then I ate the liver and roe, which actually tasted better than the flesh of the fish, as well as being richer in vitamins and minerals. Later I ate part of the meat, putting aside the remainder in the shade of the compass for the next day's meal. I was pleased at having saved a whole day's ration.

The seas had grown stronger, bending the wooden frame-work of the boat with each wave. Because the air tubes were not fully inflated, there was a creaking, groaning sound in the boat. I began to feel that my own bones were making these unhappy sounds. Yet the foldboat sailed better now than ear-lier; sometimes she ran before combers like a Hawaiian surf-board. The *Liberia III* had certain advantages over the *Liberia II;* I found it easier to set her sails, and in calm weather I could read because she rolled less. Now the trade winds blew with full power, and the whole ocean appeared to move toward the west.

Fortunately for me, the nights were quieter than the days. At night I skimmed through a sea of bioluminescence, which enchanted me with its beauty and variety and reassured me of the ocean's fertility.

October 29

Around midnight, the wind, calming for an hour or so, al-lowed me a little sleep. Then it returned, from the northeast, blowing with a force of twenty-five miles an hour. The outrig-ger slipped, and in the dawn a big breaker pushed it completely out of place. I waited for more light before repairing the dam-age. Then I took down the sails, forced myself out of the spray cover, readjusted the course, and stretched out over the outrig-ger. I was pushing it back into position when suddenly an enormous, steep green wall towered above me. It hovered briefly and then crashed over me and the boat. I gasped for air. Because I had all my weight on the outrigger, the boat did not capsize, but it was half swamped with water. I climbed back in during a few seconds of calm and sat down in water. I adjusted my course so that the bow soon pointed west again; then I hauled out my little pot and bailed. I got up the last of the water with the rubber syringe. One hour later the inside of the boat was drier, but I was still soaked through.

The sea roared and stormed with such violence I was unable to take the noon position. A school of dolphins passed by, but I lost sight of them quickly in the rough water. Later that morning I spotted a few albacores.

I reacted to my enforced inactivity like a schoolboy; I squirmed on my seat, I wriggled, I moved first one way, then another, changing positions every few minutes.

For ten days the trade winds had blown steadily. Had I hitched a ride with them that would take me directly to St. Thomas? In that case I could expect to make the crossing in fifty-five days. That evening rain squalls hit the *Liberia*, and with the help of the mizzen sail I caught three quarts on a plastic layer of my spray cover. I drank one quart immediately and put the rest aside in an aluminum container.

October 30

Eleven days at sea. Now the trade winds appeared exhausted. The night was calm. An Atlantic swell of more than twenty-four feet rolled under the boat, heaving the *Liberia* up to a peak, from which she slid gently down into the next valley. At noon I enjoyed a thorough hygiene hour. I washed all my clothing in the sea, drying it on a quickly installed clothesline. My knees and thighs were covered with small pustulae. I opened them with a needle, removed the pus and let them dry out in the sun. I fished purple snails from the water. As I crushed them, they stained my fingers with the dye that was once used to color the togas of emperors and kings.

October 31

I had my first night of flat calm. The cans still took up too much room for me to stretch out my legs in sleep though. The rudder already had a free play of more than 20 degrees, considerably more than I expected from my previous experience at sea. From the southeast a few small breaths wafted over a lazy ocean. I noticed a great deal of plankton, but as yet had seen no triggerfish or water striders. The wind veered to the south, and a rainfall brought me more drinking water.

November 1

My thirteenth day at sea, and the winds, of course, were contrary. My watch stopped working, but it was no great misfortune, for the chronometer would replace it. A bad squall, coming from the southeast, broke the boom, as I laughingly called the stick no thicker than a finger to which the sail was attached. I repaired it with ease, but the sails no longer fitted as exactly. Before the twenty-four hours of the thirteenth day had passed, I suffered an attack of stomach cramps. My relaxation exercises brought some relief.

That afternoon the contrary wind stiffened. I had no sail up, but I was still blown back toward the east. So as not to drift too rapidly off course, I took down the paddle that served as a mizzenmast. For the first time on the voyage I threw the sea anchor out over the stern. The boat held herself surprisingly well, hardly swinging around at all. I attributed it to a good job of trimming the boat.

November 2

For a whole day I lay to on the sea anchor. The boat shipped a great deal of water, since we were no longer sailing with the waves or before the sea. Big waves ran pitilessly over the deck. I bailed at least once every hour, until I was so tired of it that I pulled up the anchor, so that I was again before the wind. I now faced the direction I came from. The only advantage was less water in the *Liberia*.

Around noon, the wind calmed. The latitude showed me that in two days I had been driven almost forty miles northward. But when I compared it to the three thousand I had to cover, forty did not overly disturb me.

A giant swell, indicative of a real storm, rolled down from the North Atlantic. I perched proudly on the washboard, enjoying my hygiene hour and watching a little dolphin, hunted by three larger brothers, take refuge in the shakedown of my boat. The little fish, not much longer than my foot, waited quietly under the air tube, but his hunters spotted him. One attacked but the little fish escaped. Now I watched a life and death chase. They swam around the rudder, showing very little respect for my boat. Finally one succeeded in capturing his prey. It was hardly an evenly matched contest. The three older dolphins measured three and a half feet to the little fish's paltry inches. However, they must have enjoyed the chase, for they started beating the bottom of the boat with their tails. They approached, turned on their sides and smacked the keel. Although they in no way threatened the safety of the *Liberia*, I was indignant over their lack of respect. In a momentary rage I grabbed my grappling iron, stabbed and wounded the first, then I thrust at the second, but broke the aluminum point of the iron in the process. The third dolphin continued his cavorting until I drove my knife into his body. I could have caught them easily with my underwater gun, but they were really too large to bring aboard without damaging the boat.

November 3 and 4

The trade winds returned during the night. The sky was cloudy and later a roaring, blustering, and hurling squall poured rain on the sea, ironing it flat with its force. I caught fresh water in my spray cover. In the past sixteen days I had collected more than I was able to throughout the first crossing.

The wind whistled through the shrouds, and at night I dozed only from time to time. I was beginning to feel tired. During the night of the sixteenth day I had the strange impression that the ocean ran toward the east. I could not rid myself of this kinetic illusion. I put my hand into the water and, sure enough, it ran eastward. The clouds stood still, and I believed that my boat was being carried back to the African coast. I shone a flashlight on the compass. It showed west. I knew who I was; I knew where I wanted to go, but heaven help me, how was I to rid myself of this certainty that I was going backwards? Everyone has experienced the same kind of sensation sitting in a stationary train, when the train beside him moves, and he has the illusion that he is moving. But this hallucination in a small boat was unexpected. Then a comber washed over the boat, sweeping away with it this mysterious sensation. With complete assurance I knew now I was sailing west.

I almost always kept the mizzen sail up. Sailors will wonder why, but it afforded me such fine protection against cold winds that I overlooked the less advantageous steering.

The wind was still fresh, so the night was unpleasant. But the seabirds enjoyed it, for it made their flight easier and freer. I saw several Manx shearwaters. There were more of them this year than last, and this time I had no trouble identifying them. Because of their skillful aerial acrobatics, I nicknamed them "the mad flyers." My good friends from the first crossing, the Madeira petrels and the Mediterranean shearwaters, joined me once again. I saw only isolated tropicbirds. On my previous voyage I had sailed closer to the Cape Verde Islands, where they appear more frequently. A trained zoologist, by looking at the seabirds and at fish, can roughly tell his location on the high seas without recourse to the stars.

The rough sea had forced me to do without my daily hygiene hour. Without a sun bath to dry the pustulae on my thighs, I had to wipe them off with a handkerchief. I used my thigh muscles less than any others, and properly I should have massaged them daily. However, the erupting exanthemas made massage too painful, even though I realized that without it the muscles might shrink. Between my two voyages I intentionally gained weight so that I would use up excess fat rather than muscle tissue at sea.

"How much weight will you lose?" Jim asked me in Las Palmas. "About ten pounds?"

I told him I expected to lose at least forty-five pounds, and he pointed out that I could afford it, whereas with his skinny frame he could never stand such a loss.

November 6

Finally the wind abated; the first trade wind clouds appeared in the sky. I put out all my wet possessions to dry in the sun: books, cameras, sea charts and, of course, my clothes. I knew I had sufficient drinking water to avoid dehydration and could afford the luxury of a long exposure to the sun. I noted with interest that this light exertion brought my pulse up to forty-eight beats per minute, whereas before it had been thirty-four.

So far nothing unforeseen had occurred. The voyage had gone as I expected, based on my previous experience, except for less stable weather. My natural optimism took over. I planned new voyages or daydreamed of a farm in the tropics, always a pet idea of mine. During the first two weeks a woman appeared in my dreams of the perfect life, but as the voyage continued I rejected her completely. I was even baking my own bread. Food—I thought mainly of food, mostly of sweets. My special favorite is a cake with whipped cream. There, in mid-Atlantic, food played the foremost role in my daydreams.

November 7

The trade winds lay dormant; only rain clouds and soft gusts remained unchanged. As I bailed the boat, I discovered that one tin of milk had corroded. In the afternoon a swarm of triggerfish plundered the first barnacles off the boat bottom. It was an odd sensation to feel them under me, first snapping at the barnacles, then diving deeper and slapping the boat with their tails. My body was so much a part of the boat that I had the sensation they were attacking me.

To one who uses his eyes, life at sea offers endless variety. Very seldom is one day like the next, but my twentieth day differed not at all from the day before: weak winds from the northeast, the same birds, and the same swarm of triggerfish rolled under the keel.

I am an optimist—I have to be—so I celebrated the end of the first third of the voyage. Celebrated with what? There was not much choice; I could either drink an extra can of milk or an extra beer. I chose milk. I had also taken with me a pound of honey for each week of the crossing. I had not touched it yet, but as soon as I remembered its presence on the boat I pulled it out and in minutes a half week's ration was gone. It was difficult to hold to the rations I had planned for. During the first week I was sometimes hungry, but after that, hunger left me, and I suffered only from thirst. Surely I took with me the least amount of food of any boat that has ever made the Atlantic crossing, at least much less than Alain Bombard.

November 9

As long as the nights were calm, I was always able to catnap and renew my strength. During these naps my feet controlled the rudder; although I sometimes found myself off course, still the foldboat managed to stay with the waves.

I saw my first water striders. It is not unusual to find them in the ocean far away from land, although these were a different species from those I had seen in the Gulf of Guinea. The first swarm of flying fish swam and leaped alongside the boat.

I was approaching the tropics and expected to be south of the Tropic of Cancer that night. I made several attempts to spear some triggerfish with my knife but only succeeded in wounding them. In the evening the wind freshened. The shearwaters' activity increased, while the petrels behaved with the abandon of children released from school. Heavy seas in the early evening forced me to sail with care, lest the boat broach.

November 10

The entry into the tropics brought no visible change; wind gusts were still fierce, identical birds and fish accompanied me, and the sea, as ever, was full of twists and surprises. The wind had beaten the surface, stirred it up, finally turning it into a boiling inferno. Trade winds drew their breath of life from squalls and gusts, which every now and again rushed over the water. My heart felt for my boat, which had to make its way over a sea as rough and as full of bumps as an ancient cobblestone road.

I had to replace the bulb of my flashlight that evening, but my boat was so well organized that I was able to find it at once. Day or night, I knew exactly where to find every spare part.

November 11

Sunday, and my thoughts turned to the coffee and cake being served at home. Familiar church bells rang in my ears. Warm air wafted toward me from the southwest. I had decided to indulge in a Sunday treat of canned carrots; when I opened the can I was overjoyed to find Danish meatballs. My mistake came from the trademark on the outside, which looked like two crossed carrots. I had suffered horribly from boils during my first crossing and, thinking they might have come from a meat diet, I took no meat with me on this trip. I had also chosen to take beer, hoping its vitamin B content would help prevent furunculosis.

Later that day I fell into a flat calm. With a quiet surface I was always made aware of the plankton "dust" that floats near the surface of the water. I caught a little pilot fish with seven dark rings around its body; a good start for an aquarium, but unfortunately not in my present situation. Triggerfish returned. I hung a thin nylon line from the paddle support of the outrigger. It barely touched the water, and the triggerfish were fascinated by this dangling object. Every one of them wanted to snap at it, giving me a fine opportunity to catch some. I tried spearing them with my knife, but only succeeded in inflicting wounds. My hand proved more agile, so with a quick scoop I caught one around the head. At first it stayed motionless, but after a few seconds, it grunted a little reproachfully, as if to say, "You broke the law of the sea. I am taboo as food." But it was mistaken. Its organs had a wonderful flavor. Under their fins, triggerfish have red meat that tastes like meat from mammals, which I preferred to their white meat. I ate the brain of the poor creature, although it was not much bigger than the tip of my little finger. When we eat protein such as fish our body needs additional liquid to excrete the salts and urea, but there is no available liquid in meat, unless it is pressed out. The eyes, the brain, the blood, and the spinal fluids do supply us with some water, but it is not enough to carry on the process of excretion. Therefore a castaway should not eat protein if he is dehydrated, for it will aggravate his condition.

November 14

For four days the wind blew from the west. It was not strong, but I knew it was delaying my progress considerably. I was no longer alone on the *Liberia*. A crab had made its home on the port side of the boat. At noon every day he came out of a little hole and warmed himself in the sun. But he was a cautious companion, scuttling for shelter whenever I bent over to have a closer look at him.

I caught another triggerfish with my hands. This fellow had little transparent long-tailed parasites on his fins. A pilot fish popped out as I slit his stomach. With fresh bait I caught a dolphin. I sent an arrow from my underwater gun through his body, but could not pull him up on deck until I had killed him with my knife. I could only haul in a fish as big as this one when he was dead, otherwise he would damage the boat. This fellow had many dark spots on his skin that looked like bugs. They were parasites and, under them, the fish's skin had retained its light color.

I threw more bait overboard and caught another dolphin. But then my attention was attracted by the behavior of the rest of the swarm, which suddenly collected on the port side. A shark! Only three yards away from the boat a shark waited, and halfway between the shark and the boat my poor victim dangled from the line, fighting for his life. It looked as though the shark would attack the fish, but he was evidently afraid of my strange craft and did not dare approach. So I pulled the dolphin into the boat, killing him outright with a knife thrust between the eyes. The shark, lolling behind the boat, obviously had been attracted by the struggles of my victim. It was a fully grown shark, about twelve feet long, easily twice the weight of my boat, contents and crew. As the shark seemed as timid as I, I was less nervous, although I was glad to see it turn away. I looked over my catch. In the stomach of one I found a remora, a sucking fish, and in the other fish only my bait. I ate their organs first, then drank their blood mixed with a little rain water.

When I curled up to nap in calm weather, I could feel the snaking movements of my boat right through the rubber. But I trusted the strength of the material. At that point in the voyage my mood was one of utter confidence; no disaster would touch me. I asked myself, "Why should I concern myself with something that has not happened yet and that I could not change anyway?" Although the calm dampened my hopes, I still expected to arrive in St. Thomas by Christmas.

November 15

A warm breath blew over the ocean from the west. The atmosphere felt sticky and, unlike windier days, the air was empty of birds. Probably they were resting on the water, storing up strength. I ate some more of my catch. It stayed edible for twenty-four hours if I kept it in the shade; thereafter it soured. Fish can be kept longer if it is sliced and dried in the sun, and no water is allowed to touch it.

My attention was attracted by the snorting of a single whale. Then I saw his body, a black patch in the high swell. Occasionally a Madeira petrel fluttered listlessly in the humidity. Only two tropicbirds retained their energy, flying high above me. Then once again a loud snort sounded across the water, and I saw a huge spout shoot into the air. I heard the whale take several shallow breaths, then one loud, deep breath. With that he plunged into the depths, his tail fin erect in the water. There is a whale skeleton on display in the Oceanographic Museum in Monaco, into whose abdominal cage the *Liberia III*, with hoisted sail, could fit quite comfortably.

Slowly, slowly I paddled into the breath blowing against me from the west. The sea boasted a pretty shingled pattern. I did about one knot with my paddle. I tired quickly and rested often. Without warning, a shark appeared beside me. It was about nine feet long, the average size for a high-sea shark. It stared at me out of its round, pig eyes, so close I could have reached out and touched it. I found my camera and took pictures while the fish dawdled under and around the rubber canoe. I had time to get at my movie camera, because the shark continued circling around the air tubes, surrounded by a host of pilot fish. I was neither particularly eager to have a shark near me, nor very sure of how to get rid of it. Watching it closely until it came within reach, I hit it on the head with the paddle. My action had no effect whatsoever. After a while, however, it swam off, leaving me convinced that it had no bad intentions toward me. It behaved as a zoologist would have expected.

My sea anchor line was no thicker than a pencil, but it never occurred to a fish to bite through it. They do not destroy for the sake of destroying, nor do they plan or reason. They never thought of capsizing the boat and then attacking me.

I was worried about my right knee, which was swollen just below the knee cap and very sensitive to the touch. A similar swelling in any other place would have caused me less concern, but the knee joint merits special care and attention.

For the first time since the beginning of the voyage, I trimmed the boat; I took twenty-five pounds of food from the front and stowed it behind my seat. As I still had a west wind, the bow now went better into the wind.

I drew an empty bottle smelling of gasoline out of the water, cleaned it carefully and stored it away.

November 16

Again the wind came from the west. For nine days now I had had contrary winds. The air was heavy, my body dehydrated, my saliva thick and sticky. My tongue stuck to the roof of my mouth. I was roused by seven Mediterranean shearwaters, flying on the starboard side. I had never heard them make such a loud noise before, and the harsh metallic sound of their wings frightened me. Seven in a group—I had never seen so many together.

The swelling on my knee had gone up. I injected penicillin into it.

The terrible west wind frustrated my whole being. It tried my patience, made me nervous, ill at ease, and irritable. I was ready to start an argument with myself. Of course, I knew these symptoms to be common to people in a state of starvation or to castaways, but knowledge did not help me. Again dreams of a farm and of pastry topped by mountains of whipped cream brought release from tension. Nothing else interested me just then. In my mind I was either working on my farm cleaning out the chicken coop, eating marzipan cake, planting trees, or whipping cream. My God! What a Philistine I was at heart.

Another bottle, covered with big barnacles and crabs, floated by. It must have spent weeks in the water. I ate two crabs, thoroughly chewing the hard shell to protect my mucous membranes. A huge swarm of pilot fish had adopted the fold-boat. They made daring side trips to the outrigger, behaving as nervously as though they were crossing an ocean.

In the afternoon I spotted a sea serpent. I heard a quiet snort on the port side from a comber. I looked and behold—the fabled sea serpent. The swell took me to the exact spot, and there I saw four black curves, the first curve had a black fin. After the next swell I saw three more fins. Four little whales or porpoises swimming after each other made an impressive sea serpent. Soon they disappeared behind the high swell, and with them went every sea serpent legend I had ever heard of or read.

November 17

During the night the wind freshened. I dozed for only seconds. The weather did not look promising; a dark ominous wall of clouds concentrated in the east. My eyes turned to it constantly. Thunder rumbled across the water, lightning zigzagged through the cloud bank. I was still at 21 degrees north and at a longitude of around 30 degrees west. I had sailed more than a thousand miles from Las Palmas.

Darkness came too fast and too early for my taste; in a few minutes I sat in a pitch blackness, through which white foam caps glowed, ghostly and insubstantial. The wind strengthened. I had already taken in the foresail. Now it thundered and lightninged all around me. The wind was more powerful than ever before on this trip. I still felt confident but no longer as cheerful.

November 18

I passed a cruel night. Every few seconds I had to beam the flashlight at the compass to check on my course. I experienced the darkness of the blind, the thunder of the gods. I was battered, cold, wet, and exhausted. The morning found me as empty and lifeless as a doll. Looking at the heavy seas I was afraid they might devour me. It was only fear—the fundamental fear of death—that forced me to stay awake, to use every last possible reserve of energy. Tropical rains smashed down, pounding the boiling sea. It was a storm of major proportions. Threatening clouds obscured the sky. I peered behind the mizzen sail, hoping to find a small crack in the gray sky, but the blue of the sky seemed to have vanished forever, and even the sun no longer existed. The wind raged at more than forty miles an hour. As soon as the rains stopped, the seas reared up to a height of twenty-five to thirty feet; some of the waves that rushed under me seemed even twice that height. I was surprised but pleased to discover that my mizzen sail was just the right size for such a storm.

My average speed through this boiling sea and frequent rain squalls was close to three knots, a good speed from the *Liberia III*. Most of the breakers, when they came from aft, pushed me forward without washing over me. On the other hand, when they came from starboard or port, the *Liberia* disappeared into a mountain of water. She could only go with the waves. It was an amazing spectacle of nature: the beating rain, peppering and battering at the water, turned it from green to white. When the rain ceased, giant combers overlaid the surface with white froth and foam. I felt I was in a supernatural elevator that descended rapidly to an inferno at the bottom of the sea, to rise again with incredible speed, into the sky. But the rubber boat wound her way through all danger. It was impossible for her to keep a straight course with rear winds and mizzen sail. After each rise and fall I had to look out like a watchdog to keep on course. Cross waves washed over the boat, but her buoyancy brought her up every time. My shoulders were battered by mighty combers hitting from the rear, they broke and foamed over the deck, stopping thirty to sixty feet in front of me. Any nerve-racking backward glance showed me combers capable of knocking down a house. A forward glance onto the backs of the waves was less discouraging and dangerous. The trick was to hold to the westward course! Waves could not destroy a rubber-and-canvas boat as long as it went with the wind. The waves coming from aft had less power to do damage as long as they could carry the boat on their backs. Waves broke under the boat, oblivious of the 440 pounds they carried. I had the feeling that I swam in a cigar-shaped life belt.

The spray cover took on a great deal of water in this raging hell. I bailed every hour. My hands were soon bleached to a snow white from rain water, the calluses on them soaked and swollen. When I did little repair jobs, my hands were easily scratched, but later the cuts healed without complications.

Despite the storm I had time to give thought to my companions; Mediterranean shearwaters flashed high in the air, dashed down again, rushing at the wave crest and making me think they had never felt better in their lives. Madeira petrels danced on the waves, touched the surface lightly with small black claws and obviously enjoyed the weather. Two big dolphins jumped out of the water, then let themselves fall back in, bending their bodies sideways in a fashion that always astonished me. My little triggerfish were busy cleaning barnacles off the boat bottom. These creatures behaved as always, taking delight in the storm; only the man in the rubber boat was ill at ease and worried.

The rudder had a free play of about 40 degrees. This, combined with the mizzen sail, made it difficult to hold to the western course. I thought about the advisability of throwing out the sea anchor. I absolutely had to sleep in the coming night; without sleep I could not survive the storm. But I could never wholly forget the great danger of capsizing if I did not stay constantly on the alert. Then, there was a strong possibility that I might lose the rudder in such high seas, for the line of the sea anchor, stretching behind the boat, could simply lift it out. It was a difficult decision, but finally I threw out the anchor and, in a few seconds, the boat lay in a good position. I took in the mizzen sail and drew the spray cover up high, leaving only face and chest free. I never fastened the cover over my stomach, as some foldboat users do in mountain rivers; it would have given me a trapped feeling and made it difficult to free myself if I ever capsized.

I thought about the famous voyage of Franz Romer, another story of suffering at sea. In 1928 he sailed in a foldboat, especially made for him, from Lisbon to San Juan in Puerto Rico. He was the first to do it. He left Lisbon at the end of March, shortly afterward he was thrown ashore by a storm in the south of Portugal. He sailed from there to the Canary Islands in eleven days and from there made the voyage, in fifty-eight days of unbelievable torture, to St. Thomas. In St. Thomas he had to be pulled out of his boat. During the roughest part of the trip he could sleep—or better catnap—only between crests of high waves, then he was forced to awaken to control his rudder. To me the story of Romer's voyage is the greatest of all sea stories.

Franz Romer in his foldboat and I in mine had to control our boats every minute. They were very narrow and had no keels, so without control they would have capsized. But I had the advantage of setting out a sea anchor, which Romer did not dare to do for fear of damaging the rubber of his boat or the rudder.

Only a man who knows these foldboats can imagine the torture that Romer must have withstood. Eight weeks of sitting or lying, almost always wet, with never a possibility of standing upright, surrounded only by waves and combers. Eight weeks condemned to a cockpit, to suffering, shouting, and prayer. In 1928 Romer did not have the medicines of today against pustulae, ulcers, and boils. He had only one asset: the patience of a yogi and the energy of a man possessed by an idea. Anyone who has ever tried sitting for twelve hours in a foldboat knows of the cramping pain, but he has no idea how this aches when one's body is covered with ulcers, which do not heal, which exude pus and burn like the fires of hell. Whenever Romer wanted to eat or adjust his sails, he had to open his spray cover and—splash—a bucket of water was flung in his face.

At the very end, Romer, a former ship's officer, made the fatal mistake. He left San Juan in September, the hurricane month of the Caribbean. He had been warned, but he was determined to go farther. Shortly after he left, a bad hurricane swept the area. Romer was never heard from again, nor did any part of his boat drift ashore.

Now I lay behind a sea anchor, more exposed to the combers than when I went under sail, because the boat did not go with the waves. Romer's spray cover was destroyed by a breaking comber. I had protected myself against a similar disaster by laying thin planks over the washboard and putting air cushions over them.

The night was black and stormy, but I felt an unusual exhilaration as I lay in the boat, listening to the roaring, howling, and boiling that went on around me, while I sat inside, curled up for a short nap. I fell asleep in a few minutes. Then I awoke, all my instincts working, and without conscious thought, I bailed.

November 19

The night was endless. Heavy dark storm clouds would not let the daylight through. Only rain squalls, thunder, lightning and bailing kept me alert. As I expected and feared, I lost my rudder. The steering cables responded heavily to my feet; then suddenly they turned light to the touch, letting me know the rudder had left me. Fortunately I had brought a spare. I dug my chronometer out from its rubber bag and checked the time. Daylight was half an hour overdue.

It came at last, but the monotony of dark gray skies between masses of heaving gray-green water remained unbroken. Without a rudder, the *Liberia* could not hold a course to the waves, so I shipped even more water. My hands looked bad. I peeled off the sodden calluses.

The rise and fall of the boat during the night had made it hard for me to rest. I was still very, very tired. I crouched and laid my head on the washboard, too frightened to sleep, and as I lay there I heard the spray cover whisper to me.

"Now come," it said, "be reasonable and lie down. Forget everything. Leave it. Let others do something. You don't have to do everything."

At first this conversation seemed perfectly normal, until I remembered I was alone on board. Often as I awoke, I looked around for my companion, not realizing at once that there was nobody else with me. My sense of reality had changed in an odd way. I spoke to myself, of course, and I talked to the sails and the outrigger, but the noises around me also belonged to human beings; the breaking sea snorted at me, whistled, called to me, shouted and breathed at me with the rage and fury of a living being.

I had to wait for the storm to lessen before putting on my spare rudder. The sky still threatened. From time to time it thundered and lightninged. Tropical downpours and combers emptied buckets of water into the boat. I bailed mechanically and patiently. I gave up worry and thought. The storm had shown me that I could have confidence in my boat. It is only after a man has lived through a storm with his boat that he knows exactly what to expect from her.

November 20

This was my thirty-second day at sea. The night was restless, but the wind had weakened. I decided to replace the rudder. With the wick of the rudder between my teeth and the blade tied to my right wrist, I slipped, fully dressed, into the water. The waves were still fifteen to twenty feet high, the temperature of the water lukewarm. With difficulty I swam to the stern. One moment I was under the stern, then the boat hit my head, and the next instant the stern was before me. So I took the stern firmly under my left arm, changed the rudder blade into my left hand, when suddenly a big wave tore it away. I cannot describe the shock; it was unimaginable. I reacted quickly, grabbed for the blade and luckily caught hold of the string attached to it. I could feel the sweat of delayed fright coming up inside me. The next attempt was successful; with my right hand I pushed in the wick, fastened it once more with string, and crawled back into the boat. I tried to undress, but the seas, with winds still blowing at twenty-five miles an hour, were too high. Water had entered the boat while I worked on the rudder, dragging the cushions out of place. I righted them and sat down again. With the steering cables I again controlled the rudder. My new rudder was the standard size, whereas the one I had lost in the storm was only two-thirds as big. Back in Las Palmas I had decided that my heavily loaded boat did not need a whole blade and that a standard size would exert too much pull on the rubber stern. I pulled in the sea anchor, fastened it behind the mizzenmast, and set the little square sail.

Now my legs shook from delayed shock. It would take time for my nerves to calm down. But I felt as though I had won a battle and, after the bailing was finished, I treated myself to an extra portion of milk. The seas still roared around me, the wind blew furiously across a slightly clearer sky. The sun was circled by a big rainbow, a sign of intense humidity in the atmosphere.

November 23

Little by little, the wind eased. I hoisted the gaff sail. But the weather did not improve. Squalls chased each other across the water, squeezing rain out of the clouds onto the suffering fold-boat below. Every few minutes I looked behind the mizzen to be sure that no bad squall approached, which would force me to take down the big sail. A chart of my course would have looked like the movements of a snake. I was 30 degrees too far to starboard one minute; in the next, a wave pushed me 30 degrees to the south on the port side; but on the whole I managed to keep west.

Two great big dolphins had followed me for several days. Whenever the wind abated, they beat their tails against the bottom of the boat and then swam slowly off. They could easily be caught, I thought, especially when their heads came above water. Though I knew they were too big for my boat, I had a strong desire to get one. I loaded the underwater gun. My first shot was a bull's-eye. The arrow landed on the fish's skull. He jumped, he leaped into the air and lifted the outrigger as he did so. Quickly I jerked at the line and held an empty arrow in my hand. The hooks of the arrow had not taken hold in the hard skull. Perhaps it was better this way!

As the sun went down—1,400 miles from the Canary Islands, I saw a butterfly flutter in the air. Only the trade winds could have brought it this far.

My knees had improved!

November 24

Tropicbirds, Mediterranean shearwaters, petrels, and Manx shearwaters flew around me again. The wind was very tired, and all my sails were hoisted. Suddenly, the port-side backstay broke. I took down the gaff sail and, to my horror, saw a huge, dark box only a half mile away. A ship had come up on me without my hearing anything. I had no idea what they wanted. Had they stopped to pick me up? I waved my hands and signaled that I was all right. Evidently they missed my hand signals; I was too far away. They made a turn around the *Liberia*. Stubbornly, I kept the sail hoisted. As the freighter came port side for a second time, I could even distinguish faces on the bridge, crew and a few passengers following with interest my boat's maneuvers. I took pictures and shot film. A young officer jumped from the bridge to the main deck, megaphone in hand.

"Don't you want to come alongside?" he shouted.

"No, thank you," I answered, without giving myself time to think.

"Do you need food?" came the next question, and again I replied, "No!"

He asked my name, and I asked him for the exact longitude. After giving orders to have the bridge reckon the position, he inquired where I came from.

"From Las Palmas. Thirty-six days at sea and with course to St. Thomas," I informed him.

"Would you like me to announce your arrival at the yacht club there?" he wanted to know.

I told him, yes, and gave him my nationality. He gave me the exact position: 56.28 degrees longitude, 20.16 degrees latitude. The young officer found it hard to believe that I didn't need food, but at my insistence the freighter slowly got under way. The captain shouted a last "good luck" from the bridge; the engines started carefully so as not to endanger my fragile boat. Then the steamer, the *Blitar* from Rotterdam, took up her western course.

The meeting left me dizzy. My quick decision to refuse food was unnatural. Evidently my mental discipline combined with the auto suggestions, "Don't take any assistance," had forced my out of hand refusal. I thought about their reactions on the freighter as they stumbled on my funny, small craft— which obviously could not hold enough food for a crossing—in mid-Atlantic. The ready offer of help from the captain made me happy. It showed me that men are never alone, that castaways can always hope and that there are men all over the world who help others.

My latitude was exact, my longitude was a few degrees too far west. Thus even in a foldboat one can take the latitude accurately, although I knew that in a high swell and with heavy weather, it is not absolutely correct.

Tropical rains came down in torrents that night. I caught five quarts of fresh water, perhaps to compensate a little for my firm "no."

November 25

A steamer passed at nine in the morning within three miles but with contrary course. In the high seas and winds of twenty-five miles an hour, they could not see me.

I wondered when the famous stable and sunny trade winds would start. Only at noon did the weather clear for a short time. Another butterfly lay on the water. Dolphins hunted flying fish, and tropicbirds circled above the boat.

For the past two weeks some of my canned milk had been sour, but only a little had really spoiled. I discovered some cans with small holes in them and decided that the metal was too thin. The sour milk turned into an excellent aid to my bowels. On a small boat, a badly functioning digestive system can become a real nuisance. Somehow or other, I had to solve the problem every five to seven days. When I found that my turned milk helped, I no longer worried about the taste.

November 26

I counted my pulse rate at night; that night it was thirty-two, lower than the usual thirty-four. My body adapted itself more easily to the hazardous ordeal than did my mind. I was still convinced of a successful crossing, but sometimes I became restless and dissatisfied, cursing at the unstable weather conditions. On my thirty-eighth day, a typical stormy squall rushed to the west. In the northeast, explosive masses of dark clouds gathered.

December 5

Two bad nights. Several times waves struck the boat crosswise. I sailed the correct western course. Heavy seas coming from the beam nearly capsized me. I was saved by my outrigger. The whole foreship plowed the water in heavy seas, sometimes taking water over as far as the mast, though the narrow bow projected far out of the sea. It was good I had a mizzen sail; with a foresail the bow would have dug deeper into the water, and I would have run the danger of somersaulting. Rain squall followed rain squall, while the wind, coming powerfully from the north, drove tons of water over the westwardly running *Liberia*. Another day's ration saved by eating fish.

December 6

For five days the weather belonged to the wind. My body was constantly wet. Everything ached: knees, elbows, shoulders, and—as one would expect—buttocks.

My attention was caught by three small articles floating on the water, one of which looked like a mousetrap.

December 7

I was too exhausted to sail all night as I wanted to. Once again I heard voices speaking to me from various parts of the boat, and I answered them.

"Where are you?" I asked the knife. "Come on, don't hide from me. I've got work for you to do."

To the outrigger, as a heavy cross sea tried to push it out of place, "Great! Show the sea what a half tire is worth. Don't, please, make a fool of me. And don't forget, you and I have to stick together in this. If you go, I go."

The imagination plays extraordinary tricks on tired ears; the breaking waves shouted, praising or cursing me. They whispered and talked to each other, to the boat, to the lonely sailor. It was clear I needed sleep. I put out the sea anchor and curled up to take catnaps.

In the morning the weather looked no friendlier; stormy squalls rushed over me, some wet, some dry. A northern wind took command and pushed me south. I tried to sail west, but it became dangerous. I was lucky I had not yet capsized; several times the outrigger plunged deep into the water. I touched wood and took the precaution of putting out the sea anchor so that I could sleep a little.

December 11

The weather did not change. Dangerous clouds gathered in the north. The air was sticky, and the wind sleepy. Sargasso weed floated past me, but I did not allow myself any false hopes, although in these latitudes it is generally found near the Caribbean. My longitude measurements were rough but reliable, and I knew where I was. My noon position indicated a climb to the north. Menacing weather from the north interrupted my hygiene hour. My practiced eye discerned a siege of bad weather ahead.

At three that afternoon it was still calm and flat. At six the clouds exploded.

The sea roared and tropical rains hammered at the water. I felt like giving up on the trade winds. Should I sail southward? In a vile humor, I threw over the sea anchor. A nylon line, no thicker than a pencil, held it to the boat. A shark's bite and the line would be finished. But I knew this was unlikely. I remembered with amusement the statement I had read in an old book in St. Croix about a shark's taste buds. The author, stating that in the Caribbean sharks attack a Frenchman rather than an Englishman, gave as his explanation the fact that the fish were repelled by the latter's meat diet. I was sure that a fish with such epicurean tastes would never be interested in a nylon line.

December 13

The trade winds blew at thirty miles an hour. Feelings of discouragement and disappointment took hold of me, and I found myself wishing for a taste of the fine favorable winds I had had during the last three weeks of my previous trip. I comforted myself with the knowledge that these ugly winds would have to stop sometime.

Twenty dolphins, flashing blue and green in the water, gathered around the *Liberia*. There was no time to watch them. My rudder needed my full attention; again it had too much play, and I had to concentrate to stay on course. I was surprised to see so many dolphins at once. Were they chased by a shark and looking for protection?

I avoided backward glances, for they showed me terrifying seas and towering breakers heading straight for my frail *Liberia*. Once I narrowly missed disaster. An enormous breaker, coming from the rear, left me gasping for air as it poured water onto the boat. We were taken thirty to forty-five feet high into the air and then flung down with a hard bump. It was my first experience with such violence, and I had no desire to repeat it.

To what did I owe that fact that I was still afloat? Luck? Was it only luck that I still lived? I refused to answer my own question. I knew I was well prepared, well trained, and beyond that, I would not analyze my situation. But I had to admit that these giant breakers caused me concern. They did not come often: in a span of twenty-four hours they might pass only once, perhaps twice, with full strength—but the mere prospect unnerved me.

In the dusk I spotted a red light, a little later a green light and then both together. At first I could make neither head nor tail of them. When suddenly I realized that a steamer was bearing straight down on me. In a panic I flashed my flashlight on and off against the mizzen sail, put the paddle beside me ready for use. The ship gave the impression of coming at me head on. I watched with extreme relief as she passed about fifty yards away. I noticed that she rolled even more than I in the heavy seas.

December 14

I sailed all night through. I had no recollection or feeling that I had ever slept. I knew only that I was tired, terribly tired! Often during the day my eyes closed and my mind wandered. A tropicbird from the western Atlantic, approaching that morning, gave me comfort. The first American to greet me on the voyage. Though I knew, of course, that they fly far from land, I welcomed him and cheered up. The wind blew from thirty to forty miles an hour. I forgot the beautiful white bird and thought solely of my discomfort and my fears. I felt so small, so insignificant, and so helpless in these powerful seas. The unusual name that a Fanti fisherman in Liberia had given his canoe repeated itself endlessly in my mind. "Who are You, Seapower?" My God, Fanti fisherman, I thought, come and look at these waves, and you will feel as small as I. All at once a huge steamer loomed to port; it had come up without my noticing it. What do they want, I asked myself, and waved at them.

"Everything is fine here," I shouted. Then I saw a man, megaphone in hand, calling to me.

"My dear Lindemann," rang across the water, "don't be a stubborn fool . . ." And the rest of his words drowned in the roar of the waves. The words were spoken in German, and the voice was familiar. And then I knew who he was. It was the voice of a newspaper man whom I had met when I returned from my last trip. I remembered him clearly because he had arrived before the others to interview me. He was a former ship's officer, but I could tell at the time from the manner in which he questioned me that he hated the sea. And why was it this voice that shouted at me from the steamer?

The ship made a circle around me, putting oil on her course. But I continued sailing, passing by the oil slicks. The small breakers lessened, and the surface appeared smoother; but the high combers were not impressed by the oil and thundered on. Another squall swept the sea and kept my hands and feet occupied steering the boat in a westerly direction. The steamer, circling around, confused me. I forgot to head west. I took pictures of it, and then there it was, alongside once again. A young officer made a despairing gesture in my direction. Could he not help me? smiling, I waved "no" at him, but my smile was a parody, a horrible grimace. I had begun to realize that anything could happen to me in such stormy trade winds, that factors I had not reckoned with could overtake me. The ship veered off close to the boat, its waves mingling with wind waves and splashing over my deck. Then I found myself in its wake, forcing me to be on my guard to avoid the log line of the ship. On her stern I read, *Eaglesdale, London.* The meeting cheered me, for it was fine to know that people wanted to help even though I would not give them the opportunity. Perhaps I should have accepted. Give up after eight weeks, after fifty-five days at sea? I had to succeed by myself. I would make it all right. I was determined.

The German voice coming to me from an English steamer puzzled me. Had I really heard it? Could the man have resolved his hate/love for the sea by returning to it? I would have to write to the ship and find out who had spoken. (After my arrival in St. Thomas I wrote the captain of the *Eaglesdale*, who replied with a friendly note, congratulating me on having survived "such bad weather." But the German voice was a hallucination. My eyes had reacted correctly, but my ears had deceived me.) As the ship left she put oil out to calm the seas and prolong my life.

December 15

I passed a night of hell. Again I had no sleep. I was afraid to throw out the sea anchor, because in these heavy seas, its line would threaten the rudder. I knew I must not lose it, but I also knew I simply had to have sleep. I could not overestimate my energy; I had to be fresh enough to stay on course. On the other hand, I could not afford to sleep even for an instant in that boiling sea. The problem looked quite different here at sea than it had on shore. At sea I could only stay awake for four days and nights. On shore, with short catnaps, I had managed it for longer stretches. And now I felt my eyes closing. I dozed, I dreamed, I became the prey of imaginations and hallucinations. And then I put my last energy into staying alert. I began to sing. Slowly, I ground out a tune, only to find that something in my body cut off my voice. Then I counted, one . . . two . . . three . . . four, and suddenly I could not find the next number; it was lost; it was simply not there any more. I knew only one thing: the boat had to go into a garage, somewhere I had to shelter her and lie down beside her and sleep.

The mizzen sail beat against my shoulders. A warning? I flashed the light onto the compass and found I was headed too far north.

I had the feeling that behind me stood a barn in whose lee the waves were flatter, while farther out on both sides, the sea still raged. As soon as I left the protected lee, masses of water washed over the deck. Ah yes! The barn would protect me . . . stay in its lee . . . where it was calm, cal-me-r and then . . . water . . . I swam . . . what was it? The shock awakened me, I flashed the light onto the compass; too far south. I did not hear the breaker that swamped me, it was simply there. I bailed, I had to bail . . . I must bail. Why wasn't I doing it?

I was invited on a hunt. A Negro servant called for me. Lovely! I trusted him, he knew where we had to go. I sat comfortably in a kind of rickshaw. I saw big white lines ahead, and they worried me a little.

"Boy," I asked, "where are we going?"

"It is all right. We have to go through the surf," he answered, and as he spoke we plunged through. The deck was under water and came up again. I looked at the boy to the left. He wore black and snorted like a whale or horse, but he worked without talking back.

"Boy, where do you boys live?"

"In the west."

West! The word reminded me of something. I knew it, and then I remembered the compass. Again I was off course. I looked at the boy on the left, but he had gone. A black horse rode there now, pushing the boat. Horses know the way home. I could rely on a horse . . . satisfied, I relaxed . . . then suddenly I seemed awake, slowly and instinctively I came to myself. But who was I? No answer. What was my name? No name. What was happening? West, west—and no more stayed with me. Again I remembered the compass. The flashlight lit it up. Again, off course. Then a sound came into my consciousness, the sea still roared. I was cold, although sail and spray cover provided ample protection. Then I clearly heard the voice of Mephisto, "I do not see your water lies." I looked for my black boy and black horse at port side and saw only black outrigger. It must be more than a lifeless object. It had to have spirit and soul.

During the morning a real storm with winds of forty miles an hour had developed. I looked with disbelief into the face of the waves. "Such waves cannot exist," I thought.

A little later I screamed and shouted, "I will get through. I will make it, I will make it."

As if to confirm my optimism, I saw a frigatebird, an American frigatebird, sailing high through the air. According to my calculations, I was still four hundred miles from the Caribbean islands; but frigates rarely fly more than one hundred and fifty miles from their land base, and I could have made a mistake. What a lively mistake! It meant landfall within four days. This called for a double ration of food right away. I had starved myself enough. Now began the good life. Every day I would eat double rations from now on. I would celebrate Christmas on land. Lucky, lucky man. When I threw out the sea anchor I did it with happiness and sense of relief. My secret aim was to celebrate Christmas on shore. I bailed and dreamed of Christmas pudding. The storm was at its peak. The boat had trouble sticking with the waves. As she had lightened considerably, she might now be badly trimmed. I should have done something about inner ballast, but both water containers, provided for that purpose, had developed holes. So I forgot it.

I woke up and bailed, napped again. I sat, the spray cover drawn over my head. The time was nine in the evening.

All at once a huge wall rose starboard . . . nothing more . . . out . . . empty . . . dead? No, I gasped for breath, beat with hands and feet, and then they were free. I had capsized, was in the water. "I must reach the boat, the waves must not separate us," went through my head.

The hull stood high over the surface. It felt slippery. My mouth tasted of salt. At last I caught hold of the outrigger. The boat lay across the waves. I pushed her into the right direction. Would the storm ever stop? What could I do? I thought back to the time when my boat had capsized near Madeira on one of my shorter previous foldboat voyages, and I remembered the difficulty I had had then in righting her. I found myself between outrigger and boat, with only my head out of water. The storm showed no signs of subsiding. The waves rumbled, roared and thundered as before, mercilessly. In the sea, my body felt bitterly cold. Then I climbed onto the hull, my right hand on the paddle to the outrigger, the left cramped to the edge of the boat. The wind hurtled over the hull, comber after comber washed over me. Still I was terribly cold. Only my head, protected by a woolen cap with a hood over it, stayed warm.

Was this the end? No! I would not allow it to be the end. I willed the *Liberia* to stay afloat. Would I sail the rest of the way to the islands, perched on the hull? Waves, warmer than the winds, broke over my back. I glanced at the stars. Orion was not even in the zenith, so it was not yet midnight. I knew I had to wait until daybreak to right the boat. I faced seven hours precariously balanced on the hull. The stiff winds chilled my body, I slipped back into the water. My body curled, and with cramped hands I held tight to the outrigger paddle. Every movement stirred up cold water between my skin and clothing. I forced myself to remain motionless. During the night the sea calmed, but big waves still made giant shadows. I felt sick. I vomited—I must have swallowed sea water. My hands clutched the paddle. How strong they were! To keep my body in the right direction, I had to tread water constantly. I froze.

I thought of home and of my parents; they knew nothing of this voyage. They could not imagine what had happened to their child. Self-pity engulfed me.

December 16

It was midnight. Nothing had changed, except that I was even colder than before. Then one of my feet kicked against something. What was interested in my feet? Anxiety attacked me. I scrambled up onto the hull, my legs gripping the westward-pointing stern.

Two in the morning Orion descended in the west. I had slid back into the water, forced there by the extreme cold. The pitiless winds had reduced me to a shivering, chattering skeleton. I thought back to a voyage I had made in the Straits of Gibraltar one winter, when the wind blew so cold that my hands were unable to hold the paddle. The wind, that time,

blew me into a harbor around midnight, and I had been offered a drink. That was what I needed now.

Suddenly I heard the sound of bells. They reminded me of
church bells at home, the same bells that I had rung as a child.
Did they ring now for my funeral? They must know, surely,
that I could not die now, that I would get through? I was quiet,
my muscles held on, instinctively, and demonstrated that deep
in my subconscious there was still life. What did the heavy,
brutal combers want of me? Didn't they realize that they could
not touch me? That I was taboo? That I would survive, that I
could make it, must make it? I had not lost my faith, nor had
my subconscious or my instincts betrayed me.

At four in the morning Orion was about 45 degrees west. I
dozed on the hull. Once a voice invited me to go to a nearby
farmhouse, to have a drink and sink deep into a feather bed.

"Where is the house?" I asked.

"Over there, in the west, behind the hill," came the answer.

Then I awoke. My sense of hearing had returned, I could
feel the numbing cold again. I heard myself repeating aloud,
"Never give up, never give up, I'll make it." I dared not sleep.
Deep sleep meant certain death. I knew the sea devours everything, leaves no trace, draws even the dead downward. In the
water again, I floated, dead, empty of feeling, at time deliri-
ous. But something survived, the lighthouse that guided me
was my determination to succeed. As long as I had that, I lived.
Sometimes, the lighthouse darkened; then there was nothing—
only muscles, an animal without thoughts, all instinct—until
the lighthouse suddenly lit up for me again. Loud and bright,
it warned me not to give in, to keep on fighting. It shouted at
me, "You will make it." Then I awoke, my senses returned, first
hearing, then feeling, then speech. I heard death in my ears,
sea and storm beat upon my body, salt stung my eyes, cold
shook my bones. I was grateful for my lighthouse, it made me a
slave who was not allowed to die, a slave to an idea.

I lay on the hull, my head pressed against the slippery
rubber. I thought at times that I belonged to another world but
knew not which. A happier world, where no one froze, where
salt did not sting the eyes. But my hands clung to this world,
and for this I thanked God.

Finally, a shy dawn came to my rescue. For the past two hours I had lain on the hull. Hands and legs held fast while my mind wandered. I could no longer control it: dreams and thoughts, reality and hallucination, I could no longer tell the difference . . . a concentration on nothingness . . . but still I stayed alive.

The wind had not lessened its force, but I had to try to right the boat. I could wait no longer. I fixed a long line to the outrigger and pulling from the opposite side, I managed to right her. As the stern pointed westward, I pushed it east. Waves filled the boat. I found to my relief that the compass and my bailing pot had stayed on. The bow pointed far out of the water, the stern just floated. The mizzenmast was broken at its base, the sea anchor lost. I climbed into the boat as waves washed over my face. I looked for three air cushions to push under the stern. I found the first, inflated it, and pushed it far back of the aft washboard. There were the two others, and they followed the first. I began to recover, I drew the spray cover up to my shoulders, untied my pot, and bailed. The boat was not yet stable, and I had to sit close to the outrigger.

Big waves ran over the deck, but slowly I put myself in control. I continued bailing. My pot, which held quite a few quarts, struck me as a most useful object. Then I set the course for the west. I bailed until the pot no longer scooped up water, and I finished the job with a sponge.

An hour later the boat was empty, but for some fifty quarts I left in for ballast. Then I checked the sails, which were in the water on the starboard side. I put them on deck and fastened them. I checked the inside of the boat; every single one of my cans of food had gone, my food supply for the last part of the voyage had vanished. I had had emergency rations of eleven cans of milk, which I kept in a bag tied to the mast. Where was the flashlight? One had gone, but I found my spare and beamed light at the bow. Clothes and watertight rubber bags lay in chaos. My beam picked out something red. It was the bag full of milk cans. I looked for the two bags that held the Leica, one with black and white film, the other with color. They were gone. The bag with my spare parts was gone. My night glasses, my fluid compass (although I found it later in St. Thomas), the toilet articles, the grappling iron, all these now floated somewhere in the Atlantic.

The port-side shroud of the mainstay was torn from the deck canvas, the line for the foresails were in such bad shape that I could not use them without repairing them first.

The frigatebird that had consoled me earlier flew over again. I had to be close to shore. Then I remembered to check my sextant and found it wet in its bag. The chronometer was also full of water but ran the minute I touched it. I took my position before it was too late. The trade winds still blew the storms of yesterday, the storms they might continue to blow for many days to come. The nautical almanac was soaked through; I handled the pages carefully. My latitude was approximately 18 degrees and 20 minutes, it could not be too far off. My good knife had disappeared. My cans! Gone, too! But I was alive and well, and what more did I want? I did not hoist the sail, as the storm and the wind pushed me to the west. In the late afternoon I shot a triggerfish with the underwater gun. Its meat tasted better than ever before—and my bottles of rain water had stayed with me.

December 17

The weather did not change; the sea roared, the storm howled, fish and birds gathered around me again. I was dead tired. During the night my body had shivered uncontrollably. Now at last it was warmer, and the sun shone. Shortly before noon, a wave whistled beside me, reminding me of an old sailor's legend my grandfather had told me when I was a child. The legend of the disaster that a whistling wave brings, springs from the story of a shipwrecked sailor, the sole survivor of a ship that went down shortly after a whistling wave had gone by. The sailors heard it, just as I heard it then. Was the whistling wave an omen for me, too? What did I have to lose? Only my life. But I will make it.

Under the water I could see living creatures move; two dolphins. They were small but edible. I shot them, jerked them up on deck, beat them to death with my round knife and devoured them whole. My stomach was still in an unsettled condition, but I ignored its complaints.

Air . . . nothing . . . air at last. I was capsized again! Again I clung to the boat; it was slippery from long thin algae, and the few barnacles that were left did not offer much hold. I pushed the boat in the right direction, and there on the bow was a small bulge on the rubber. It was the line from the outrigger, which I had deliberately left there, under the boat. It was easy to right the *Liberia* with the line. Soon I was climbing inside again. I bailed while my elbows held the spray cover high. How had it happened again? My underwater gun had slipped away. I had not had a chance to fasten it after the last dolphin. That was bad. I continued bailing. The islands had to be close by now. Even without the gun I would succeed. I realized that I had capsized over the outrigger each time. Were the Polynesians right when they put it on the windward side? Both times I had felt no shock. It could have been such a sweet death. "Bail, Hannes, bail!" There was a bulge in the rubber. It must have been made by something pointed. I decided to try leaving more water in the boat, if the wooden frame could stand it.

I still sat in water. It was not cold; I felt nothing. I had to rig the mizzen sail. It would give the boat speed and lessen the danger of being capsized by angry waves for the third time. With my knife I sharpened the point of the mizzenmast and put the paddle mast on it. It was shaky, but it held. Then I hoisted my sail, relieved to be under sail again and ready to celebrate Christmas then and there.

December 19

It still stormed. I was empty, a shell, unthinking, kept going only by a complete concentration on the words, "Keep going west, never give up, I'll make it." I dozed. Sometimes, while meditating, I felt happy; I was somewhere where I could take refuge in irresponsible happiness, where I could escape my ego and my consciousness.

Then I had to find my eleven cans of milk in their red rubber bag near the foremast. Only eleven cans! I felt like drinking two a day. The islands had to be close, I told myself, but these cans were emergency rations, and they had to remain that. There was always the possibility that I might capsize again, that I might have trouble with the rudder; I had to save my milk. I would have to drink the water in my bottles; there was still enough to last for a few days. I knew of castaways who had survived more than fourteen days by drinking only one glass of water a day.

A sudden shock awakened me. The steering mechanism no longer worked, I looked back, drew at the steering cables and—to my horror—found the rudder blade barely hanging on. With a paddle I guided the port-side cable over the stern and pulled the rudder in starboard out of the water. Now I urgently needed a sea anchor. The rudder wick was broken. Small wonder in such weather, but I now faced the problem of a new wick. My spare parts were all gone. Inspiration came to me when I remembered the small wire on top of the mizzen that kept the sail in shape. It was the very thing I needed. With my paddle I kept the boat more or less on course, pulled the wire into the right shape for a wick, slid fully clothed into the water and fastened the rudder blade. My clothes were now completely drenched, but then they had not been fully dry for days. A pathetic afternoon sun occasionally dried me out here and there. At night I invariably sat in water. It was a miracle that my buttocks were not more painful. Was my skin accustomed to the constant immersion?

Clearly before me, in a mind's eye sharpened by danger, I could see the red roofs and green palms of Phillipsburg.

December 21

I made a sea anchor of my last pieces of string tied to a seabag. But I did not use it, and I hoped I would not have to, for it could only hold me back. A terrible sense of urgency took hold of me, forcing me to calm my nerves with consoling speeches.

"I'll make it; keep going west," I repeated endlessly.

When my mind wandered I felt gay and lighthearted, whereas my conscious moments brought tension and worry. There were times when I forgot everything, when I removed myself to a place where there was nothing but an eternal stillness, where I hardly existed, and the noise of the storm could not follow.

Frigatebirds, circling the *Liberia*, announced my imminent arrival; I knew I was not far from the islands.

My strength lay in my foldboat. Taunting the sea, she resisted all combers that sought to destroy her. The sea sensed the *Liberia's* defiance, and the giant waves hounded me for it, doing their best to catch me.

"As long as the mizzen is hoisted, you won't get me," I shouted at them.

Yesterday I drank a can of milk, and today I was greedy for a second. I scanned the sky for clouds that would indicate an island. Nothing! Tomorrow might bring better luck.

During the night I froze; my teeth chattered, my arms shook, and I suffered from terrible cramps. "I will make it," I repeated, as I prayed for alert senses. All my life I have prayed and meditated; now, in meditation, I concentrated on my arrival in St. Martin, with its colorful houses and fat, green palms. But the picture that developed before my mind's eye was gray.

Why not take a can of milk? I would still have nine left. But what if I had another accident? On a sudden impulse and with the indifference of an exhausted man, I grabbed for a can, beat with my knife at the edge and sucked out the milk. Only after I had emptied the can, did I have the strength to feel ashamed of my weakness.

December 24 and 25

The days seemed shorter, the nights longer; nighttime belonged to the devil, while the days belonged to hope. Trade winds blew at thirty to forty miles an hour, bringing with them towering waves. How long had I sailed with no sleep? Many, many days, and God alone knew how many nights. It could have been weeks. The passage of time no longer held meaning for me. Time, Philistine word, a modern, sick word; time, the disease of today!

And today was Christmas Eve. Last year I had discovered my America on this very night. I felt certain it would happen again. "I am lucky," I thought, "and twice I will arrive on Christmas Eve. Royal terns squealed and quarreled around me; my Christmas present, a frigatebird, flew by. I sang Christmas carols.

I wondered which island lay ahead. I could be near Antigua, of course, as I had been last year, but I desperately wanted to arrive in St. Martin. I had set my heart on Phillipsburg.

I checked the sextant; it had rusted and was out of order. Still, I intended to land in Phillipsburg. I was determined. I could not put my hand on the movie camera, but as it was probably useless by now, I decided it didn't matter. I had wanted to take beautiful pictures of waves, to show a storm, even take a picture of a wave running over the boat. What difference did all my lost plans make now?

Christmas Eve. I thought of Christmas trees, of all the great variety of trees I had seen in my lifetime of travel, decorated as Christmas trees. In Liberia, one friend had taken a dead tree and decorated it with seaweed, making, in this fashion, one of the prettiest Christmas trees that I had ever seen. I decided on my Christmas present for that night: a can of evaporated milk. I would drink it at dusk to remind me of my childhood, when I had always received my presents at twilight on Christmas Eve. I still had seven cans. Should I drink two? After all, I might reach Antigua during the night.

The rudder! Something was wrong. I looked back and saw the rudder was gone. Empty hinges stared back at me. The paddle! I had to steer the boat with a paddle, as I had done off the coast of the Sahara the year before. Why, why did this have to happen on Christmas Eve? Better not ask. I did not dare ask. My feet were free for the first time since my departure from Las Palmas. They had accustomed themselves to holding the westward course and were unused to their new liberty. With the paddle my speed decreased considerably. One shoulder felt the brunt of the wind side. The seams of my jacket had burst there, and rheumatic twinges shot through my upper arm, necessitating a change of paddle from starboard to port. It was difficult to keep on course—more so now than ever.

Dusk set in. I punched a small hole in the milk can, nothing came out when I raised it to my lips. The milk had curdled. I banged the can against the metal tip of the paddle and enlarged the hole. The end of my paddle smelled of walnut. How I love walnut cake! Walnut cake with marzipan will always send me back to Germany.

A streak of light glimmered in the sky. The lights of St. John's in Antigua? One voice said yes, urging me to take another can of milk. Another voice urged caution; don't be rash, it counseled. At least, at St. John's I would find English toffee. Then the lights went out, the sky darkened. What a pity, for my sake, that the inhabitants went to bed so early; they could have stayed up a little longer. Tomorrow, I would hit St. John's. Tomorrow—all day long—I would chew on English toffee.

The boat ran backward. I could not understand it, right there, before Antigua. I was attacked by a dizzy spell; with cramped hands I held the flashlight over the compass. West, it answered me. Then I knew nothing could go wrong. Two flying fish fell into the boat. Should I eat them? No! Not on Christmas Eve, tomorrow I would have all the food I needed in Antigua so I threw them back into the water. A big comber pushed me forward, then another pulled me back. With both hands I clung to the washboard. The world spun around me. Through my dizziness I could not hear, but knew I was still going back and back. Again two flying fish landed on the boat.

"I warned you," I told them, "not to try this again," and I bit into one. It was full of scales. I scraped them off with my thumb and ate both fish. The sensation of sailing backward was confirmed when I put my hands into the water, although I knew it was an illusion brought on by weariness. My course was west. Again a big comber rushed over the boat, shaking my senses into some kind of reality.

The African had returned.

"Where are we going this time?"

"To the west," he reassured me.

I threw the sea anchor. Everywhere I saw that flat shadows of shrubs and bushes . . . it was flat there, the surf washed over the boat, once, twice . . . oh God, how many times . . . yes! It was so flat there that land had to be somewhere near. My eyes saw what was not there to be seen; my ears heard sounds that did not exist. Suddenly all was quiet. I heard no crash of surf or sound of waves. Why this silence? Why? Why? Only when I talked with my boy or when he answered did I hear anything. How hard he worked. I was happy, endlessly happy, in another world. In a world where the sun shone, where neither body nor spirit existed, a world of ether that surrounded me with irrational joy. I sank even deeper into my mind.

Then I heard again the roaring of the sea, first from the distance, but coming slowly closer. Now it was fresh, menacing, and rumbling in my ears. I no longer saw any lights of Antigua. I was awake, alert as never before. My sextant was not working. I concentrated with all my powers on thoughts of Phillipsburg—on the great bay—and the roaring of the sea dimmed. I saw the church, a little church with its roof just over the water and men taking shelter under it. Gray, gray, everything looked gray. Why?

December 26

I awoke with a dismal sense of oppression. Could I have passed the islands without noticing them? I would not be the first to have missed them. There ought to be land nearby. The day before I had seen nine frigatebirds and royal terns, a sure sign of land. It had to be somewhere. Should I change course? But how? For a long time now I had not known my exact latitude. I knew I could not be too far to the north, for the trade winds had continually pushed me southward. Still, I decided I would turn south on the first of January. I gave myself five more days to reach St. Martin on the present course.

I still had five cans of milk and a little rain water, brackish but drinkable. Under my skin there still lay a little fat. Oh! I was rich! I could reach the mainland, if necessary. I would make it. Sargasso weed floated on the surface. I caught some, shook it out over my spray cover and feasted off the delicate seafood I found. Several small crabs and two sargasso fish also fell out of the weed, but even in my present situation they had too little flavor to be palatable. However, I enjoyed some little shrimps that I wiped off the plastic cover with my sponge.

Trade winds blew in gusts of twenty-five miles an hour. The easing of the stiff wind made me strong and happy, confident that even without a sextant, I would hit Phillipsburg.

December 28

There was not longer any doubt that I had missed the islands; frigatebirds and terns decreased in number, sargasso weed thinned out. I saw few Madeira petrels or tropicbirds. A booby bird visited me. I tried hard to find out where these birds came from, but I never succeeded. They simply arrived.

December twenty-eighth was my birthday. I was hardly aware of it except for passing thoughts of my birthday cake. Cake and Phillipsburg chased each other through my mind.

December 29

I sat on the *Liberia*, nursing four cans of milk and a hope that never faded. Trade winds had softened to twenty miles an hour or less, the sun shone. It was unbelievable after the long period of stormy seas. Was the sea, at last, becoming reasonable? Soon I expected to sit upon the washboard and enjoy my hour of hygiene again. During the day I bailed until my seat was dry once more. But it did not really matter; I was happy—full of hope—and buoyed by the certainty that I would succeed.

Close to noon I noticed a shadow on the horizon to port. A shadow of a cloud, such as I had seen before. No? Yes? I was sure, suddenly, that it was an island. I could see the island, but I could not be sure which one it was. It lay, solitary, on the horizon. I could see it and no other. Strange! I continued sailing through the night, although the island disappeared behind a bank of clouds.

December 30

I passed a quiet night. I had to sail athwart and to the south to be certain of being in position for the island I had sighted. I was overwhelmed at the thought of seeing land. The island emerged with the sun, bare and broken up by rocks. To starboard lay great bare rocks; to the north I sighted my actual goal. In the background I could make out another shadow, which I recognized as Saba, the volcanic island. That meant that St. Bartholomew lay ahead of me.

I would land in the bay of Phillipsburg. Now at last I was sure. To the west of St. Martin lies the Anegade Passage, which I would have to cross to reach St. Thomas. It is not easy sailing, and I knew I would have to put my sails and equipment in order, before attempting it.

A last squall stirred the surface of the sea. Slowly I paddled toward St. Martin and rising ahead of me I saw the reality of my dreams: a little church, red roofs, and green palms behind a gray veil of rain. I looked on peace and calm. It was late afternoon as I entered the harbor, paddling close to the wharf where a crowd was sheltered from the rain. I sailed straight through the surf up onto the beach.

Forgotten were my seventy-two days, forgotten my discomforts, my fright, and my despair. As I climbed out of the boat, a breaker poured a bucket of water into it, my knees buckled, and I held onto the edge of the boat. Turning her on her bow, I tried to pull the stern out of the water. I went to grab the bow, but I stumbled and fell into the last licks of the surf. I tried again, and again I fell, until at last people came over from the wharf and carried the *Liberia* ten yards up the beach to where the water could not reach her. They asked me where I came from. "Las Palmas," I answered, but it meant nothing to them, and they ran back to their dry shelter.

I made a stab at clearing up the sails until I was interrupted by a voice from the pier; a police officer wanted to see my papers, so I drew a watertight bag from under the forepart of the spray cover and stumbled over to him. I handed him my passport and answered his questions. The crowd listened to my story and, after they had grasped the extent of my voyage, insisted on escorting me to the hotel. But the boat was still my first concern. I made my way awkwardly back to her, fastened the sails, closed the spray-cover opening and took out a few of my possessions. Then, very slowly, I walked to the hotel. Questions were thrown at me from all sides, but I hardly heard them. "Seventy-two days at sea, seventy-two days at sea!" repeated itself rhythmically in my mind. I could not believe that I was finally and at last stumbling through the streets of Phillipsburg. Although I walked shakily, like an old man, I did not need support from anyone.

At the hotel, the manager told me that word of my arrival had reached the governor, who had made me a guest of the island. Someone found clothes for me, and I was led to a shower. Staring back at me, from the old cracked mirror, was a face I did not recognize: sunken eyes, hollow cheeks, and unkempt blond beard. Good Lord! Was that my face?

I showered, and then, prepared to face a barrage of questions, I returned to the main room of the hotel, which was crowded with visitors. I sat down to eat and was offered—a cake! a beautiful coconut cake! I gulped three slices. As I ate, more and more people crowded into the room, stared at me shyly, shaking their heads in disbelief.

Later that day I investigated my movie camera and found it had corroded, although I hoped to be able to save some of the film. I spread my possessions all over the hotel room to dry before I lay down to sleep. But, still in the grip of immense tension, I could not sleep. At midnight I got up and walked down to the beach, where a small, dark lonely shape lay on the sand. The *Liberia*, a nothing without me. So I sat beside her in unspoken companionship listening to the surf, whose endless roar calmed me more than the unusual stillness of the hotel bedroom. The next day a mechanic fixed the rudder, I rigged the boat, stowed away new food supplies and, after another night's rest, left the hospitable island of St. Martin. After fifty hours of comfortable, relaxed sailing, I was before St. Thomas, exactly seventy-six days after I left the Canary Islands. As I paddled into the yacht basin, against the wind, I saw my friends ready to welcome me. They had evidently seen me coming into the harbor. Their first teasing words of greeting reached me as I pulled up alongside the mole. Slowly, with their help, I climbed out of the boat. Someone came over and whispered in my ear, "Didn't you tell me last time that you never intended to do this again?" But as she said it she took my right hand in both of hers, as if to say, I understand you.

I heard later how my friends happened to be gathered at the St. Thomas Yacht basin to see me arrive. I had sent one of them a letter from Las Palmas in which I mentioned that I expected to be with them around Christmas but without saying how I planned to get there. And then one morning a cockleshell sailed from the ocean into the bay of Charlotte Amalie, someone spotted it, and word went around at once, "Here comes Hannes. Have your cameras ready." Thus not only was I warmly greeted on my arrival but I now have in my possession two treasured unposed pictures of myself at that moment.

I spent a few weeks in St. Thomas, regaining my strength and avoiding the present-day Caribbean pirates, who saw a way of making money out of my voyage. For the first few days I had to take antibiotics against abscesses around my knees, but soon they disappeared, and I swam and danced again. At the hospital I spent my money in check-ups only to find that there was nothing extraordinary in my physical condition. My weight had gone down by some forty-three pounds. But as the hospital examination occurred five days after my arrival, I think I probably lost nearly fifty pounds, most of them during the last few days of the crossing.

I retain fond memories of my interview with the chief of immigration in St. Thomas. I had to go to him to obtain a visa for the United States, which entailed filling out an official questionnaire for Washington, D.C. "How would you describe your boat?" he asked, "motorboat, freighter, or steamer?"

"Just put down 'other,' again."

"What is the boat's tonnage, and how much water does she draw?"

"She weighs fifty-nine pounds, full she draws eight inches, empty about two inches."

Despite my startling answers I was given a visa, and shortly thereafter the *Liberia* and I flew back to New York.

I sat in the plane, looking down on the blue canvas of the sea, on which the wind painted white foam ridges. How harmless they looked from above! But I knew what these combers meant. The motors of the plane ran smoothly and rhythmically, passengers read and dozed, a pretty girl came down the aisles, carrying coffee to the pilots. But what, I wondered, would happen to these people if the motors failed, and the plane was forced to ditch?

During my two trips—two hundred days and nights alone at sea—I had learned a great deal that could help castaways. I know now that the mind succumbs before the body, that although lack of sleep, thirst, or hunger weaken the body, it is the undisciplined mind that drives the castaway to panic and heedless action. He must learn command of himself and, of course, of his boat, which is often his strongest and most resilient ally. Morale is the single most important factor in survival. Prayer, which brings hope and, with hope, optimism and relaxation, is a powerful aid in self-mastery. I cannot overemphasize the importance I place on auto-suggestions such as those I repeated to myself during the second voyage. Hunger brings on quarrelsomeness, suspicion, and irritation, so it is well to remember to watch one's neighbor, who may suddenly become the victim of dangerous hallucinations. He may think he sees a food store near the boat and jump overboard to reach it. I had this urge myself several times.

Stimulants are harmful for they are usually followed by a breakdown. Sleep is a vitally important factor, for lack of it leads to delirium, as I know from experience. The castaway should try to sleep, if only for a few minutes at a time. Seconds of sleep may save his life.

Fresh water is another key to survival. Research has been done that proves that a man can survive for three days in the tropics and nine days in temperate zones without food and water. We know that in the last war, a man survived for eleven days in the temperate zone under these conditions. I feel very strongly that no one who wishes to survive should drink salt water. If there is sufficient fresh water on board, a small amount of salt water may be drunk as a salt replacement, but that is all. Salt water is never a substitute for fresh water. If a castaway should happen to have milk or beer on his life raft, he can consider himself fortunate, for both these fluids will give him necessary calories. A skilled fisherman can keep himself supplied with all the solid foods he needs on a life raft, but he must be careful to balance his solid food intake with liquid intake. Only the eyes, blood, and spinal liquids of fish supplied me with fluids; to extract liquid from the rest of a fish's body one needs specially built presses.

Above all, my advice to the castaway is never to give up hope; on my second voyage, for example, I met no steamers in regions that are not crossed by shipping lanes.

Many of these thoughts about my own survival crossed my mind as I sat in the plane from St. Thomas to New York, traversing in a few hours a large stretch of the Atlantic Ocean. And why, I wondered, had I felt challenged to cross the Atlantic in a dugout and a foldboat, when I could have done it with ease and safety in a plane or a steamship? What drove me to test my strength of mind and body to the utmost? I realized that no one answer would satisfy me; the urge for adventure, the quest for scientific knowledge—both played a part. I told myself that man has always searched for the new frontier, pushed for further boundaries and that I, as a man, would have to accept that for my answer.

As a youngster, HANNES LINDEMANN loved the sea and sailing. His grandfather, a captain from the old windjammer days, stirred his imagination with the lore of sailing and the legends of the sea. Under his guidance, Hannes first learned how to handle a boat. This led to longer trips in sailboats and folding kayaks—small boats with collapsible wooden frames and rubberized canvas covers.

Out of these nautical experiences evolved the idea for crossing the Atlantic alone in 1956, first in a self-built African canoe and then, a few months later, in a folding kayak.

Since 1959, Lindemann has worked as a medical doctor for preventive medicine. Author of several successful books, Dr. Lindemann taught psycho-hygiene at Bonn University, Bonn, West Germany, before his recent retirement. He no longer sea kayaks. His hobbies are drawing and painting.

FRANK GOODMAN

Seven Tales for Seven Lives

Most canoeing (sea kayaking is known as canoeing in England) involves a journey, even if it is only a couple of hundred yards of turbulent rapid, and it is very easy to imagine significant emotional experiences at every breakout. Whether these experiences do "build character" is questionable.

I am quite clear that many claims made for canoeing experiences in terms of educational, moral, and character-building benefits are totally unfounded. But it is also true that it is difficult to prove that any single subject at school or college does much, in general terms, to the public working within the program. Yet there is no doubt that you can spot an educated person easily. Maybe we have a classic example here of, "The whole is greater than the sum of the parts." I suspect that it is the way the individual handles new experiences that is the significant factor, and this depends on the character that is already there.

The stories related here actually happened, and as far as I know, I have recorded them as truthfully as possible. Whether my own bias has changed the emphases, or distorted them, I cannot tell. Maybe if the people who were involved in the incidents read them now, they would neither recognize the situation nor themselves.

The stories are in chronological order. Most of them seemed quite unimportant at the time, but took on more meaning later, when memory, that uncertain ally, had no doubt reworked some of the scenes with a wash tinted with nostalgia.

Of course, the best stories are seldom told, as they are usually about people who find themselves unable to tolerate the stress of unfamilar surroundings. Under these conditions, bizarre—potentially dangerous—behavior becomes the norm with some individuals. Usually, after a trip under poor circumstances, the perpetrators are blissfully unaware of their idiosyncratic behavior, and the others are so relieved to be alive that they take a vow of eternal silence. It's simpler!

I would hate to make exaggerated claims for canoeing. The phrase "paddle your own canoe," however, has stayed with us for generations, and once afloat, you have to rely on yourself a little more than in other sports. The counter indicator is the phrase, "up the creek without a paddle." More seriously, a friend of mine who worked with delinquents, teaching them many different sports, did feel that canoeing modified their behavior more powerfully than other disciplines.

It is perfectly possible to have an eminently satisfactory life without any canoeing activity at all . . . but how do you *prove* it?

Twenty-five years ago I made a sailing dinghy with a group of students. In doing so I discovered that fairing off sheets of marine ply was beyond the average student. So I was particularly interested when I heard of a new method of building boats by stitching the edge of ply sheets together with copper wire and then sealing them with a glassfiber tape: a well-proven method today, but revolutionary in 1960.

I decided to make a couple of kayaks with the students, as I reasoned with devilish cunning, that if a student could manage the method, with a bit of luck children in school could manage it too, thus making it possible to introduce a boat-building program into schools. I was slightly interested in sailing, totally uninterested in canoeing, and very much immersed in educational method at the time.

I built the kayaks with a group of students, and I was impressed with the construction process. But, after giving them to the physical education department in the college, I forgot about them. It never occurred to me to actually get in one.

About a year later my colleague in the physical education department mentioned that the two kayaks we made had been in his storage room and had never been used. I promised to try out one of the kayaks on a nice sandy beach in Wales where I was taking my annual family vacation.

The fact that I knew absolutely nothing about kayaks did not worry me at all. I just thought I would have a little play in the boat within the shelter of the bay. Anyway I was a strong swimmer! I was tying the kayak onto the car roof rack at the end of the summer term when I was handed a strange piece of waterproof cloth.

"You'll probably need this," I was told.

"What is it?"

"It's a spraydeck: you pull it around your waist and then clip it onto the cockpit of the kayak."

"I don't know whether I'd like to be held into the boat," I said, "but I'll take it just in case I decide to try it."

I put a pair of split paddles into the car. I noticed that there were two positions on the join, but knowing nothing of "feather" the significance was lost on me.

Borth, Wales, is a small town just to the south of the Aberdovey Estuary. The caravan site was just to the north, behind a line of sand dunes. It was an ideal spot for a family with young children—ours were seven and two—one swimmer and one splasher! The weather was good, and we spent the first few days in general family play on the beach before I eventually lifted the kayak off the car.

It was a beautiful, hot day with a slight sea breeze pushing some small surf onto the gently sloping beach. It was all of twelve inches high at maximum, but I looked at it with apprehension. I made a mental note that I must keep the boat head-on to the waves. I had read this important piece of seamanship in a novel once.

I sat in the boat on the beach and spent five minutes getting the spraydeck onto the cockpit coaming. The next problem was to get to the water. Luckily the tide was coming in, and several grazed knuckles later I was afloat.

The waves that quivered away from the boat in all directions as I tried to stay upright were slightly bigger than the surf. It took a short time to get the feel of the boat, and ten minutes later I was making my way out through the surf, head-on to the waves, of course, and just about managing to keep the boat straight. In 1964 even slalom boats were very buoyant and only one breaking wave came more than a foot or so along the deck before it slid away over the gunwales. As I had suspected the spraydeck was of no importance. "Just for keeping the drips from the paddle shafts off your legs," I thought!

Once beyond the breaking waves it was very calm, and I soon found it quite relaxing to move around under the sun. After half an hour of gentle paddling my arms felt tired. Time to go in. Keeping the boat straight suddenly became difficult and, just before I came to the breaking water, I found I had broached broadside to the beach.

And then it happened. Out to sea one wave considerably bigger than any of the others was coming up fast. Suddenly I realized it was going to break before the others. It was towering eighteen inches above me as I sat there transfixed! I saw the sky gleaming brilliantly through the thin top of the wave in that moment before it crashed onto the gunwale of the boat.

With a wild movement of desperation I plunged paddle and body seaward, toward deeper water to avoid hitting my head on the beach. But it never happened. With my elbow and paddle totally submerged I was lifted up and trolled toward the beach broadside on! Amazing! Exhilarating! Suddenly I wasn't tired in the least.

No one on the beach seemed to have seen this extraordinary event. I quickly paddled out again—even strokes on both sides—and turned the boat. Here's a big one. Lean into it. Yes, another happy dash toward the sandcastles. Again, quick! Again and again! I was exhausted, but I still had the energy to climb from the boat and find my family. My wife and two daughters stood at the water's edge. I was disappointed that the two-year-old was not the least bit interested, but the other two were suitably impressed!

If this was canoeing—I was hooked. Looking back now I realize that those moments changed my life, and the laugh was, I thought I had invented the high brace singlehanded.

We had gathered, all eight of us, at the lifeboat station that overlooked Ramsey Sound off the Southeast coast of Wales. A very small cleft in the cliffs housed the boathouse and the steep ramp that allowed the lifeboat to hurtle down to the sea in times of emergency.

This was one of the few places where it was possible to launch a kayak along this coast. It also was an ideal starting point for a circumnavigation of Ramsey Island, a short journey of some seven miles, but with spectacular cliff scenery and the notorious "Bitches" to negotiate—a broken dike of igneous rock that pushes out from Ramsey Island almost a quarter of the way across the sound toward the mainland of Wales. This rock takes the full force of the tidal current that sweeps north and south.

We were not very punctual, and for over twenty minutes cars came clattering down the track to the boathouse. We lifted our kayaks from the cars and carried them the short distance down to the water.

It was obvious that conditions were not going to be easy. Though there was very little wind, a long, lazy swell was heaving and sighing in the cove like a giant pair of bellows. A long wave only a couple of feet high in this sheltered spot meant a swell of eight or maybe ten feet outside Ramsey Island. The addition of this to the swirling vortices, which sweep through Ramsey Sound at over six knots on springs, meant unstable waves collapsing in all directions.

Geoff was first in his boat and allowed a wave to lift him gently from the lifeboat ramp. We watched, his boat rising and falling to the long period swells. We had begun to get into our own boats in the restricted space available when Geoff suddenly returned to the rocks and climbed out.

"Sorry chaps," he said, "I can't go today. I'm frightened. I'll watch you from the cliffs and meet you back here in about four hours."

I looked at his face and saw it was pale, not from seasickness but from a fear of the relentless heaving of the sea that spoke of unquenchable power. Geoff lifted his boat onto his shoulder and walked back up the path and out of sight.

There was a very long silence, indeed.

"Come on," someone said, "We'll be eons late for the tide if we don't go."

What had the silence really said? Had they all felt that Geoff was a coward? I had the impression that the other paddlers thought that he should have doused his fears and carried on in spite of them. But in my book it would be almost as frightening to stand in front of one's peers and admit fear when everyone else seemed confident, as it would be to press on. Had he become trapped between the two fears and merely chosen to expose himself to the lesser? Certainly no easy thing to do. I wondered whether I would have the guts to withstand the derision of my peers. There was no doubt in my mind that Geoff had made the right decision, for there is nothing more dangerous than a tense, frightened person on the sea. I hoped that the others felt the same as I did, though I knew this was not the time to ask. Their feelings would become vocal soon enough, but now we had our own forebodings to attend to. Maybe Geoff's departure helped them to steady their own qualms. Were they tightening their resolve by unfairly condemning his behavior? The group moved out and into the heightening swell. Within the deserted cove the dark waters moved restlessly.

On that morning when five of us set out to circumnavigate Anglesey Island—a distance of twenty-seven miles—in a wind that was blowing a steady force four, I wasn't thinking of Geoff at all. Within hours, though, I would be. We pushed against the last of the flood as we paddled westwards down the coast towards Holyhead Bay. We moved out wide, almost to the Skerries, to make sure we didn't get caught in the eddy, which always flows easterly there at any tide. Even so it was a long, hard pull into the strong southwesterly breeze, and we were thankful when we began to feel the ebb tide sucking up past North Stack.

"Four hours gone already," I said to Martin, "if we make it at all, it will be a slow journey."

"You're right," he returned, "South Stack will be big today with spring ebb against a four."

It was no exaggeration. South Stack is an island separated

from Holy Island by a thin sliver of water maybe twenty yards across. High overhead is a narrow suspension footbridge that serves the lighthouse perched atop the two-hundred-foot cliffs. These cliffs are a well-known rendezvous for climbers, but not one was visible as we crept closer.

The South Stack race was well formed by now, and the advantage of a five-knot push seemed dubious to me as I saw four- to five-foot seas suddenly grow to enormous size. I was even less happy when I saw that the top three or four feet of water was continually peeling off and careening down the face of the waves until it was reabsorbed in the trough.

Martin must have seen my face. "Don't worry, it's only the odd one that really collapses. Look! Don't get under one like that!"

I watched as one wave towered above its neighbors, held its form for an age, and then suddenly exploded from within, with a welter of foam and a deep-throated roar.

I did not have time to ask how to avoid such a maelstrom as Martin was already digging his paddles deep and moving away. There was no escape anyhow—the current was pulling us inexorably forward, and I knew I was committed. I felt my mouth go dry and that hollow form in my stomach.

"No sweat," I told myself. "You've surfed stuff like this before. Check your specs—are they tied on tight enough? Grip your paddles; no sense in letting the wind snatch them away from you now."

I crouched forward in my seat and settled to a slow, deliberate style of paddling—paddles deep in the water and ready to brace if required. I had told myself a lie. I had never surfed waves as big as this. The first crest slipped under my boat almost unnoticed, but behind it the trough almost made me dizzy with its depth. Down, down I sank—surely the boat would never rise to the next face. It must just go on down and down through the surface and then on, ever downwards into the quiet, cold depths where storms could not reach it. The thought was almost comforting. I felt lethargic, almost at peace. This was the end—the whimper. I was jolted alert by the shadow of the next face that was nearly ahead of me . . . the bow rising, steeper and steeper. The top two feet of water hissed toward me. But my rhythm was secure. Push,

push. Don't alter pace. Steady, steady, head down, thrust deep. The bow burst through the crest, and a shaft of sunlight diamonded the spray.

"That was considerate of it," I said to myself, and the next trough sank away from me. The rhythm established itself: sink into the abyss, rise to the crest, push through and repeat. I relaxed a little. The adrenalin was still high as I watched for the big one that could catch me unawares, but the nearest thing to total collapse was a five-foot wall of foam that smothered me but allowed the kayak to cut through it without problems.

Fear turned to exhilaration as we swept along, well separated for safety. What the true height actually was, I could not really judge, but I knew it was big when I noticed that the lighthouse, perched above the cliffs, continually disappeared from view. But as quickly as we had entered the race we were through. The wave height was back to a normal four feet, the wind died to a three, and the sun shone. But where was the ebb? There was little evidence of movement now. The south wind had applied brakes.

We moved down the west coast of Holy Island and rafted up for a snack in the shelter of some rocky islets beyond Rhoscolyn Head. We had been on the water for five hours and had made twenty five miles. Not good, considering the tides. We finished our lunch and pushed on.

As we came clear from the shelter of the islands I realized that things had changed for the worse. The wind speed was increasing fast. We were now parallel to the waves that began to lose their tops regularly. Paddle, paddle, brace, paddle, paddle, brace. Not difficult but more tiring than normal paddling. I mused about our chances now. It was 4:00 P.M. Three hours to the entrance of the Menai Straits, one hour paddling in the dark. Increasing wind speed—up to five, gusting six already with no help now from the tide. I knew that the west coast of Anglesey Island was a series of cliffs interspersed with surfing beaches. No fun surfing into an unknown bay in the dark and hoping to run up the sand without hitting rocks. Worse still to be caught on the base of the cliffs!

I looked at the others—impassive faces, upper bodies swinging steadily to their strokes. How were they feeling? I could get no answer from their expressions, but I knew I wasn't up to the challenge. There really wasn't any stigma in knowing when to cry off; Geoff had taught me that a year ago. Why hadn't the others spoken? Was it easier than I thought? Was it all in the mind? Well, I was the old man of the group, so they could think what they liked. I wasn't going on.

I shouted and waved until we had drawn close.

"I'm sorry chaps," I said, "I'm not going on. That narrow channel in the cliffs there is a passage through to a bay . . . Borthwen I think it's called, and that's the last sheltered takeout between here and the Menai Straits. I don't fancy the west coast in this weather, or in the dark. You go on. I'll hitch a lift back to the car on my own and find you in the morning."

No one spoke so I turned away and moved toward the surging waters of the channel leading through to safety. Behind me there was a clash of paddles. Two kayaks shot past on the right and there was a bump to port as someone else began to overtake me. I was nearly killed in the rush. Only one voice had been raised. The vote had been silent, but the decision was unanimous.

Because of my distrust of regimented systems I was a little chary of helping out John with the youth group he was taking on a week-long canoeing trip in Scotland. Fond of him as I was, I still found the military precision with which he ran his canoeing group quite distasteful and at odds with my philosophy of freedom and development through personal choice.

"Does them good, that type of lad," said John.

I had to admit that most of his group were a pretty rough lot; happy to steal, bully, vandalize, and generally create havoc wherever they went. Maybe "good" could come from John's style of leadership, though personally I was not convinced.

"You help him out," my wife told me. "Maybe you'll learn something yourself."

I was conceited enough to think it unlikely that I would change my mind, but my wife is a very discerning person so I agreed to go.

I admired the care and patience John put into the holiday for those lads. We spent a lot of time planning routes; talking about the weather and tides; checking camping gear; dividing rations into one-man packs; teaching everyone how to use the cooking stoves; not to mention how to care for the kayaks and how to pack waterproof bags with equipment.

Throughout these training weeks I never once saw John out of patience. Many of the disruptive boys came from deprived homes, and often their intellectual capacity was not extensive. But John was content to go over things again and again until everyone had grasped the essentials.

Though I helped out here, most of my time was spent on the water with the lads. I had had experience with delinquent boys years before when I taught in school, and little had changed in the intervening years. Some of the boys were quite skillful, but they could change very quickly from bullying braggarts to cringing crybabies.

"*You* fell out, not me, so *you* get your boat and your paddle and try again," I'd say to the lad foul mouthing it on the bank.

The logic of it would penetrate. Maybe the saying, "paddle your own canoe," has a special significance for people who can so easily find reasons why their problems should be solved by others. My years as a teacher stood me well, and the lads respected me because I was a much better canoeist than they were. Even so I found them a singularly unattractive bunch.

John calmed my fears. "Don't worry about them. If you saw their parents you'd think they'd done well."

I knew this to be true, but a whole week with that lot? Daunting thought!

"I get them away from everything they're used to," explained John. "That's why I make it an expedition. The whole group has to be self-sufficient. They don't get to see a shop or the television, and that's a shaker for most of them. In fact I dare not take them near a town. I made that mistake the first year. They shoplifted 50 percent of the display in the village store, stripped the trees of apples within a two-mile radius, and got so drunk that I had to ask the local landlord to ban them from the pub. Most of them were underage, anyway. So now we go to the wilderness."

The journey north was uneventful. There were the usual high jinks during the first night because, of course, the lads

Frank Goodman

were very excited in spite of the juvenile mask of unconcern. I was happy to find everybody breakfasted and packed for a 10:00 A.M. start the next morning. The weather was perfect, and we moved off down the coast in easy stages. An early lunch stop and then a final landing before four in the afternoon was planned.

"I'm glad you agree with me, Frank. Nothing's worse than taking beginners too far. It's easy to forget how knackering the first day can be."

The south coast of Mull Island, with its high cliffs, looks intimidating from a distance, but a closer inspection shows that under the cliff is a raised beach—so common on the west coast of Scotland. This ancient feature has created a minicliff at sea level, about ten feet high, but the sea has broken through this in many places, and for the canoeist these coves provide ideal sheltered landing spots along the shore. John knew the coast intimately, and the campsite he had chosen was a dream—a sheltered cove for the canoes, with an entrance only a few feet wide opening onto a circular shingle beach. Above the miniature cliff, the old raised beach, now grassy, formed a beautiful level area for the tents.

Each boy shared a two-man tent, and each tent had a cooking stove. Every person had his own day's rations, issued by John every morning. They could either take turns using the stove or pool their rations and cook in pairs.

Tents were pitched, and soon stoves were hissing as water began to boil. Simple, freeze-dried menus were the order.

"Easy for them to cook, and better than they get at home for the most part," said John.

The commotion began at the far end of the line of tents.

"Piss off! You're not getting any of mine."

"I've told you, I'll smash your face in if you don't bugger off."

A lad came up to John, red faced and angry. "Bill won't share his food with me," complained Sam.

"Why should he?" queried John.

"Look at this mess!"

Sam held out a horrible soggy mess of freeze-dried "ham and egg pie" that had been thoroughly soused in sea water and was totally inedible.

"How did that happen?"

"I forgot to fasten the clip on my waterproof bag, and I put it behind my seat instead of in the hatch—so I could get it quick," explained Sam.

"Well that's a shame," said John, "but you know the routine as well as any. Don't do it again."

"But what are you going to do about it?" shouted Sam.

"Me? Nothing."

"Nothing! Make that sodding Bill share."

"No, I won't. Sorry, Sam, but next ration handout is at 7:00 A.M. tomorrow morning."

"Tomorrow!" shrieked Sam. "What about me tonight?"

"Hard cheese," said John. "It won't hurt you to go without tonight. You won't starve, and it'll remind you to fasten your bags up properly and put them in the proper place."

"You bastard! You bloody horrible bastard," screamed Sam. "I'll get you, you swine. Wait till I tell 'em back home. I'll show you."

John took all of this very calmly, and when Sam ran out of breath John said, very quietly, though the whole campsite heard every word, "Well, all right Sam, I can see you're upset. Calm down. Take this and get yourself some fish and chips."

John reached into his trouser pocket and slapped a pound coin into Sam's palm. Sam's jaw fell open to his knees, and the expressions that moved across his face were incredible. The entire group got the picture. Poor Sam! He had spent most of his life somehow trying to collect money for fags, chips, and fodder for one-armed bandits. Now, here he was with money, given to him, not stolen! There, in his grasp, a small fortune. He looked around at the sweep of hills and the lowering sun dipping toward the Inner Hebrides. The nearest fish and chips shop was not twenty yards away but twenty miles away—as the crow flies!

Sam looked again. One pound, solid in his hand, and for the first time in his life utterly worthless. The other boys sniggered, casting sidelong glances at each other, and turned purposefully to their meal. My first emotional response was to leap to Sam's defense. He was a poor creature really, and no match for John's rigorous detachment. But I saw in a flash what John was doing. In the miniature drama ending in that single, stark action he had jolted Sam to understand something of the nature of responsibility and simultaneously proved to him that money has no intrinsic value.

It was brilliant—poetic, dramatic, utterly simple, and yet searing in the clarity of its message. I, too, turned away silently. Growth, I knew, was often painful.

"I thought you would learn something," grinned my wife when I told her the story.

"Sam and me both," I said.

I'm not sure that I know where holidays stop and expeditions begin. Certainly I've been on holidays that have turned into epics, and I've been on expeditions that weren't worthy of the name. What is it that makes people happy to exchange the comfort of a canoe picnic on a nice day for an uncomfortable journey in adverse conditions?

The Hobbit crystallized adventures nicely when he said they were nasty, cold, wet things that made you late for tea. Personally, I don't like being cold though I am not adverse to being wet or late for tea. For me, an expedition means the thrill of new experiences, meeting new people, wondering at the spectacular scenery and wildlife. But all this can be done without undertaking an expedition.

One of the most important reasons for setting up a trip, as far as I am concerned, is to see if I can actually do it. It is a very private thing, a test of oneself, a check on what sort of person one really is, or maybe even an attempt to change one's character. On second thought, though, these reasons are quite superficial. Why should we need to prove ourselves to ourselves? When I trace the development of my own most committing expedition—the journey around Cape Horn, the motives seem very sparse indeed.

It began when two friends suggested an interesting canoe trip somewhere remote and in an exciting part of the world. The biggest problem was money. We needed to raise money in order to indulge ourselves, therefore we had to offer something to a potential sponsor. Often this need be no more than a well-publicized link between the sponsor's name and the image of the expedition. But sometimes it demands a great deal of time and effort if, for example, equipment is to be properly evaluated for a sponsoring company. One idea we had for our expedition was to paddle as far north as possible along the coast of Greenland, but this seemed a woolly affair—there was no real goal. Nothing for a sponsor to latch onto.

We needed a firm clear goal with the right image. Mountaineers have it easy: they need only to say, "climb Mount Everest," and the scenario is clear.

Was there a similar goal for the canoeist? We racked our brains for weeks until someone said, "What about Cape Horn?" I cannot honestly remember whose idea it was now, though I have a sneaky feeling it was mine! But there it was: Cape Horn. It was so obvious! It had been staring us in the face all the while, and we had not recognized it.

There it was—an image of vicious weather and horrendous seas with that isolated cliff rearing up above the spume.

But that was an image only. What of the reality? We had no idea, but we agreed it was worth finding out. What were conditions really like at the end of the South American continent? Was it feasible to make a kayak journey there? Did we stand a chance of getting "around the Horn?"

It was not easy, as we had imagined, to get information. We could find very little by way of useful photographs, drawings, or other indication of conditions near that remote headland. Only the *South America Pilot* and a very small-scale chart gave us anything at all, and it was only after we had bought these that we at last realized the trip was possible. One thing we did discover was that the reality, as far as we could judge, was only a little less daunting than the image. We were happily embarking on an expedition that, however optimistically we looked at it, must contain more than its fair share of cold, danger, and deprivation.

It was quite clear that we were determined to go. But why? I would suggest that the basic reason is anxiety! A fundamentally anxious person has a need to channel anxiety from the general to the particular, and what better way than to shed, for a time at any rate, the half-understood worries of normal living and focus on pressing and solvable problems presented by an expedition?

A lot has been said about the freedom available to the canoeist at whatever level he is paddling, but I am convinced this is a fallacy. A paddler's choice of action is limited, indeed, and his freedoms, likewise, are extremely circumscribed. We should not talk, in this instance, about freedom of choice, but rather of freedom from choice. Once the basic logistics of a trip have been dealt with and a general target raised in the sights, there are only a couple of problems: the weather and the tides. When we were on Cape Horn the weather was so overriding in importance that we dismissed the rather small tidal movement.

Our anxiety was nicely channeled into a concrete form, and it felt like freedom! In reality, the adrenalin flow that is the consequence of partaking in any risky activity is oil on the troubled waters of the mind. I am sure this is true of myself and of all my companions who undertake committing journeys by kayak. And from reading the stories of the great adventurers there are strong indications that they, too, were the victims of vague phantoms of stress, which needed to be transformed into an individual ogre before they could be tackled.

Although I believe this to be true, the evidence does not come from an analysis of my own emotions. Even after important decisions have been made there is precious little feeling of relief, but rather the nagging doubt that the decision was the wrong one!

The worst time for me was the gap between making the decision to go and the commencement of actually paddling. I really did have nightmares about being out of my kayak and being lifted up on enormous waves and hurled toward a harsh rock face rearing vertically from the ocean. Many times I saw this rock surface rush toward me until every detail of its crystal-line structure was clearly defined inches from my eyes. At the point of impact I awoke with a pounding heart, gulping in lungfuls of air. Even so I felt that the scene owed more to Hollywood than to any real situation.

Once the journey began, however, my fears receded, and I found the required singleness of purpose most satisfying. On the day we began the circumnavigation of Cape Horn, however, satisfaction gave way to apprehension! The journey began from Hershal Island at 5:00 A.M. on December 22, 1977. The vicious westerly gale that had howled for two days had died away, and only a few white horses creamed along the channel that separated us from the north shore of Cape Horn Island just two miles away. The cloud base that had dipped to the skyline the previous day had evaporated, and we could even see the pinnacles that perch so strangely on the eastern flank of Cape Horn some seven miles away to the south.

We knew that before long we had to pass under those pinnacles after traversing the western shore, three hours of the most exposed paddling in the world. Only a gentle breeze stirred the tussock grass as we slipped into our kayaks. The snap of the well-fitting spraydeck as it clipped onto the cockpit rim was reassuring. I felt secure and comfortable.

High cirrus clouds were already sliding in from the west as we moved out from the shore through the encircling kelp. In the open channel a very long, lazy swell lifted us gently. It was not more than a foot or two high, and very smooth—but the frequency was astonishingly low. It made me apprehensive. As we paddled west, the channel gradually widened, and slowly the stacks of the northwest corner of the island began to separate themselves from the stern cliffs. We could see a wreath of white foam around the base of the stacks, but it looked small. Maybe we were in luck, maybe the seas had abated in the night. But how could they? The fetch to the west of Cape Horn encircles the globe, and a full gale had blown for two days. What did the graphs in the books tell us about wave height? I could not remember. But I knew that it should be considerably more than a foot or two. What was wrong?

Then I recalled the training trip in Scotland when we decided to run for cover in big seas just south of Cape Wrath. The cove we were aiming for was a shallow one with its mouth open to the full force of the wind and waves. As we entered the cove the waves breaking along the north wall were some eight feet high, but that solid cliff was draining away the energy from the ends of the waves, reducing their height dramatically. Instead of finding fiercely breaking surf near the shore, we were carried up onto a dank bed of rotting seaweed at the back of the cove on waves just eighteen inches high.

Here was a similar situation; the cliffs on either side of the channel were draining energy out of the waves. Even though we were paddling due west into open water, and the channel was now at least three miles wide, the conditions were easy. But the wave period was so long! Then I realized that the stacks were a long ways away. The answer was staring me in the face. I had seen it many times before, but once again I failed to recognize its distorted features. The answer was scale! The small stacks close to us were, in fact, stacks still a mile away. I felt my eyes suddenly refocus as my brain added more messages to the purely visual one, and I saw!

Nobody spoke until Jim said, "Come on—it's going to blow." I knew then that he was nervous. Even so we were totally unprepared for the swift change that hit us. Suddenly we were lifted in a huge swell—not eight feet as when we were preparing for this in Scotland, but over sixteen feet of cold, smooth slopes that rose slowly until the crest, ruffled by the local breeze, slapped and tickled the hulls of our kayaks before we sank down again into the glassy trough.

We looked out between the stacks. Always go the shortest way if you can! But we did not have to discuss it. Between the fangs of rock the uneven reflections had turned the surface into a host of white-clad warriors performing a horrifying war dance. They crouched low then sprang high in the air, flicking their streaming headdresses to the left and the right; stamping and surging to and fro in their amphitheater. There was no coherent pattern to their gyrations. Maybe some underlying polyrhythm, some hidden, surging percussive force was controlling the chaos. But all we were aware of was the deep roar of a thousand war cries bellowing at random, echoing from cliff to cliff—warning us to keep away.

We circled around outside the stacks. Not too close; the farther out to sea the calmer the water. Yet experience told us that this size of reflected wave could travel miles out to sea, quite a distance from the cliffs that caused it. Still no one spoke. There was no need. The wind was calm. We had to paddle.

Now we could see due south. The waves had taken on a new, even more frightening aspect: as they reached the shore they were breaking hard, trapping air between their curling fronts and the base of the cliffs. It was as though howitzers were attacking the island. We could feel the jolt of the impact in the hulls of our kayaks, though we couldn't see the waves themselves as a fifty-foot-high wall of spray drifted lazily along the foot of the cliffs, hiding both rock and surf.

These are the most nerve-racking conditions to paddle in. The large swell was easy enough except that it was impossible to see where we were going. But superimposed on the back of these waves was the clapotis—the dreaded reflecting waves from the shore that have no rhythm. They just held their station, leaping up and down, their faces so steep that capsize seemed inevitable. Cape Horn spawns giant clapotis, eight feet of solid water roaring upward with such speed that the top bursts away from the body of the wave and lands, cold and heavy, on your head. We tottered forward, bracing when the water rose past us and balancing when the surface suddenly sucked down, leaving our paddles in midair.

There was no alternative, no decision to make. We had to go on. It lasted three hours. Then, slowly, the reflections died away as we approached the southern tip of the island. The waves were rolling past the shore, not confronting it. A rhythm returned to our paddling as we saw the dark cliff, crisp against a brilliant blue sky. We could take photographs, but a sudden puff of cold air caught our paddles. It would be foolish to dawdle. It was 9:30 A.M.

Now we had to discover a landing spot on the east coast. We swept along in the huge swell. I remember seeing Nigel completely framed by a background of white as a huge wave swept up the rocks onshore. We felt we were almost clear, yet the sheer size of the waves was staggering. There could be no survival if such a monster caught us too close to shore. Soon we found a resting spot—a beach of large gray boulders sheltered by kelp, facing east and almost calm. The sun was hot in the cove as we lay there on the stones.

What did we feel? What had we learned? We had been apprehensive paddling through the clapotis, and although we had not exchanged more than monosyllables, we understood each other's mood perfectly. We would turn south as one man, toward that daunting west coast, and we knew that no one would turn away. But now, where was the elation, the sense of achievement? We were drained! Only a sense of relief flooded through us, coupled with a real sense of awe at the power of those exposed waters.

Expeditions allow little time for rumination. The blue sky was gone, and the wind began to suck and swirl around our boats. Time to find a spot for the tent. Time to think about the next big crossing back to Navarino Island and the relative safety of the Beagle Channel.

After a poor night's sleep in the rocky east cove of Cape Horn Island, we realized that the gale was still roaring over the cliffs and swirling down on us, pressing the rain fly from alternate sides as though intent on prizing us from the ground like a buried tent peg.

Barry and I had promised ourselves a climb to the top of Cape Horn itself and, as the island is only a few miles across, and the cliff is only 1,400 feet high, it didn't seem too big a task even in the gale. The bogs that lay over the impervious rocks were much drier than we had expected, and on some of the flatter areas we made good progress. But as we approached the steeper ground, which swept up from the center of the island to that notorious cliff, we found the going suddenly much more difficult.

The ubiquitous vegetation of the southern end of Patagonia is the evergreen beech tree. In a sheltered location it can grow thirty to forty feet and form a dense forest, but its height is effected by the wind just as surely as the temperature affects the height of a column of mercury in a thermometer. On a west-facing slope the perpetual blast can bonsai the beech trees into miniatures just a couple of inches high.

Our path lay up a slope across which the wind had howled for hundreds of years, and the beech trees had been clipped down to a height of about three feet. The sturdy beech do not give in to the wind easily. To compensate for their lack of stature they had crowded together to form a low but solid bulwark, and although no single twig could survive if it were the merest fraction above its neighbor, all of them were packed so tightly together that it was difficult to see how the leaves could find space to grow.

To walk through this barrier was a problem. The tops of the twigs could not support our weight. Our feet would hold for several seconds but then would slide down through the mass to ground level some three feet below. It was as though we were walking through deep soft snow with neither skis nor snowshoes.

It felt as though I had to lift my ankle to my ear for every step—and it was tiring. Barry plodded ahead with a steady rhythm that spoke of his many seasons as a Himalayan climber, and I began to wonder whether I was going to make it. My legs were deadly tired, and the same twigs that allowed my feet to plummet through them to ground level were there to hook onto my boots and trousers so that extraction was a momentous effort.

"Bloody hell," said Barry, in exasperation. "This is the hardest low-angle climb I've ever done."

I could have hugged him, but I contented myself with a grin.

"Thank goodness you said that," I replied. "I thought it was just my legs that wouldn't respond."

"Don't you believe it. This is hard!"

The sharing of a problem, even as simple as this one, really does halve the load, and we seemed to make better progress after that. I mused on the effect of this simple communication. I obviously was not a loner. Some sort of sharing was essential to me. Could I have made the climb had I been alone? Probably not. More likely I would not have begun it. Any journey without a companion to say, "Look at this" or "Did you see that?" is a dull one indeed.

The going became easier as the beech trees gave up the unequal struggle against the wind, their place taken by tussock grass, which withstood anything this climate could conjure up. A green-winged teal startled us as it burst from the base of some rocks, caught the full blast of the wind, and curled off to the east like a slingshot.

Steeper and steeper, but then another large outcrop of greenstone was the last, and we were on top. Away in the distant northwest, the stacks and arches of that magnificent corner of the island were clearly visible, and the terrifying west coast, with its leaping foam, stretched down below our feet. To the south the vastness of the Drake Strait was lost in the spray that lifted off the torn surface of the ocean. The roar from the water below was totally drowned out by a wind so constant in its pressure that even on the cliff top it was perfectly safe to lean out at a ridiculous angle over the edge. I found my pocket wind gauge useless. It was off the scale that finished at seventy miles an hour!

Farther to the east we saw the deep curve of the bay and farther away still the cruel outcrop of Isla Deceit grayed by spray. Then the most startling image—so close under our feet that it had been overlooked until that moment—almost totally enclosed by rock walls was a corrie lake. Its jet black waters, lying calm in the wind shadow were in strange contrast to the blue-green and white of the turbulent ocean. A jewel of jet, a perfect circle, clasped in a setting of gray-green diorite, which on the south side was so thin that only a few yards separated the still black water from the blue sea.

I found the shock of discovery very intense. So much was explained: the cliffs of Cape Horn present a solid face of rock half a mile long with some strange rock pinnacles a little to the east of the summit. These pinnacles had given me an uneasy feeling as they were unlike any cliff-top rocks I had every seen before. Now all became clear; they were not just the work of the sea but had been formed by glacial action. The cliff of Cape Horn was, in fact, an arête. In just a few seconds of geological time that cliff would be eaten back a dozen more feet, and the whole of the wafer-thin eastern face would disappear.

Ever since man had rounded Cape Horn, this lake had been kept secret from him. Even from the east it remains invisible; it is perched too high to be apparent from sea level. On the poor charts of the area it is not recorded, and we found no reference to it in our readings of other explorers' descriptions of the area.

Obviously others must have discovered it, because no doubt others before us have climbed to the top of Cape Horn. It was rumored that Sir Francis Drake himself had gazed out from that southern cliff more than four hundred years ago. Yet it was a secret—not a complete secret, yet one known to only the few who had made the arduous journey. For us the secret was even more impressive because it came at the end of a wearying flight from England and a nerve-racking paddle from Puerto Williams, followed by the cruel slog up the beech-infested slopes. Here, though, was the real and metaphorical jewel of our journey. Maybe it was a jewel only because of its setting, or just because it was rare. No, it was the journey that had made it so and, to be sure, the difficulty of the route had definitely improved its quality.

Perhaps our journey had been closer to other, quite different journeys I had made occasionally in the design field. Here, too, were problems to be solved, areas to be explored, sometimes the flash of insight, the hard slog of development work— always with unexpected niggling difficulties presenting themselves—and then sometimes, with luck, a happy solution. Our journey had been crowned with a jewel, but wasn't it the nature of the journey that had made the jewel? Wasn't it always better to discover things for yourself, make your own journey, even if the jewel proved to be flawed? The Chinese proverb says it is better to travel hopefully than to arrive, and maybe that is right.

For me the fact that we were the first to round Cape Horn by kayak paled to insignificance compared with this secret black jewel. Maybe this was just a personal thing. I had never felt particularly competitive, never really had the big kick on the occasions when I had come in first in an endeavor. These were hollow victories for me, ephemeral and quickly forgotten. So being a member of the first kayaking group to round Cape Horn—beating all the others to it as it were—did not produce in me a lasting satisfaction. To me the lasting joys are twofold: the awareness of the development of physical skills during concentrated practice, and the revelation that can follow hard, concentrated thought. The jewel is sometimes very small and indeed not always rare at all, but these discoveries are everything. So much better than being told. So much better than having learned it from a book. And in the end, when you find that the experience is not unique, but has been savored by others too: how much happier to find that you are in good company, that you are not alone, and yet still an individual.

Is it really possible to be so similar to countless other individuals, yet still have a uniqueness that is yours? Maybe Cape Horn can reveal an answer!

How far is it around Cape Horn island? Maybe twenty-five miles to paddle in a kayak. How far is it along the coastline, counting every bay and smallest cove? A hundred miles? Now measure the distance and include every indentation, every rock. Another thousand miles. What happens if we take into account every pebble and the countless grains of sand that lie on that shoreline? The distance becomes infinite.

Within the finite limit is an ever-deepening dimension, an infinite variation that increases with ever-closer inspection. Here is the fascination, here is the revelation, here are the jewels—not scattered for all to see, but precious indeed to those who have made the journey.

Ailsa Craig is an island lying some ten miles off the Scottish coast in the Solway Firth. It came into existence when a volcano blasted out its lava. But as the subterranean fires cooled, the molten rock in the vent solidified, and much later, when erosion had inexorably worked on the softer material, all that was left was a hard plug of basalt. Ages afterward the sea came, and a new conflict began. Waves attacked from every side until high cliffs showed where the hard rock must inevitably give way to the attack of the ocean.

Thus Ailsa Craig sits on the flat surface of the firth, like a solitary rock bun—the last on the plate. On a clear day the island seems just a stone's throw from the shore, the ten miles of water foreshortened into a narrow gleam of light. How futile to search for an overdue canoeist here. Few inland river valleys in Scotland are ten miles across, and to suggest it is possible to see a lone vehicle from one side of the valley to the other would be foolish. Yet in the firth, that one island can distort the scale until distance melts away, and the watcher on the shore is easily inveigled into the expectation of spotting a paddler between himself and that rock. What value is a brightly colored kayak or a set of hand flares in reality? A very slim line of defense against the vastness of the ocean.

Ailsa Craig can perform other magical acts. Not only can it cause space to disappear but also, conversely, it can make visible the unseen air. Westerly winds flowing in from the Atlantic move up and over this rocky sentinel and, in so doing, force moisture to condense. A cloud traces out the invisible movement of air. It is always changing and can fascinate those who have time to stare. To the local fishermen this cloud that still hovers—ever changing—over the island has more than simple beauty. It is a barometer and a personal weather-forecasting kit! The speed, moisture content, and temperature of the air are all revealed to the initiated by this lingering cloud, and predictions based on its form have proved reliable.

We had gathered on the mainland shore and watched Ailsa's cloud evaporate—a sure sign of fine weather. The gentle breeze from the south was no hindrance as we paddled slowly toward this lump of rock. For two hours we seemed to stand still, but then the island began to open up across the horizon. This slow version of the "ground rush" experienced by free-fall parachutists does not spell the danger of a late pull of the rip cord, but rather the subtle pleasure of a temporary rest.

We landed easily in the slight sea and walked up the steep path to the lighthouse. The keepers were delighted with the daily papers and *T.V. Times* we had brought them. We knew these would be the most welcome items for the isolated men.

Then it was back to the canoes for a quick lunch before our circumnavigation of the island—only a mile or so. As we moved around clockwise the cliffs heightened, and we noticed that the contraction of the rocks, as they had cooled those thousands of years before, had left its telltale mark: six-sided columns of rock cracked in regular lines from the parent mass.

The height of a cliff is difficult to judge from an inshore canoe because of the intense foreshortening. But we were helped in an unexpected way. We had noticed areas of the rock whitened over by the droppings of some large bird, and then suddenly, we were among them. Gannets! Every column of rock was occupied by a gannet's nest—thousands of them—and thousands of birds were wheeling above us, too.

It would be untrue to say that they blanked out the light, but certainly they darkened the sky—layer upon layer of them. Some were low enough for us to hear air hissing past their feathers, and then up and up, smaller and smaller, until the ever-circling specks lost definition. Invisible height and space were revealed by that purposeful chaos. Farther away from the base of the cliff they were fishing. They thudded into the water at speed, their white wings furled back, their yellow heads, with their murderously sharp beaks, splashing as they sliced downward to the doomed fish below the surface.

Totally undisturbed by our presence, they were giving serious attention to the built-in duties of their swirling lifestyle. Meter-long wings moved imperceptibly as they deftly used the air masses lifting up over the cliffs. Close to and low down they were white, but with height and distance they slowly changed to dark silhouettes against the bright sky, forming a complex system of size matched to shades of gray. It was stunning to watch, yet it was no display. There was serious purpose in their effortless spirals. How could they show off to us when we were not part of their world? Yet inadvertently they showed us the space we were sharing, the very air that encircled us was made visible.

Strangely their presence heightened our isolation, too, and

it felt good. The gannets needed those dizzy, remote hexagonal perches rising above the cold ocean in order to survive at all. We can manage well enough in softer realms, but maybe some moments of remoteness, some revelation of the space and time around us is essential for our complete development.

It was one of those summers for which England is justly famous—rain almost every day, clouds keeping the daytime temperature so low that at least one woolly was always needed. Charles II was right when he said that the English summer was two fine days and a thunderstorm. This year we hadn't even had the two fine days! But suddenly there was that rare transformation to remind us that England is a good place to live in after all. Here was a calm, bright, beautiful morning with sunshine, but not too hot—the perfect day.

There must be no delay. It may last for twelve hours, or it could dissolve in clouds within an hour or two. Make decisions quickly, or it may be too late. Our decision was instantaneous. My wife Doreen and I put a flask of coffee and some food into the hamper, the hamper into the car and we followed. Our double Canadian canoe was on the roof rack, and in ten minutes we were at the river's edge.

The River Trent has been a navigation for hundreds of years, and every three or four miles there is a weir bypassed by a couple of locks for bigger rivercraft. The commercial traffic has completely disappeared, and only weekends are busy with pleasure craft.

Long before man had begun to stabilize the river, it had rushed headlong across the country from the high peaks of northwestern Wales to the Fens of the eastern counties carrying away the melting ice of the last glaciation, which had stamped its pattern on the landscape. Here, beneath our feet, were the gravels that still carry the remnants of early man mixed in with mammoths and woolly rhinoceros. But today the river is only a shadow of its earlier self. Its headwaters were diverted north by the River Dee thousands of years ago, and the Humber claimed the middle section for its own, too. Only the marl bluffs, defining the present floodplain, remind us of the vigorous meanders that once scoured away the surface.

We scrunched down through the gravel to the river's edge and slid our boat into the water. My wife was the bow paddle and made a drawstroke downstream while I pushed off and stepped into the stern. The reeds shook at the margin as a water vole retreated from our presence. He was not unduly alarmed; only dogs were his sworn enemies.

Cat's-paws touched the surface at regular intervals, but mostly the water was mirror calm. We paddled slowly, listening sensuously to the "stritch" of droplets tracing the arc of our paddles' return before they dipped. We felt the gentle but firm acceleration in the small of our backs.

A heron, standing stock-still until we were almost upon him, opened his gray wings and moved away downstream then curved around only inches above the water to return again to his favorite fishing spot. We turned to watch him. He banked across our wake, a precisely angled V with small wavelets all held at exactly the correct angle along its line. When we swung into the bank and stopped, our wake caught up with us, and the reeds nodded their approval of our presence.

There was no need for any comment until a kingfisher burst away in front of us—a turquoise comet of only a few seconds—and curled away to the steep, sandy bank where sand martins were nesting.

"There's been a pair here for the last two years," I said.

"Speaks well for the general improvement in water quality," returned Doreen.

"Well, look at the number of fishermen on the banks. There are even a few salmon trying to make it upstream these days."

We paddled on again. The next bend swept close to the bluff. Bright red cliffs rose maybe a hundred feet high, the less steep parts cloaked in elm trees that had fortunately escaped the ravages of the Dutch Elm disease, which had decimated the species farther south.

As the ground flattened out again we pulled into the bank. The flow was imperceptible, but close inshore a grass stem broke the surface, and the ripple around it showed that, in fact, gravity was still at work. A perfect miniature V wake from the stem mimicked that of the canoe, but not precisely. Here the ripples intersected the V at an opposite angle to the waves of the larger wake. We peered at it closely, enjoying this microcosmic reminder of the mathematical basis of our world.

"Gravity versus surface tension," I volunteered, but I didn't want to labor the point. It was the sun that was important, as was the clean air and the rich, dry grass we were sitting on.

Even the flies knew their place. They provided background "musak" but never presumed to settle on us. No mosquitoes visited, and the only disturbance was the occasional scrape from a grasshopper who had not yet learned to blend with the ensemble.

"Give him time, give him time," said my wife.

A stolen kiss in the long grass of a riverbank is always worth having, even when it has been available for over thirty years. Two teenagers coming through the bushes were somewhat disconcerted to see old-uns kissing in secret.

"They think we have to give it up at forty—by law," I remarked.

We laughed so much that concentric ripples marked our launching spot, and we giggled like schoolchildren on our return journey.

"Taken to its logical conclusion we should have stayed in bed," said Doreen.

"Taken to its logical conclusion," I said with philosophical gravity, "everything is either absurd or obscene."

"Or both," said Doreen, laughing at the implications.

"You'll tip us over if you don't watch out," I called.

We sobered up and soon the canoe was back on the roof rack.

"Only ten minutes to go," I said. "We'll be back before dusk."

We had traveled less than five miles by car and even less by water, there had been no rapids to shoot and no tidal streams to breast, yet our contentment seemed absolute.

"Why is it so much better to go picnicking from a boat than from a car?" Doreen asked as we turned into the garage.

"It's the change of element, isn't it?" I suggested. "A sort of alchemy, like transmuting lead into gold. No, that's not right, more of a primeval need to extend our territory, to broaden our horizons. It doesn't have to be wildly exciting, just doing it is enough."

"Yes, that's right," replied my wife, "it's a symbolic conquest moving to a new land without the need to dispossess the natives."

"That's it exactly. Perhaps it's the reenactment of an essential human activity that reinforces our sense of well-being."

We mused on the accuracy of this observation as we closed the garage, but as we glanced down the garden we noticed that clouds were already darkening the sky. They were extending vertically very quickly, and already they had altered the quality of the sunlight until the green of the shrubbery glowed more richly than under the clear sky of the early afternoon.

"Here comes the thunderstorm," Doreen commented.

"And after only one fine day," I replied. "Never mind, this one was perfect."

FRANK GOODMAN took up canoeing in 1965 and designed his first kayak a year later. In 1970, after twenty years as an art teacher and lecturer, he started Valley Canoe Products. His most famous kayak is the Nordkapp sea kayak.

In addition to being a competitive slalomist and kayak surfer, Goodman has paddled wild-water rivers throughout the United States and Europe. In 1977 he was a member of a four-man kayaking team to first round Cape Horn.

In 1979 he organized a kayak-building course with the Inuit of Baffin Island and returned in the summer of 1980 to paddle with the Inuit from Frobisher Bay to Allen Island.

LARRY RICE

Rocks, Ice, and White Whales

The flight from Montreal's modern, bustling airport to the
gravel runway at Pang took eight hours, 1,500 miles, and three
plane changes. Upon arrival we were not merely tired, we felt
as if we had entered a space portal back through time. There
was an unbalanced, disturbing blend of the ancient and the
high-tech. Young native mothers wearing caribou skin mukluks
and knee-length anoraks with babies on their backs roared up
and down dirt roads on three-wheeled, all-terrain motorcycles.
A chain link fence encircling a satellite station was festooned
with dozens of stretched and drying seal skins. Canvas shelters
housing entire families stood side-by-side next to prefabricated
government-built homes and modern fiberglass offices. The
new environment heightened our enthusiasm for the three-
week journey that lay ahead.

Gathering our gear at the one-room airport terminal, we
hired the only "taxi" in town to take us to a small public campground a mile outside of Pang. The campground was not much
more than a loosely defined patch of treeless, lumpy tundra
with one outhouse and a nearby creek for drinking water. Nevertheless, it was a welcome place to get organized after spending two days in transit.

The view from our tent door, which overlooked the magnificent steep-sided Pangnirtung Fjord, made up for the campground's lack of visitor services. To the south, a number of

miles distant, were the frigid waters of Cumberland Sound. To the north, toward the head of the fjord, were lofty mountains lost in clouds. Hidden beneath the mist, according to our map, were the chiseled granite peaks of Mount Odin, Thor Peak, and Mount Asgard, to name a few, and the vast, frozen wasteland of the Penny Ice Cap.

Lying only fifteen miles north of Pang, this 2,200-square-mile block of ice is one of the largest of its kind in the northern hemisphere. It also forms the nucleus of the 8,290-square-mile Auyuittuq National Park (I-you-we-tuk, "the land that never melts"), Canada's northernmost national park, whose southern boundary is within hiking distance of town. Established in 1972, Auyuittuq preserves an arctic wilderness of jagged mountains, glacier-carved valleys, and ice-choked fjords.

The campground was hardly crowded, in fact there were only a half-dozen tents besides our own. This came as no surprise; only three hundred to five hundred climbers and hikers visit Auyuittuq's backcountry each year. We would have enjoyed talking with someone just returning from the park, but despite the gear there was no one around.

Of course, even if we had chatted with a park visitor, they probably would not have been able to help us with our own plans. The 180-mile round-trip sea route we had mapped out through Cumberland Sound's islands, inlets, and mountain-ringed bays was entirely outside Auyuittuq's boundaries. Our trip would be through Crown Lands, which, we found out, were in many ways more pristine than the park itself. But because oil drilling, mining and other development schemes are slowly encroaching upon Canada's Arctic, we were overjoyed to later learn that plans are being made to nearly double Auyuittuq's size, which would extend protection to the wilderness we explored.

Besides paddling through an area seen by only a few *Kablunas* (an Inuit term for Caucasians, meaning "the ones with the large eyebrows"), we were enticed by the possibility of observing the beluga whales that spend the summer in a remote fjord about seventy miles northwest of Pang. I had been fascinated by whales in particular long before I made wildlife biology into a career. Judy shared a desire to learn more about the belugas, and we both acknowledged that whale watching was one of the integral reasons for making the long journey north.

After pitching camp, we assembled our Klepper kayak, a seventeen-foot, two-seat folding model that we transported aboard the airlines as regular baggage. The Klepper is not only portable, it is extremely seaworthy. Its rubber and canvas skin fits tautly over a framework of wooden ribs and, along with air sponsons and sprayskirts, it is virtually unsinkable.

The Klepper has been chosen for many serious expeditions and has even been paddled solo across the Atlantic Ocean. The only drawback to using a Klepper is in packing it for long trips. Bulky, waterproof cargo bags can be placed quickly in the open cockpit; however, the protruding wooden ribs and the lack of easy access complicate the insertion of storage bags into the streamlined bow and stern. Careful planning and lightweight gear are required to get three weeks of supplies stowed under the deck. Even so, it's always a source of wonder that there is enough space for two paddlers when the boat is loaded for a long tour.

With chores out of the way, we followed the gravel road back to town to discuss our plans with the park staff. At the Auyuittuq Park headquarters, a modular fiberglass and Plexiglas building at the outskirts of town, we talked to site superintendent Clément Bédard. Clean-cut, friendly, and with a ruggedly handsome face, Bédard, in his mid-30s, looked like he just walked off a national parks recruiting poster. He was not a kayaker, but was keenly interested in the type of trip we had planned.

"In the few years since I've been stationed here, you're the first sea kayakers I've seen; this area is still relatively unknown to paddlers from the south. Don't be surprised if your boat attracts a bit of attention; Baffin's Inuits long ago traded their kayaks for outboard-powered freighter canoes."

Had we arrived two weeks earlier, Bédard told us, we would have found a solid ice sheet on Pangnirtung Fjord instead of deep, open water.

"Break-up in this area usually occurs from early to mid-July, but it may vary by a few weeks either way. You still might run into scattered pack ice and bergs on Cumberland Sound, but if you get trapped just sit tight—the next tide will generally carry the ice away."

Our final question dealt with polar bears. Judy and I had camped and kayaked in grizzly country many times before

Camp on Clearwater Fiord

without incident, but we were still leery of the burly white
giants. Bédard told us that polar bears can be found throughout the island. This time of year, however, they *usually* were
not in the area we were going. When the sea ice goes out, the
bears concentrate along the Davis Strait coastline to the east
where there are more seals. Still, because of recent mishaps
between bears and Inuits camped along Baffin's shoreline, we
were cautioned to store all food away from our tent and to
prepare ourselves for an encounter. Polar bears are as fast as
race horses on land and could probably swim faster than we
could paddle.

We turned in early that evening, to our luck. Those first
few hours of sleep were all we got. At midnight, the sound of
rising winds and waves crashing on shore woke us. We tried to
relax and fall back asleep, but it was hopeless. With the tent fly
cracking like a bullwhip, all I could think about was how exposed our campsite was on the barren tundra, and how difficult (or impossible) kayaking would be in these conditions.

By 1:00 A.M. the gusts had increased in velocity. Wide
awake and shivering from the cold, I got out to inspect the tent

pegs. To my dismay, I found that half of them had pulled loose from the mossy ground. I staked out the tent as best I could and even tied it to the kayak for added security before crashing back inside to get warm. Judy, in the meantime, had put on her foul-weather gear and was ready for action. Good thing. A few minutes later we held our breaths as a tremendous roar whistled down from the head of Pangnirtung Fjord. The williwaw had arrived.

Created by up and down drafts near glaciers, large bodies of water, and open tundra, williwaws are violent winds that can reach velocities of a hundred miles per hour. In this case, the windstorm was produced by a cold air mass surging off the Penny Ice Cap and gusting down to sea level.

Our dome tent, which had withstood many an Alaskan tempest, was blasted by the gale. For four hours we braced against the billowing nylon walls to keep the aluminum tent poles from snapping. In the dim glow of the arctic dawn, we watched in fascination and dread as the yellow side panels expanded and contracted. It felt as if we were trapped inside a blacksmith's bellows. I began to wonder what the hell we were doing here. Maybe we should have vacationed in the Caribbean, at least there we would be sheltered by palm trees.

At first light we unzipped the tent door a crack and gazed wide-eyed out on the fjord. The sky was gray and brooding. Out on the water nature was even more chaotic. Closely spaced whitecaps, blown horizontally into hissing sheets of spray, galloped down the mile-wide channel. We had the utmost confidence in our kayak, but if caught in such a maelstrom, we would not stand a chance.

Fortunately, williwaws usually are not long-lived; this one died to a gentle breeze by 7:00 A.M. Nearly calm seas and a temperature of 38 degrees Fahrenheit now made travel possible.

Anxious to get moving while conditions were good, we downed granola bars and a few quick cups of tea. Refreshed, but feeling the effects of a night without sleep, we tore down camp and hastily stuffed a huge assortment of gear—cold-weather clothes, seventy-five pounds of prepackaged food, cooking gear, tent, tarp, sleeping bags and pads, books, cameras, binoculars, repair kit, and innumerable odds and ends—

into two tapered, waterproof bags that slid under the bow and stern decks, and into another pair of large dry bags that would nestle beneath our bent legs. We had learned long ago to pack the kayak at the water's edge. When fully loaded, the boat is too heavy to haul from camp.

With barely enough room for the two of us to squeeze inside, we fastened the sprayskirt, grabbed our feathered eight-foot paddles, and launched the kayak into the pale green sea. A somber sky still cast a pall over the land, and salt water cold enough to wake the dead sprayed in our faces. But, it was grand to be under way as we followed long and narrow Pangnirtung Fjord out of Cumberland Sound.

As always, when starting a kayak trip, a tingle of excitement swept over me. Only now the sensation was more pronounced than ever before. Perhaps it was because we were heading into a region full of mystery, or maybe it was due to the uncertainties of kayaking among rocks, ice, and white whales. Whatever the reason, at that moment, feeling snug and secure in our little portable home, there was nothing on earth I would have rather been doing. No conversation, no words of interpretation were needed between Judy and me. The fact that we were both here, on another kayaking odyssey, was evidence of our mutual feelings.

The surrounding country was wilderness in the truest sense. Rocks, clouds, water, birds, everything radiated brilliance in the unpolluted, crystalline air. We were Lilliputians kayaking in a land without scale. After scooting across the half-mile-wide fjord, we cruised past mile after mile of polished boulders and ledges at the water's edge. Eclipsing the rugged shoreline were thousand-foot ridges and broad plateaus that rose straight and treeless up from the deep channel. Patches of snow still clung to the mountainsides, reminding us that Baffin Island's kayaking season does not last long.

We settled into the familiar routine of paddling. Rhythmically—pull right, push left, pull left, push right—we dipped our blades into the slightly choppy sea. This was one of those rare times when both tide and wind was in our favor. Knowing that conditions on the ocean change by the minute, not by the hour, we pushed ourselves hard to make good time.

Four hours later we rounded Nasauya Point, at the mouth of Pangnirtung Fjord. Ahead were the wide-open waters of

Cumberland Sound, called *Tinikjaukvik* or "Place of the Big Running Out" by the Inuit, referring to the strong twenty-five-foot tides. And there, like strange clouds set upon the sea, we met our first icebergs—huge pillars towering a hundred feet high. A few bergs lay close to shore, a dozen more were imposingly silhouetted against the seaward horizon. During two previous Alaska kayak trips, in Glacier Bay and at the face of Hubbard Glacier, Judy and I had been exposed to icebergs for days on end. However, the icebergs of Cumberland Sound were the type that might have sunk the *Titanic* and transcended anything we previously had seen.

Cautiously, we edged our kayak into this Alice-in-Wonderland sea of sculptured ice. Many of the bergs had quaint and familiar shapes. One resembled a large two-funnel ocean liner, complete in every detail except for the smoke. Another was a replica of the rock of Gibraltar. And there was even a medieval castle adorned with battlements, turrets, and spires. We paddled closer to a few of the bergs, but not too close; these floating islands of ice are notoriously unstable and can topple over easily.

There are few colors as vivid as that of an iceberg. Through its frosted cobalt blue surface we could see small boulders and rocks deep inside. And surrounding the iceberg was water that looked as if it had been stained with blue dye. The effect was startling. I felt as if our paddles were brushes, and with each stroke we were dipping them into a bucket of paint.

The bergs were scalloped and pockmarked with shallow caves, and each had its own assortment of miniature waterfalls. We drew alongside one of the rivulets and filled a cup. The liquid was fresh and pure, as water should be upon being unfrozen after 10,000 years. These bergs had probably calved off a Greenland or Ellesmere Island glacier, taking a year or more to drift two thousand miles down the "iceberg alley" of Davis Strait and back up into Cumberland Sound. Most of the giants near shore were hung up on the shallow ocean bottom and, like beached whales, were doomed to a slow death on land.

We slid over lazy oceanic swells, far different than the bouncy chop found in the fjord. Although the crests were three to four feet high, the waves were gentle and relaxing. At times like this we appreciated our beamy, two-person Klepper. While not as sleek as the newer rigid kayaks, the folding boat excels in stability. With two double-bladed paddles churning away in harmony, and a foot-operated rudder for steering, we cut through the water at a respectable two to three miles per hour, fast enough for our relaxed expedition.

Right now, of more concern to us than speed was the continuous line of jagged rocks off to starboard. If forced aground here in rough water, we would likely face serious trouble. With a kayak damaged beyond the capabilities of our repair kit, our options would be to hike back to Pang—a formidable task—or try to hitch a ride on one of the native canoes that cruise by infrequently. Except in unusual circumstances, no government vessels cruise Cumberland Sound. In any case, we could rely on our three smoke flares to alert passing boats; we did not carry radios or emergency locating beacons.

Boat traffic was not the only rare commodity in Cumberland Sound; there were also long rocky stretches where coves and harbors were in distressingly short supply.

Several hours slipped by as we proceeded on course. It felt good to glide along effortlessly. Our pretrip training program of daily jogging, pull-ups, push-ups, and occasional paddling workouts was paying off. My philosophy on physical preparedness is simple: I would much rather suffer from sore and strained muscles while at home than be laid up or in pain in the backcountry when the stakes are high.

It wasn't until well past 7:00 P.M. that we found a break in the rocky shoreline that led to a bowl-shaped grassy clearing above high tide. Perched about thirty feet above the water, the campsite was not the easiest place to reach, but we welcomed the opportunity to stretch our legs. It took four trips to carry the boat, waterproof bags, and odds and ends through the slippery boulders and up to the tundra meadow. A cold, dreary rain began to fall, momentarily dampening our spirits, but hot drinks and freeze-dried stew a little later chased the chill away.

After dinner we took a stroll behind our campsite. Not expecting anything out of the ordinary, we were both surprised and delighted to discover that ancient peoples had also used this site. The remains of an old village were plainly visible in the grassy bowl. At one end of the sheltered clearing were half a dozen stone rings, circles of rocks once used to anchor animal skin tents; at the other end were a dozen pit-type excavations,

Cumberland Sound

and approximately nine by four feet, littered with piled stones and whale ribs once used for walls and rafters. The village apparently belonged to the Thules—forerunners of today's Inuits—who occupied coastal Baffin Island from A.D. 1200 to A.D. 1800.

We had done some library research about the Thules before we left for Baffin, but it wasn't until our return to Pang that we learned the sketchy details about this abandoned village. An Inuit park warden explained that there are many such Thule whale-hunting camps adjacent to Cumberland Sound. The vast majority, he pointed out, are known to only a small number of Inuit hunters and have never been examined by archaeologists.

Standing among the ruins was a heady experience. But it was more than just the fact that we were using a centuries-old campsite that made us feel that way. The Thules were among the first kayakers. We empathized with their nomadic way of life and admired their ability to survive in such a harsh, unforgiving land. For the Thules, kayak forays out on Cumberland Sound determined whether their families would eat or starve.

Evidence gleaned from sites like this one suggest that the Thules were skilled maritime hunters. In summer they used skin-covered kayaks and umiaks to pursue sea mammals as large as bowhead whales, and during freeze-up they used sled dogs in their search for polar bears and seals. During the "Little Ice-Age," a climatic cooling period that lasted from approximately A.D. 1600 to A.D. 1850, the Thules were forced to abandon their whaling life and to become increasingly dependent on seal, caribou, and fish. Anthropologists consider this transition to be the origin of the modern Inuit culture.

Each pit we examined looked as if it could house four to five people in what must have been extremely close, dark, and damp quarters. According to polar explorer Wally Herbert in his book *A World of Men:*

> . . . the Thules lived in turf and stone huts where a visitor would enter through a long, low tunnel crawling on his hands and knees—a hut almost circular, dingy inside, where the only light came from the tunnel and a window-pane made from the split intestines of a bearded seal . . . The hut would be bare of furniture of the conventional type, with only a platform of stone a few feet off the floor, a communal bed covered in skins, and a perch in the daytime for the women who sat making clothes for their family from bird skins, seal skins, and polar bear fur. A winter hut was lit by a blubber lamp and tended with care by the wife of the hunter, but the hut would be abandoned in spring after its roof of flat stone had been stripped off to let in the crisp, pure air to drive out the odor of wintering—the odor of blubber, putrid meat, and stale urine."

With insatiable curiosity, we eagerly explored along the fringes of the village site where we came upon two graves—one an open ring of stone, three feet by two, and a weathered skull and skeleton inside; the other a pile of gray lichenous rocks the size needed to cover a small child. When we peered through the chinks at this last grave, we were stunned to see a section of skull with tatters of braided golden hair! Only then did we recall a theory about blonde-haired Vikings discovering a country west of Greenland between 1,000 B.C. and the middle of the fifteenth century. As recorded in Leif Erickson's saga, the new territory was called Helluland, meaning "The Land of Flat Stones." It was described as being with "no grass . . . but with great icefields, and all that lay between the sea and the icefields looked like one great slab." Some researchers believe Helluland and Baffin Island are the same, but as yet, no definitive evidence of Vikings having visited Baffin has been found.

With more questions than answers, we left the site and returned to the familiarity of our own camp. The discovery had left us quiet and reflective. The spirits of the Thules were still around.

Due to persistent rains and rough seas, not uncommon to Baffin Island in late summer, we laid over the following day and roamed the low mountains behind camp. We actually welcomed the inclement weather, as it allowed us to acclimate a bit more to this foreign land before moving on.

As paddlers, Judy and I enjoy sunny weather and blue skies as much as anyone else, but we also rank foggy, rainy, what many consider lousy days right up there with some of the best. Our senses come alive under overcast skies, sharpened by mood and mist. I have been on kayak trips with individuals whose attitude turns sour after a day of foul weather. To my way of thinking, nothing short of a natural disaster can ruin an expedition quicker. Judy and I were fortunate in that the worse the weather became, be it a gale that kept us tentbound for three days or paddling in a downpour, the closer we became.

The next day the wind lightened, and the rain turned to scattered fog, so we loaded the kayak and continued heading up Cumberland Sound. American Harbor, sixteen miles away in the shadow of dome-shaped Usualuk Mountain, was our next goal.

My thoughts drifted back and forth throughout the morning, like currents on an ebb and flood tide. On an easy day, as this was, paddling became a mechanical form of movement that required little concentration. Sometimes an hour would pass like a minute as I daydreamed about people, places, and events of the past, of sea kayak trips I would take in the future. Then, as quickly as I fell into my reverie, I would snap awake, blink, and be fully cognizant of where I was and who I was. The wooden paddle would suddenly come alive in my hands, responding to my slightest direction. I listened to the kayak and understood its every creak and groan. Much more than a conglomerate of rubber, canvas, and wood, the kayak, like the shell of a sea turtle, protected me and was part of me. On the water I was helpless without it, with it I was strong.

As the day wore on, I found myself gazing more and more over the wavy green water to the openness of Cumberland Sound. The refraction of light played weird tricks when the sun peeked through the mist. Cloud banks looked like land. Icebergs looming to our port side masqueraded as islands. Sometimes the bergs appeared to be hanging upside down in the sky and, at a distance, looked as if they were right before our eyes. The clarity found in this pristine region was startling. To bring me back to reality I had to transfer my gaze back to shore, where the sight of land was always reassuring.

One of the nice things about sea kayaking is encountering the many seabirds. Northern fulmars, black guillemots, red-throated loons, common eiders, and glaucous-winged gulls soared, swam, and buzzed by us all day. The fulmars and guillemots circled us for hours, apparently looking for a shrimp plankton and the small fish that we stirred up with our paddles. Baffin Island's cliffs and rocky coastline provide nest sites for a number of northern species.

Since leaving Pangnirtung Fjord, we had been aware of a line of pack ice four to five miles away on Cumberland Sound. Little by little, the ice had moved toward land as a result of wind and tides. When it was only two miles from shore we began to be concerned.

Pack ice might be described as a gigantic jigsaw puzzle devised by nature. In a "loose pack," the parts of the puzzle have drifted slightly apart, and a kayak can usually weave in between the floes. In a "close pack," the ice gets pressed together, the congested areas grow larger, and the parts of the puzzle become fused. In either case, small-boat travel in pack ice is a white-knuckled affair.

About halfway to American Harbor, the change of tide pushed the pack ice in to surround us. Suddenly, we were paddling in a North Pole scene. Mazelike leads were followed through small bergs, rowboat-sized growlers, and pancake floes. The wind and currents kept everything in constant motion; lanes opened and closed shut with dangerous rapidity.

Judy pushed away another chunk of ice with her paddle, then turned around to face me. "Larry, I was just thinking," she said, with an unaccustomed tenseness to her voice. "Aren't these exactly the conditions that polar bears like? I mean, I don't want to sound as if I'm worried, but every time I hear a chunk of ice splash into the water, I half expect a polar bear to suddenly appear."

"Naw, no way," I replied with forced assurance, but the exact same thoughts were racing through my mind. From what we had learned about *Ursus maritimus*, the Great White Hunter, pack ice like this suited them fine. What is more, the dead seal we had seen on the beach earlier in the day, with half its midsection ripped out, only increased our apprehensions. We had taken along a 12-gauge shotgun for emergency use, but sealed in a waterproof case, wedged under the bow, and generally unavailable, it offered no immediate protection.

Fortunately, the ice never became a close pack, and any polar bears in the vicinity must have been on the prowl elsewhere. Like mice in a maze, we managed to squeeze through in our chosen direction.

The hours rolled past; the hazy sun drooped lower and lower on the horizon. At 9:00 P.M., under an ethereal twilit sky, we finally found a place to land. Our long day of kayaking was repaid with a pretty island campsite. A gently sloping sand beach, the first of its kind we had encountered thus far, led to a flat ledge among blue lupines and spongy moss. Lichens—gray, black, orange, yellow, red, and green—coated the rocks and boulders above high tide; their phosphorescent glow cheered the scene.

We had not drunk much since breakfast, and after the exertion of unloading the boat, our thirst became keen. Our water bottles were nearly empty, but to fill them we did not have far to go. As in most arctic areas, locating drinking water was not a problem. Permafrost underlies the ground and keeps precipitation on the surface. A short walk brought us to a rock basin where the liquid was painfully cold and gin clear. A little later, snug in our sheltered niche, we prepared dinner as a parade of "bergybits"—icebergs about the size of small cottages—floated by.

A full stomach and a vista of serene expansive waters and low austere ridges do wonders for philosophical contemplation. I almost felt like pinching myself to make sure this was not a dream. Looking out on the arctic landscape, thoughts of the exploits of great explorers—Peary, Franklin, Stefansson, Nansen, Amundsen, and others—of the frozen north flooded my mind. Their skill, determination, courage, and accomplishments set a benchmark that is rarely obtained by today's wilderness travelers. While I have had no delusions about being an explorer of their magnitude, I have wanted to make discoveries in my own personal way. Backpacking and canoeing in remote lands has satisfied this desire to an extent, but sea kayaking has permitted me to experience an entirely new world in a novel and exciting way.

Flood tide arrived at 11:30 A.M. the next morning—our signal to move on. The temperature was 55 degrees, with fleecy clouds sailing above an oily calm ocean. As we cruised between dozens of small islets and the fifteen-mile-long Kekertelung Island, it occurred to us that we were not exactly sure where we were. We knew our location within a mile or so; but because of the region's hazy maps and confusing channels, that was the best we could figure. In other words, as seat-of-the-pants navigators are prone to say, we were "temporarily misdirected."

At times like this we admired the route-finding skills of the native Baffin Islanders and appreciated the importance of the scattered Inukshuks they had constructed. These man-shaped stone pillars, built by both Thules and Inuits, once served as landmarks for travelers coming in from the open sea. We spotted a number of the monuments on ridges and hilltops, silhouetted against the horizon. Rather than serving as beacons, the stone figures now stand guard over a vast uninhabited land, reminders of a people and a way of life long gone.

I temporarily forgot about the Inukshuks as we wove our way from one island channel to the next. Off our bow passed low mounds of rock without even a blade of grass, ground smoothed by wave action and past glaciers. Other islands were substantial affairs, gradually sloping a thousand feet or more above the ocean, and carpeted with a brown-green mat of ground-hugging grass, forbs, and eight-inch willows. When our view to the west was not obstructed, we would see that Cumberland Sound was slowly becoming narrower as we paddled up its mouth. On the far shore, twenty miles away, was a curving, low-lying land mass that appeared much closer. The Drum Islands were also visible on the horizon. These flat-topped plateaus looked just like their name. And with only a few distant icebergs floating serenely on the ocean, and no pack ice at all, the tension we had felt earlier vanished.

Sheltered from the wind, we paddled with ease through the archipelago. My eyes never strayed far from the map and compass as I tried to maintain a northwest course. Despite my calculations an element of doubt always persisted. If our predictions were accurate, in a few days we would reach the head of Cumberland Sound. Soon after we would coast into Clearwater Fjord. This deep-water inlet—fifteen miles long and one to two miles wide, indented with three bays and enclosed by thousand-foot mountains and known for its beluga whales—would serve as our home for the next five nights. We could not afford to miss it.

Two days and sixteen hours of paddling later, we leaned back in the kayak with a sigh of relief. A mile ahead was the mountain-walled entrance to Clearwater Fjord.

"Well, we finally made it," I said to Judy, with satisfaction in my voice. "I'd offer a toast, but I forgot the champagne."

Even if we had the bubbly there would have been no time to drink it. A tidal current grabbed the boat, and we raced along at nearly double our paddling speed.

Up until now we had seen no marine mammals save one lone ringed seal. Suddenly, all that changed. We heard a whoooosh! of air, followed closely by another and another. A flash of two white backs breaking the surface and explosive jets of sun-glistening steam confirmed our hopes. Belugas! This was our first-ever sighting of this arctic cetacean. A kid who had just seen Santa Claus would not have been more excited.

The miniature whales swam into the fjord and disappeared around the bend. We made a futile attempt to keep up, then followed inside to find a campsite.

After a peaceful evening sandwiched between a cliff face and a jumble of seaside rocks, we arose early to catch the 7:30

A.M. incoming tide. To our surprise, the good weather was holding—42 degrees, clear, and with only a mild breeze. We could
not ask for a better whale-watching day.

A few minutes after we put on the water, a steady "put-
put-put" reached our ears. Angling toward us was a green
freighter canoe, piloted by a weathered old Inuit with two boys
at his side. We had seen a score of these handsome wooden
boats—used by the Inuits for seal hunting and coastal travel—
from a distance out on Cumberland Sound, but this was the
first time we had been approached.

"Hi, there!" I called out as the canoe pulled alongside. A
big, toothless smile from the old man and shy, deadpan stares
from the kids greeted us. It soon became apparent that our
"conversation" was going to be a pantomime of hand gestures
and signs. Except for a few English words known by the oldest
boy, they spoke only Inuktitut, an Inuit language of tongue
clicks and guttural sounds.

By tracing each other's routes on our map, we learned they
had come from Pang and were headed far up the fjord for a
combination seal-hunting and camping vacation. Likewise,
they learned we were headed for Millut Bay, an offshoot of
Clearwater Fjord, to study the white whales. As park superintendent Bédard had predicted, the old man was keenly interested in our kayak. His ageless face and coal black eyes spoke of
childhood memories when he undoubtedly had used a kayak.
The Inuit caressed the canvas deck, ran his creased brown fingers along the rubber hull, and touched the wooden ribs below.
I handed him my paddle. He clutched it like a long lost friend.

"*Nutjialarjiudebropnak, Aaaaaaaaaayyyy,*" he sing-
songed, his body alive with animation. Then, after returning
the paddle, he pointed to the kayak and clucked.
"*Qualiurinamistisbaqilsay, Numutsliaristuljiitremanicip,
Aaaaaayyyyy! Nutjiatlarjiutdebropnak, Aaaaaayyyy.*"

"What did he say?" we asked the eldest boy.

"Nice boat," he translated, with a face that would have
made a straight comic proud.

After a few more minutes discussing polar bears (we
learned that one ambled into an Inuit camp on Pang Fjord a
few days earlier), whales, seals, ice, and the weather, the Inuits
prepared to leave. Before shoving off, the old man reached

back in the canoe, pulled out a large arctic char and offered it to us. Since we already had adequate food and there was no spare room in the kayak, I politely declined.

We waved to each other and said our respective good-byes. Barely a hundred yards away, the Inuits suddenly reversed direction and sped back toward us.

"Maybe they're upset about me refusing the fish," I said, a little uneasily.

But when they pulled alongside, the oldest boy, looking not the least embarrassed, took out an instamatic camera and began to shoot! After we were immortalized on Hudson Bay film, the trio waved and sped off, leaving our "primitive" kayak bobbing in their wake.

With the drone of the outboard gone, we began to hear beluga music. Besides the usual gurgles and popping of blowholes, we listened in amazement to an unearthly symphony of high-pitches squeaks, whistles, squeals, and slurps. Early whalers nicknamed belugas "canaries of the sea," and for good reason. The constant stream of ultrasonic trills were not only finchlike, but sounded as if someone was trying to tune in a shortwave radio. Across the fjord, between Shilmilik and Millut bays, we counted at least fifty whales spouting and breaching over the mirror-flat surface. The surrounding cliff faces amplified their chatter.

A search for a campsite closer to the whale action led us across the fjord to a new spot some thirty feet above the west shore of Millut Bay. The rock slab wasn't the easiest place to reach with our kayak and gear, but the shelf provided a fantastic overlook to spy on the belugas. I couldn't believe our good fortune to have the entire bay to ourselves. It was just us and the white whales.

Once situated, we scanned the waters through binoculars. This time we counted not fifty whales but hundreds. A constant succession of white backs and vapor plumes glistened in the sunlight, joined by a steady "whoosh, whoosh, whoosh" as the slow-swimming belugas surfaced to breathe. With the entire area to ourselves, an area of intense wildlife activity among a wilderness as beautiful as any we have ever seen, we felt as though we had stumbled into sea kayaker's heaven.

Belugas are shallow-water whales, most at home in the icy arctic waters of northern bays and coastal inlets. They are not averse, however, to life in fresh water far from the sea. They have been observed 1,240 miles up the Amur River in Asia and 600 miles inland in the Yukon River. With a robust body, relatively small head, no dorsal fin, and a series of small bumps on their backs—plus the fact that they are the world's only all-white whales—belugas (*belyi* is the Russian word for "white"; *ukha* is a suffix meaning "large" or "big") are easy to distinguish from its two close relatives, the narwhal and the orca, which also share Baffin Island's waters.

A mile up from the campsite was the mouth of the Ranger River, a large-volume glacial stream that tumbles down from the coastal mountains. The silt and gravel it carries transforms much of Clearwater Fjord from deep blue to dishwater gray. Belugas are drawn to estuaries like this to spend the brief arctic summer and raise their young. As yet, no one knows the reason for this behavior although theories abound. Some biologists speculate that reduced salinity in the estuary attracts the whales. Others believe that poor underwater visibility minimizes attacks on the belugas by orcas. Or perhaps it is simply that cod, salmon, and marine invertebrates, such as squid, are found near the estuaries in greater numbers than in the open ocean.

The latest theory is more complex. It suggests that belugas get some energetic benefit from the warmer river water. Calves born in late July and in August do not have enough blubber to withstand the extremely cold water of the open sea, which does not get much warmer than 34 degrees. By spending the summer in this polar "hot tub," fed by 42-degree river water, it is possible that their survival into adulthood is increased. Whatever the reason, we had plenty of whales cavorting before us.

Canadian marine biologists estimate that about five hundred belugas inhabit Cumberland Sound, with the majority of them spending most of the summer in Clearwater Fjord. As high as this number sounds, it is small compared to the number of whales seen in the past. The beluga population is much lower than it was in the 1920s and before, largely due to commercial hunts that lasted until the late 1950s and early 1960s.

During the commercial whaling era, beluga products were used as ingredients in margarine and as mink food for fur ranches. Today, these white whales are still an important resource for the Inuit, providing food for people and dogs, and oil for heat and light. The village of Pangnirtung is allowed to take forty beluga whales from the Cumberland Sound stock each year—twenty-five of those at the floe edge or in open waters of the sound, and fifteen in a managed hunt in Clearwater Fjord. Although this harvest represents only 1.5 to 3 percent of the estimated Cumberland Sound population, it may be that these whales are hunted elsewhere as well and that further protection is warranted.

That evening the estuary was smooth as glass, and the weather was pleasant and clear, perfect conditions for mingling with the whales. We launched the kayak at slack tide, carrying with us only life jackets, binoculars, and camera. Soon we merged with the Ranger River's flow. We pulled our paddles in and drifted out of the bay with the current. By remaining motionless and quiet we entered the whale pod without frightening them, a technique probably used by Thule hunters centuries before.

In a few minutes we were surrounded by belugas. A ceaseless progression of white, humped backs broke the surface as the whales came up to breathe. We felt neither fear nor apprehension, just wonderment and elation. This was a moment that we had long sought to achieve. Occasionally a whale would pop up only yards from the kayak, but generally the belugas kept their distance, curious and cautious. Lois Crisler, author of *Arctic Wild*, a book about her experiences in Alaska's Brooks Range, described moments like these as "wildlife nuggets," rare, fleeting episodes that may only be witnessed once in a lifetime of animal watching. Who knows when, or if, we would see something like this again?

Sitting in a small kayak in arctic waters, surrounded by a circling pod of whales each about the same size as our boat, was a new and heady experience for me. I wasn't scared—never has there been a recorded instance where belugas have attacked a boat. Still, the encounter had me rattled. The mammals were looking us over with beady black eyes as if they knew something we didn't, which I'm sure they did. They were talking among themselves in a strange, bizarre language known only to themselves. Outnumbered and outmaneuvered, we were the aliens here, a sensation that felt similar in many ways to what I sensed while scuba diving through a parting wave of silvery fishes. Instead of scuba tanks and neutral buoyancy I was in a kayak afloat in a gauzy dream.

The reverie abruptly ended when a beluga surfaced within a few yards of the boat, exhaled quickly and submarined, leaving a bright ring of expanding circles. The nearness of the animal was startling, but I was pleased that we were allowed to come so close. Following Judy's lead, I dipped my paddle in the swirling sea and pushed on. Our little vessel lurched forward, probing the surface tension of inner space where the white whales make their home.

We yearned to discover more about these creatures. Slowly, as the initial bubble of excitement leveled off, we began to discern some of the belugas' identifying characteristics. Scanning the pod, we noticed that most of the animals were pale white, the normal adult color. There were also a number of bluish gray adolescents. It takes five or six years for young belugas to change to pure white, and by then they are the same size as the adults, fourteen to sixteen feet long and weighing as much as 3,500 pounds. Their life-span is believed to be between thirty-five and fifty years. Watching, listening, almost touching, I could understand why so many human beings at their first close encounter with a whale feel a bond that impresses deep into the psyche. I was feeling it, too.

Around midnight, with light still bright enough to read by, the tide turned, and we paddled back to camp. As we readied for bed, the whales were still "singing" out on the fjord. Only now they were joined by the wails of red-throated loons and a clamoring of glaucous-winged gulls on a nearby cliffside roost.

During the next few days we continued to observe the belugas, except when the bay was too rough to paddle or see the whales from shore. At those times, we either kayaked a couple of miles up the Ranger River on a flood tide or hiked the high country behind our campsite.

While hiking in the U-shaped Ranger River valley, an expanse of treeless tundra flanked by knife-edged granite peaks, we saw animal signs we had missed from the seat of our boat.. Caribou tracks lined the mudbank; an arctic fox pounced after lemmings on a grassy hillside; a short-tailed weasel squared off in front of us a few feet away. While flocks of Canada geese grazed in the sedge meadows, eider duck families patrolled the stream. Ravens, snow buntings, pipits, and Lapland longspurs were a few of the land birds we saw. Central Baffin Island's cool summer temperatures and frequent strong winds usually kept the mosquitoes and black flies in check, but in that breezeless, tussock-filled river valley the biting insects acted like we were the only warm-blooded meals on the block.

Hiking the high country—only nine hundred to a thousand feet above sea level on this part of Baffin—we were overwhelmed at how much of the surrounding wilderness we could see. Down below, with steep-walled sides and unplumbed depths, was the glacier-carved fissure through which we had paddled earlier. Twenty-five miles to the east stood the majestic seven thousand-foot mountains of the island's interior. Except for those found on Ellesmere Island, these are the tallest peaks in North America, east of the Rocky Mountains. When the clouds temporarily parted, we could see part of the massive Penny Ice Cap. Its permanent snow and ice cover gleamed briefly in the sun then was quickly lost in the fog. Otherwise, the land consisted of rock and more rock, either bare or with an onion-skin veneer of lichens and moss.

Our silent inventory of the landscape surrounding us was interrupted by a "kek, kek, kek" call from a boulder field ahead. The big white gyrfalcon was not hard to spot. Larger and rarer even than the peregrine, this year-round resident of arctic mountains and plains paid no attention to us as it gazed over its domain. Although we had seen the handsome bird before in northern Alaska, we considered ourselves extremely fortunate to see one again.

As our days of wandering the valley came to a close, we began to feel a chill in the air. For sea kayakers, the Arctic in fall is not a place to linger: freezing temperatures mixed with snow are common in September; and landfast ice, or "fast ice," along the shorelines often occurs by October. The changing temperature signalled that our time was running out.

As we paddled out of Clearwater Fjord for the journey back to Pang, we received a send-off that only a place like Baffin Island could provide. Into the narrow arm came a steady procession of beluga whales heading for the Ranger River estuary we had left behind. In groups of twos and threes, a hundred belugas streamed by—a veritable cetacean freight train—blowing water and mist.

Like others before me, I had fallen under the spell of the North Atlantic Arctic, a place similar yet so different from anything I had known. Here we were, still deep within the wilderness, and I was already planning kayak tours to Ellesmere Island, Greenland, Devon Island, and a return to the northern Baffin Island, but how was I to explore all the Arctic areas I wanted to explore in just one lifetime.

"That," said Judy, "is the ultimate sea kayaker's puzzle. I guess you just have to take them one at a time."

With these thoughts to keep me company, I picked up my paddle, and dug the blade deep into the water. Not far from the kayak, a lone beluga straggler swam by. I smiled as I recalled what the Inuit elder had said just before leaving us a few days ago.

"*Akagotaur,*" I whispered to the passing whale, "see you again."

LARRY RICE has traveled extensively in search of wilderness and wildlife. His journeys, many by sea kayak, have taken him throughout the continental United States and Alaska, Canada's high arctic, Africa, southern Chile, and Argentina.

He is a contributing editor to *Canoe* magazine and has published widely in *Backpacker*, *Oceans*, *Alaska*, and other magazines.

Rice resides in Illinois, where he manages a 6,000-acre state fish and wildlife area.

GREG BLANCHETTE

Paddling around Hawaii

Cutting Teeth

Every kayak trip begins with a single, specific launch, which in terms of psychological trauma, is the kayaking equivalent of losing your virginity all over again. My 1,200-mile trip around the Hawaiian Islands began with three aborted launches, a reflection, perhaps, of my pervading squeamishness about the whole venture I was embarking upon that late May of 1985. I wanted to start the trip from Oahu and paddle upwind across the channels to the big island of Hawaii. But unseasonal high winds—northeast trades to the tune of twenty-five and thirty knots—persisted for weeks after I arrived, and there was no way I could cross the channels against that. As a stalling move, I launched on the leeward side of Oahu and battled the off-shore gusts only to give up in disappointment. I launched again on southern Oahu and fought into the winds at one mile per excruciating hour. I was exhausted. I merely looked at the flying spray off windward Oahu and was devastated. Launching was out of the question.

So I parked my boat on the lawn of Richard and Joan Findeisen, my newfound friends, and toured the island by car for a week. Had I not been locked into an unalterable plane ticket, I believe I would have given up the whole thing as a foolish notion, returned home, and chalked it up to bitter experience.

As it was, I barged the whole circus to the big island—the boat nestled lovingly in among a containerload of coffins—with the hope of salvaging at least an abbreviated trip from the wreckage of my plans.

The third "launch" did not even involve getting wet. With the boat tied on top, I dragged my rental car along a bone-jarring lava road that wound roughly toward the water and, I hoped, an appropriate launch site. The shore, when I finally got there, was a sheer, ten-foot lava cliff. My fourth and final launch came at the end of a tortuous gravel road. I stashed my boat and the gear in the shoreside bushes and returned the car, mostly intact, to the airport. Then I haughtily turned my back on all forms of complication-ridden modern transportation and gratefully hoofed it back to my primitive muscle-powered craft.

The next morning, with utmost relief, I slid the boat into the water. The trip, in whatever form, was on.

Soliloquy

It is a whole different world paddling a mile or two offshore. Gone is the ready-made entertainment of inshore paddling, the continuous procession of things to watch, the reefs and boomers and random breaking waves. Alone, you are reduced to the basics, the elements of paddling that we all started out with once upon a time in a pool or a quiet bay somewhere: body, boat, paddle, water.

As boredom creeps in, my first line of defense is singing. With no audience but the occasional bird, I am uninhibited and soon find myself howling at the top of my lungs. A continual source of amazement to me is just how long I can go on dredging up new bits of song from the moldering bottom of the barrel. Sometimes an appealing snippet will catch my fancy and last all day. I recall paddling half of Oahu to the intermittent strains of "Slip out the back, Jack . . . fifty ways to leave your lover . . . " And will forever identify Pailolo Channel with "Oh, it's good/to be bloody well dead . . . "

But singing will sustain me for only an hour, two at the most. After voice and aesthetic discrimination have given out, and the effort of paddling has taken some of the edge from my joie de vivre, armchair—or rather cockpit—philosophizing is a useful time filler. "Why am I here?" is always a popular item of business, a perennial, mostly, because it results in no satisfactory or lasting conclusion. I usually take the general approach: "Why do I exist?" "What is the purpose of the cosmos?" "Why do crackers fall jam side down in the sand?" My inquiries are conducted in a wondering, as opposed to analytical, frame of mind. My brain is off the hook—not actively searching for answers but considering them one by one as they percolate up through my consciousness. Descriptions of meditation sound a lot like that, so I suppose the state of mind must be similar.

Only after all possible entertainments have been exhausted does my favorite part of the long offshore paddle begin—the stark process of putting miles under the keel.

I have a cousin who claims I was born in the wrong century for travel, and I think she's right. I have a hard time regarding flying as real, genuine traveling. A few years ago, I sailed from Vancouver to Hawaii. It took a whole month, but I appreciated the sense of distance and felt I'd truly arrived at a foreign place. Similarly, unless I've spent several days on a lurching train, or preferably weeks on a bicycle, I can't credit myself with actually having traversed a significant portion of the earth's surface.

Real travel, for me, is intimately tied up with the passage of time. It is for this reason that I remember these long, superficially boring stretches of coastline. They represent the quintessence of my own reasons for undertaking trips like this, which is simply to cover the ground, to make the miles—everything else must follow from that. Often, at the time, the miles are almost too heartbreaking to tolerate. But somehow in the maturing of a journey, which takes place as one looks back on it over the years, those same sections become the most cherished of the trip.

A long unavoidable offshore haul forces me to think and experiment. The cliffs of western north Molokai, for example, are a dead blank wall, a thousand feet high, essentially featureless for an agonizing fifteen miles. The ocean bottom shoals gradually, so I need to travel far out to avoid the inshore chop. Worst of all, the trade wind and swell rolls in unhindered off the east Pacific dead on my quarter, so after half an hour my right shoulder aches from sweeping on that side to counter an imminent broach. I quickly begin to hate that stretch of coast. But once the foam of my rage boils off in a long string of expletives, I set about looking for ways to ease my broaching problem. To my surprise, I discover the extent to which body language can be used to control a kayak. By leaning the boat just a touch downwave at exactly the right moment, the bow will ever so slightly grip an overtaking crest, receiving an impetus that tends to defeat the broach. The effect is subtle, but when applied consistently, it takes enough load off the upper body to make a real difference.

Once the nut is cracked, I am able to explore many different ramifications of the same kind of control, to help me deal with winds and waves. I not only ease my paddling aches significantly but give myself something useful to concentrate on during otherwise boring passages. It might not sound like a simple, useful skill, but it is much more than just that; it makes me more a part of my boat, and the boat more a part of the water. And, as I practice and improve my technique, it eventually comes to have personal philosophical implications as well.

For instance, though my first 'yak had a rudder, I rarely used it and have always resisted them with suspicion and distaste. The most I can stand on my boat is a skeg, useful for "tuning" the boat to course and water conditions. But I never realized why until after northwest Molokai. If you put a rudder on a kayak, you cease to paddle it and begin merely to drive it, like you would a car. The paddler becomes little more than a power plant for a pair of single-bladed paddle-wheels. With the introduction of "push this pedal to turn this way," all the artistry went out of it, and most of the style, and with it a lot of the satisfaction. For me, that is half the point of doing something as archaic as kayaking; it is for the beauty and style of the exercise.

Yes, I admit it; I am a raving purist. That is the only way I can justify a trip like this, which makes no sense from any point of view other than style. If the unspoken rules of the trip are broken, if my personal kayaker's ethic is compromised, the trip becomes a travesty, a joke. I might as well have a forty-foot cabin cruiser following in my wake to serve hot meals at noon.

Combat Zone

I spent the whole day speeding down the east coast of Maui, constantly battling a quartering wind and sea to keep from broaching. I surfed periodically at a speed that made my skeg sing with an eerie whistle. That evening I was on the beach in Kahului Harbor nursing a stiff arm and shooting the bull with four fellows who were killing time waiting for a nearby movie theater to open. I was surreptitiously casing the beach for the night's camping spot. It had everything going for it, with one fatal flaw: patrolling the beach was the security man for the Kahului Canoe Club, a walking keg of a man with a rumbling drawl, pure Hawaiian blood, and the unlikely name of Kit Carson. Kit had a keen sense of duty and passed much time watching for ne'er-do-wells trying to camp on his beach. He knew I wanted to sleep there, and I suspected it would have to be over his corpse.

As this standoff was progressing, we all watched a big Navy ship, bristling with antennae and whirling radar dishes, as it steamed slowly around the breakwater into the harbor. When the four moviegoers told me of the ship's special assignment in Kahului, I decided with my usual magnanimous diplomacy, that I would slink anonymously off the beach after dark. This would spare the Navy the possible annoyance of discovering a foreign national paddling a low, unlighted, silent kayak in the vicinity of their top-secret communications ship on the night of a Star Wars experiment involving the space shuttle and laser beams.

An hour after sunset, conceding the victory to Kit, I quietly slipped into the water and ghosted toward the breakwater and for the deserted beaches outside the harbor. To my considerable consternation, I was not on the water more than a minute before a bullhorn barked out some command from the ship that was lost to me in its echoes among the docks and warehouses. Were they talking to me? Did they know I was here? Should I surrender myself? I found it hard to believe they had detected me, but from previous experience I knew how sensitive sonar and radar could be. I decided to push on, until something more definite happened, like searchlights, chase boats, or small arms fire.

In the dim backlight of Kahului Harbor, I could see swarms of people combing the docks and scanning the water. Somewhat nervously, I began to relish this cat-and-mouse game, pitting the utmost in modern detection electronics against the epitome of Stone Age stealth. Adopting my best seal-stalking demeanor, I slipped noiselessly across the water toward the end of the breakwater. I paddled as fast as possible, for I saw more people racing out along the breakwater, pausing to scan the water through binoculars or, for all I knew, infrared night vision scopes. It looked as if we would arrive simultaneously at the fishing light marking the quay's seaward terminus. I hunched farther down into the boat and paddled quicker.

Suddenly a flipper slapped my forearm! I nearly jumped out of the sprayskirt with fright. "Oh Jesus!" I muttered. "Frogmen! I'm done for now!" But it had been a sleeping turtle drifting on the surface and no doubt as startled as I was.

I reached the light shortly before the soldiers and pushed out a good distance offshore. Still I saw them clearly, silhouetted against the city lights as they talked into radios and peered into the night.

I paddled a long way from the harbor mouth before hitting the sand. It was a moonless night, and the only level spot I could find in the dark was right in the middle of a beach-access road. Reluctantly I pitched my tent, feverently hoping that I would not be overrun by drunken beach revelers at 4:00 A.M.; or even worse, prodded awake by the business end of a platoon of M-16 carbines. Nevertheless, I crawled into my sleeping bag somewhat pleased that my little kayak had managed to outwit all that expensive technology.

Of course, I had to admit that I was not sure they were actually looking for *me*, or if they even knew I was there—but that's kind of the point, isn't it? I mean, the best way to avoid pursuit is to avoid detection in the first place. Perhaps there is a lesson here on the virtues of simplicity in an increasingly complex world.

Despite my uneasiness, I slept deeply, and undisturbed.

Through the Looking Glass

As soon as I turned the corner, I knew I was in for a treat. Suddenly, from just slightly offshore, I could see the whole

Hawaii

fifteen-mile length of it. The colors made a first impression on me: bright earth reds from the iron in the volcanic soil; jewel-like green vegetation, almost fluorescent in the sun; the translucent blue liquid light that permeates the island waters, turning to bright foam as they are dashed against jet-black plummeting lava cliffs. Colors so vivid and alive that I can close my eyes and still conjure them up, as if they have been burned into my retinas by their sheer intensity. Colors painted onto a landform so stunning that even a jaded paddler like me, who has seen nothing but beguiling tropical coastline for weeks and weeks, can't keep from twisting my neck into a crick to take it all in.

One of the things I kayak for is to see the juxtaposition of rock and water—an ancient contest between the adamant and the compliant. There before my eyes were a thousand examples of the soft triumphing over the hard. Look at those impossibly sharp ridges, twisting like snakes into the sky. What but writhing water could have carved those sinuous valleys? Look at these cliffs, undercut and collapsed a thousand times in a million years, undercut again now. I paddled in beneath the overhang, and looked up at lava that was fresh when dinosaurs walked the earth—but careful! Those waves would not distinguish between frozen magma and tender flesh. They harbored no reservations about pounding me into my elements, even as they pounded this rock into . . . oh, God—caves!

Rock rife with faults and cracks, each weakness a cave in the making, and every minute another cave, and every cave probing back into twilight. Looking at one, there was an entrance under a waterfall. I darted through the falls and moved slowly into the darkness until I could see, in grays and blacks. It smelled like the slime on the rocks, and I could feel the breathing of the earth on my face, as waves in the back of the cave push air out and suck it in. Slower now, darker, narrower—was that light up ahead, or wet rock glistening . . . ? The slightest splash behind made me turn . . . Jesus! Heart racing, I reverse furiously, shot backward half-airborne over the crest of the spilling wave as it broke beneath me. Steering awkwardly, I backed out beneath the falls and waited for the set to pass, then jumped into the darkness again, quickly this time. At the end of the tunnel, there was a vaulted chamber with an island in the middle. Some of the roof had caved in. And it *was* light I had seen earlier, for a second cave led out of the room from the other side! I toyed with the idea of lunching on that subterranean island, a fitting activity for the mythical aquatic caveman that I somehow transmogrified into along this mythical coastline. But the leftover adrenalin had sobered me somewhat, and the surge was really too much to handle. The nymphs and spirits were cajoling me back out into the colors and cliffs and spires and caves, and all the magic of Na Pali.

Just up from Barber Point

I was two chops into it before I realized what I was doing; I had finished it completely before I realized what it meant. I am talking about my beard.

One evening, the day's paddle completed, I waited on the beach for sundown to set up my tent. Idly, I dug the signal mirror out of the cockpit bag and unfolded the tiny scissors from my pocketknife. Facing the ocean and the lowering sun, I sat down on the sand, a boat-length away from the next day's surf with the mirror propped on my knees. Squinting, I began to hack away. The beard was unruly, the result of eight weeks of salt, sun, and less-than exemplary personal hygiene. I chopped slowly, lost in a careless, meditative, almost drowsy state. As the first few tufts of facial hair scattered down the beach, the philosophical implications of what I was doing began to bubble up through my liquid state of mind. Never before, even on month-long trips, had I gone to the trouble of trimming my beard. My unspoken rule was that it could grow wild, could sprout mushrooms, could fall to my knees—but only while the trip was on. Back home, back at my "real" life, the first ritual that marked a return to normality was shaving it all off. The *barbe rampante* is one of my signals to the world (or perhaps to myself) that "This boy is passing through. He's a traveler."

But here I was, sitting on a deserted Oahu beach by a red kayak celebrating a return to . . . normalcy? Unconsciously, at that moment, this trip had suddenly become different from all its predecessors. From that point on, paddling was the new "norm." I had become a beach dweller; more than that, I had become a dweller in the world, a man whose home is carried inside himself, in a state of mind that makes wherever he happens to find himself a home. Life was no longer a dash to complete one trip and get going on to the next project. *This* was life, right here around me: this sand, this water, this moon, this kayak. I was seeing them as if for the first time.

It was a subtle moment, both a resignation and a triumph. Paddling, after that spontaneous beard trim, became more than a pastime, more than a skill, more than transportation; it became an art, like music, with its own interpretations and nuances, ghosts, moods, traditions.

Twilight Zone

I spent two days naked on Kalalau beach—relaxing, talking, swimming, exploring the caves, and contemplating my final source of worry—Niihau, the so-called Forbidden Island, which demurely peeks its peak over the horizon to the southwest. Every time I looked toward it, and I looked often, a small thrill of trepidation chased down my spine.

I worried less about the fifteen-mile channel crossing than the moniker forbidden, which combined with my almost total ignorance of the place, lent a sinister aspect. My guidebook referred to the fact the island is privately owned, having been purchased in 1864 by a Mrs. Elizabeth Sinclair, no doubt an eccentric woman. The eccentricity seems to have carried on in the family, as the two great-great-grandsons who inherited it vigorously maintain Niihau's isolation from the rest of the world. No uninvited visitors are allowed on the island, though residents can leave if they choose to (very few do). It is the only place in the world where the Hawaiian language is used on an everyday basis. It lacks all modern amenities, including electricity, telephones, and doctors. The inhabitants make their living from cattle and sheep ranching, the manufacture of charcoal, beekeeping, and exquisite handmade shell jewelry.

Today Niihau is the source of a minor legend, shrouded as it is in mystery. But several locals I met on Kauai had been there as guests. Their reports conflicted somewhat, but I gathered that beach camping, if it came to that, would be no problem. I was relieved to hear this and planned to take three days to circle the island, camping the first and last night on Lehua Rock, a small volcanic cone just off Niihau's shores (presumably not forbidden), and the middle night on as remote and inaccessible a beach as I could hopefully find on Niihau's southern shore.

This was the plan. I left late in the morning, anticipating a tranquil fifteen miles to Lehua Rock in the wind shadow of Kauai. But halfway across, a big blue twin-rotor Navy helicopter circled overhead, descending as it tried to figure out whether I was in imminent peril or not. I lay the paddle down, tried hard to look like I was enjoying life, and wracked my brains for some recognized signal for "all is well," or "no, I do *not* need help," or "go away and leave me alone." Finally, hovering a hundred feet off the water, one of the guys leaned out the open side door of the craft and gave a thumbs-up sign with a questioning shrug. I brighten, smiled, cavalierly returned the sign, and resumed paddling. They climbed away, and I assumed the incident was over until I notice their destination: Niihau.

Paddling imitates life. Now there is a profundity for you. In this case, the imitation applies because both are fraught with imponderables. I did not know if the Navy discovered me via sonar or radar and then sent the chopper to investigate or if perhaps it was abominable luck that they passed over me on a weekly run to Niihau. I only know that by the time I got to Niihau, Niihau was waiting for me.

She waited in the form of a World War II landing barge, which was idling in the water off the point I was headed for. It sidled slowly toward me when I was spotted by her captain. As I expected, he opened with the time-honored unanswerable question that plagues kayakers everywhere, "What are you doing out here?"

While I pondered that one, I examined craft and crew. It was a vintage landing barge, replete with original camouflage paint, and it was big. I had to look up five feet just to see the shoes of the man who had spoken. Tall, balding, maybe fifty years old, he had a stern but tolerant look about him. I immediately took him for one of the owners of the island. From his dress and proprietary manner, he was certainly no casual visitor. The half-dozen others onboard were a ragtag group— young, dark, very Polynesian looking.

I made some idiotic noises about my trip, where I had been so far. But I did not expect him to understand—kayaking is too much of a fringe sport for that. He shook his head in a tolerant way. "No landing is allowed on Niihau."

I got the feeling that it was a pat response, that he knew this conversation by heart from having had it so many times before with people just like me, enthusiastic, well meaning, and ignorant.

I used my encouraging voice, "Yes, I know. I'm only going to paddle around it. I'll camp tonight on Lehua Rock." I wanted him to know that I respected his sanctuary, that I would not trespass.

"No landing on Lehua Rock either."

"Some fishermen on Kauai told me there was a small beach where I could get ashore . . . ."

"The Coast Guard doesn't allow it." He genuinely regreted having to quell my enthusiasm. I began to sense the magnitude of his responsibility for maintaining Niihau's aloofness from the rest of the world. He alone was the bulwark, holding back the entire twentieth century. He looked like he might be feeling the strain.

"Well . . . do they have to know? I won't tell 'em if you won't." I, too, had a mission, which I was not about to abandon easily.

"They already know," he replied. "I told them an hour ago. Asked them to come and pick you up. You shouldn't be out here. You don't know this channel. It can blow up in no time. Last year two guys in a small sailboat disappeared on a day just like this one."

I felt that my miles in Hawaiian waters entitled me to some opinion on where I should and should not be, but I did not argue. It occurred to me that the kayaker's curse is the tendency of some people to judge the extent of one's seamanship by the size of one's vessel. They assumed that big boats required better judgment, not the inverse, as would seem to make more sense, at least to those of us in little boats.

We bartered back and forth a bit, then he went inside to radio the Coast Guard. I turned my attention to the half-dozen kids lined up at the rail of the barge, looking at me. I found them inscrutable and hard to read, partly because they were hard to see against the sky and partly because I was unfamiliar with the stoic-looking Polynesian physiognomy. All seemed curious and mightily puzzled—possibly none had seen a kayak before.

I smiled and waved tentatively. Not one expression changed, not one eye blinked. At first, I thought they might be retarded. Then it occurred to me that these people did not speak English. Only much later did I realize that they were from as alien a culture as I had ever run across; they were not even from this century. Bobbing up and down in tandem on the swell, we had little to do but watch each other.

The man reappeared. I had gathered from snatches of his conversation with the Coast Guard that they would not be coming out to "rescue" me. I assumed that there must be a steady tide of curious people setting off toward Niihau in all manner of craft, and that the authorities were just plain tired of fetching them back.

The man was not angry. Undoubtedly this had happened to him often before. He looked like an innately kind man. He could see that I was a nice guy—earnest, sincere—just out having fun. I could hear from the tone of his voice that it pained him to rain on my parade, even though his duty to do so was clear and irrevocable.

I looked up to him as he stood at the rail, a sharp silhouette carved against the tropic sky. The man was something of a minor god over on his island. To meet him out on the water . . . sun pouring down, one island before us, one island behind, each of us in our boats, each in our separate worlds, each in the grip of our separate destinies—how incredibly dramatic, what a memory to cherish like a trophy!

He leaned down and spoke, unwittingly plunging me into moral dilemma. "Come on," he said with a casual flip of his head. "I'll take you back with me. Come on."

I instantly relished the rare chance of spending an hour with this man. What a fascinating time it would be! But something nagged at me, something in his manner, his tone of voice. I was being cajoled like some recalcitrant adolescent by a man who was an expert at it. My innate distrust of authority figures, deliberately cultivated in reaction to my own vulnerability to persuasive people, set off warning bells. This was a man well used to getting his own way. He was the ultimate figure of authority, since in some sense he must have ruled the island he owned. Niihau may have been a benevolent dictatorship, but it was a dictatorship nonetheless. Again I sensed the irony of being born to a power one may not want but cannot relinquish.

He was waiting while I made up my mind. Though I dearly wanted to ride with him, it took but a few agonizing moments to decide not to. I would not be manipulated. And deep inside I knew that if I accepted this lift, I would have to abandon Niihau for good and leave my trip unfinished.

"No, thanks," I heard myself responding. "I'll paddle back myself."

He seemed surprised by my decision and offered once again. But my mind was made up. A long-distance kayaker has to have some kind of ethic to govern his activities. Mine is that wherever I go, I go under my own steam. Besides, I did not think he fully realized the problems involved in hoisting a kayak with food and water, up that high from the water.

He shook his head, perhaps astounded by my stupidity (for I was sure he really believed I was at risk) or my pigheadedness. I expected a stern warning to keep away from Niihau, but he said nothing. He merely walked to the deckhouse and backed the landing craft away. The kids, who had silently lined the rail throughout our exchange, dispersed as we separated.

The craft waited some distance off until I turned the kayak around and paddled toward Kauai, then it motored off in that same direction. In a short while, I was alone again with my thoughts.

As I paddled I argued with myself. I believed in what the Niihau "experiment" stood for, and felt morally obligated not to compromise it. On the other hand, I had come this far on my own little venture, and I owed its completion to myself. The debate raged on until, halfway back to Kauai, I threw caution to the winds. "I'm out here now," I reason. "I'll circle the damn thing nonstop! Nobody need ever know!"

It was midafternoon. I turned the boat around and struck out for Niihau once again. I knew I was in for a long slog, but I was happy to have resolved my dilemma in a satisfactory manner.

Dusk was near as I reached the island's towering southern cliffs. I kept a nervous eye out for signs of people, but could see nothing. My change of plans meant I had to dig more food and water out of the boat, so I looked for a discreet landing. I had to get ashore for a few minutes before dark.

Finally, a small pocket beach carved from the cliffs appeared, and I went in. The sand was fantastic—loamy stuff into which I sunk up to my ankles. Sand crabs the size of saucers clambered over my feet and the deck of the kayak with impunity, as I shuffled food and water into the cockpit area. I remained in the swash zone, so my footprints would be erased by the waves. I was acutely aware that I was not supposed to be there. I involuntarily scanned the kiawe thickets at the top of the beach expecting to see silent, watching faces in the fading light.

Fifteen minutes later, I was back in the cockpit with paddle in hand. But horrors—a wicked rip had swept me out of the lee of the point and, standing vertically before me, was a lone wave with my name writ large upon it. Dead in the water, I had no hope of getting through that one. Feeling sick, I folded gracefully into it as the bow of the kayak disappeared under the break. Forehead pressed to the deck, I felt my boat being picked up and thrown. With cool sarcasm, I whimsically commended myself to fate and the boatbuilder, as the stern pile drove itself into the bottom.

I rolled up in shallow water. Pushing off the sand I sprinted out beyond the surf line. I virtually tore the sprayskirt off to check for water in the boat. There was none. I twisted around to inspect the skeg. It was retracted and sustained no damage. Paddling cautiously, I watched for signs that the stern compartment might be taking on water. I wondered what the hell I was going to do if stuck with a broken boat on an island I had been distinctly warned to keep away from.

Mercifully, all was OK. Darkness was falling, and my worry slowly subsided as I turned the corner to the leeward side of the island. The paddling was smooth, but the moonless night was as dark as pitch. I steered by the sound of the surf, dodging rocks and points as they loomed out of the darkness a few feet from my bow. I was keenly aware of the irony of seeing virtually nothing of this island I was paddling around, and I began to wonder whether this was a silly stunt.

At midnight I smelled cattle, and soon heard their lowing. I passed the single yellow eye of a kerosene lantern—the only evidence I saw of the island's inhabitants.

My caffeine pills did not seem to be working. With no visible reference at all—even the stars were dim, lost in mist—I was dozing off like mad, only to jerk awake with a reflexive brace. I felt some stirrings of fear and began to curse myself for concocting such a risky scenario. My existence that night became a miserable battle to stay awake, to fight off fatigue, to figure out where to go, to cage the hounds of despair. Eventually, the interminable night relented. I turned the corner around to the windward side of the island, and Kauai appeared in the morning mist, a million miles away.

I was completely bagged—bucking into even the light chop was pure hell. It was moot, with every stroke, whether the boat was moving forward or whether my arms would be pulled out of their sockets. I did my level best to shut off my brain, to think of nothing. It was the only way to make the time pass. Cracking the occasional wry comment to myself, "So that was scenic Hawaii," I was nevertheless very conscious of being close to the hairy edge of something dangerous: if the wind were to come up later in the morning, as it often did, I possibly would not make it to Kauai.

Finally, finally, finally! I was facing the island's shore dump. I paused to eat and drink, then summoned up all my energies for one last sprint. I made it ashore without getting soaked. Prying myself from the cockpit, I left the boat by the water and literally staggered up the deserted beach. I had cunningly landed by the only suitable shade tree for miles around. I strung up the hammock, lowered my exhausted frame into it, and stared off into space for several minutes. My kayak rested on the hot sand. Niihau, the Forbidden Island, the last significant obstacle on my Hawaiian circumnavigation, sat astern of the boat. Not exactly in the way I had planned it, to be sure, but astern nonetheless.

The combination of outward exhaustion and inner elation felt odd and confusing, like being simultaneously sprayed with warm and cold streams of water.

I thought back to the previous morning when I had so blithely left this very beach. I looked at my watch, but it took me several moments to make the calculation. Twenty-seven hours. Not bad.

Closing the Circle

What a feeling, that final morning! I would never forget it. The holy dawn light streaking across the sky, giving rock and tree alike a kind of inner glow; the breeze yet to awaken from its overnight slumbers; the low restless swell sucking meditatively over the reef, disturbing the glassy inshore waters and playfully caressing the sand. And inside me, the knowledge that all obstacles were astern, that there were fifteen short miles to go, that I would finish what I had set out to do before lunch.

It is a difficult time to pin down in words—the end of a trip. How are you supposed to feel when two years of dreaming comes to fruition in the space of a morning's paddle? At once, there is the beauty and disappointment of island circumnavigation—that at some clearly defined point, it is simultaneously consummated and dissolved. Very little these days offers the possibility of such incontrovertible achievement, such a definite sense of knowing when you have *arrived*.

I was uncomfortable with this combination of triumph and relief, two emotions that do not seem to mix. The easiest thing to do was to concentrate on the exercise of paddling; on the details of Kauai slowly hardening, as the climbing sun began to tip its heat out; and to ignore the stirring in my guts. It was as if I was slowly liquefying—my joints and sinews turning more and more to water the closer and closer I got to the end of the journey. In my lightheaded state it seemed like the whole world was celebrating: a blowhole spouted rhythmically, majestically spotlighted by the sun. I brushed a school of porpoises, the young of which were practicing joyous airborne backflips, cartwheeling above the water over and over again. The world around me was holding its breath, waiting to burst into cheers when I broke the finish tape. Even the cool air hardly moved. Such moments help define the spirit of sea kayaking, its magic, its essence, its heartfelt appeal.

I love kayaking because it weaves back and forth across an interface, in several senses. It exists between two worlds without being claimed by either. The craft is useless without water, and yet a kayaker cannot survive for long without land. I can float a stone's throw out on the water and feel I inhabit a different universe completely detached from land. But a simple nudge ashore, and I am the prodigal son returning from years of wandering—people are astounded, curious, welcoming. As a vehicle, the boat itself spans the most ancient and the most modern technologies. Imagine, a millenia-old craft constructed of kevlar, vinylester resins, and carbon fiber—what a figurative meeting of minds! And here I am in twentieth-century waters, with motorboats, airplanes, automobiles—the most complicated of machines all around me—pushing my hybrid craft along using muscle power and a simple lever device perfected somewhere in the Aleutian Islands perhaps 5,000 years ago. What a titanic span of technology, of ideology, of humanity!

One last interminable offshore haul later, my patience was growing thin. Okay, I knew I would make it, but I did not want to suffer. The Nawiliwili lighthouse popped into view in its own good time, and finally I was abreast of it and headed into Lihue Harbor. This was the beam that gathered me into Kauai some weeks ago and just about this time in the morning. I greeted the old light with a mock salute, as I might greet an old friend. I had arrived. I had done it. It was over.

A Lesson in Hubris

No doubt about it. I was feeling pretty smug when it was all done. After the last mile of the last island, I dragged the kayak up under the shade trees on the Lihue beach and lay swinging in the hammock, watching the pretty girls. I read and relaxed all day and, as the short tropic twilight began, I paddled up the creek to my old spot in the swamp and pitched my tent. The "swamp" must sound like an ignominious spot to retire after the successful completion of a cruise. In the face of long stretches of inhabited beachfront, and limited landing places, I had soon learned to root out the spots where people seldom go at night. The swamp was definitely as good a campsite as I might have wished for.

The next day, ensconced again in my hammock on the beach, I reflected. It would be a whole week before I had to catch the inter-island flight back to Oahu to connect with my plane home. Though I enjoyed lazing through the days without any obligation to paddle on, I had my kayaker's pride to consider. I felt that circling Kauai one more time would give me something to do and would look good "on the record." This notion of style, a kind of celebratory loop-the-loop, grew on me steadily as the day progressed. Finally, with sunset imminent, ego flaring brightly, I paddled not toward the humble swamp, but off around the point and beyond the breakwater. I was aiming for a promising beach I had noticed on my first circuit of Kauai; it would provide a good starting point for the *next* one.

One of the very early lessons a novice kayaker learns, and it is often a painful or at least humbling lesson, is that the kayak is a creature of the sea, and the sea alone. It wants nothing to do with land and, like a sulking child, it does everything it can to make land-based operations—carrying, launching, landing—as inconveniently awkward as possible. No matter how graceful it looks dancing among the waves, there is simply no way known to land a kayak with dignity in any kind of shore break.

Such were my thoughts as I studied a particularly awkward dumping surf. It was not large enough to be dangerous, but it incorporated both an onshore component and an oblique, reflected backwash from a nearby rock ledge. As I pondered, I noticed a knot of fishermen studying me from a nearby promontory. At this, my internal warning bells should have sounded shrilly, for another early lesson is that the probability of a botched landing increases exponentially with the number of spectators present. But the sun was sinking fast, and I was more concerned with setting up camp.

The technique for getting ashore is to race up the back of the smallest wave you can find. Then as the bow gently touches the sand, quickly eject from the cockpit, and drag the boat up the beach away from the next dumper. The technique works perfectly about half the time. This occasion, however, was somewhat less auspicious. The bow touched down gently enough, but as I reached for the sprayskirt release I was unexpectedly nailed by one of the reflected waves.

Immediately things moved out of my control. Should I bail out and be swamped for sure or sit tight for the next one to wash me up the beach. This latter hope usually sustains me through a few more dousings before it dies completely. But I did not know what to do, and my mind was paralyzed by the vision of those fishermen, who were surely convulsed with laughter by now. A big one broke over my head and tore the paddle from my hands. I brushed the water from my eyes. I had to get that paddle back; the undertow was sweeping it away. I flopped down on the sand, stretching . . . my fingertips could just touch it . . . more . . . got it! The next dump filled my eyes and nose with sand, pulled my hat off, and sucked it down under the foam. Like a punch-drunk cartoon boxer, I was reeling under the blows of the oncoming waves: left, right, left, right!

Suddenly my mind cleared and, catlike in the desperation of the moment, I leaped to the standard alternative, which was to abandon any pretense of knowing what I was doing and just get the hell away from the boat. But I was still out of luck. With the skirt off, my butt up on the back deck while extracting my knees from the cockpit, I was walloped by another wave. I was knocked flat and washed up the beach spitting sand. The boat courteously joined me at the top of the swash, so chock-full of sand and water that I could not move it.

Ten minutes searching in vain for my precious hat, and another fifteen minutes bailing out the boat gave me some opportunity to contemplate the worthiness of escapades launched in hubris. It further occurred to me, while sitting in cold, wet clothes, watching the gibbous moon rise above the clifftops, that the sea does not honor one's past record, but judges and acts according to the performance of the moment.

Later, while nervously standing my ground against a large bull who had wandered down to munch on the bushes and, for all I know, defend his territory, I came to some significant and chastening conclusions regarding the necessity and desirability of another circuit of Kauai.

I remember that final night's camp spot, the whole atmosphere of the place . . . a tiny landing behind a rocky ledge, too narrow for anything but a kayak, an unexpected pond over the rise, the lowing of cattle, the pellucid, mystical quality of the light. . . . It was as close to magic as I ever expect or need to come. And my astonishment at finding a branch of wood, somehow grown into a closed triangle shape—an omen, surely, and a good one, seeing as how I had long since decided to call my next boat (a sailing craft) *Triangle Island*. What a pleasing and encouraging way to end a trip, with a happy benediction and an impetus along the next project. This is the way it should always be!

I slept fitfully the next morning. Unobserved, I launched without incident and, all things having been duly considered, proceeded humbly back around the point, to pass the rest of my week on the beach and in the swamp at Lihue.

GREG BLANCHETTE always had a deep-rooted fear of starving to death all alone in a back alley somewhere. To avoid this mishap, he was counseled to submit to the rigors of a university education. Being generally eager to please and having no great independence of spirit, he complied. Engineering. Good steady trade.

In 1981 he quit his job and acquired a kayak. Since then, he has had many memorable years of adventure: paddling, sailing, falling in love. Living.

Despite his belief that words are extremely poor tools for shaping lives, he likes what Goethe said, "Remain true to the dreams of thy youth." And Greg, raving purist, says this, "Naught by halves or thirds."

Epilogue

"Follow your bliss," advised the late mythologist Joseph Campbell in *The Power of Myth* (with Bill Moyers; Doubleday, 1988). "What we're seeking is an experience of being alive, so that our life experiences on the purely physical plane will have resonances within our own innermost being and reality, so that we actually feel the rapture of being alive."

The contributors to this anthology represent sea kayakers in tune with Campbell's philosophy. The fact that they chose to experience the wilderness by kayak is particularly relevant in terms of mythology. More than any other form of transportation, the kayak is uniquely symbolic of mankind's ingenuity in heroically meeting the demands for survival.

Through thousands of years, kayak design basically has remained the same—only construction materials have changed. In the process, kayak function has evolved from hunting to recreation as Western culture has overshadowed native culture. Yet there remains another constant despite the passage of years and change in function: the world as viewed from the seat of a kayak.

For the Western sea kayaker, traveling by kayak inspires an understanding of native reverence for the natural world. Removed from the protective cocoon of civilization, the modern paddler interacts with the dynamic sights, sounds, and spectacle of nature in the same way as did ancient man. Not surprisingly, there exists the same vibrant feeling of continuity, of being part of something larger. Time, space, the evolution of man, and wildlife within the cosmos echo through the medium of nature.

This sense of a continuum was dramatically brought home to me one summer while paddling the coastline of upper British Columbia, much of which is uninhabited and unspoiled. Being somewhat of a romanticist, I like to think that ancient man saw essentially the same environment as I do centuries later. The land and seascape become for me a sprawling stage upon which generations of mankind play their roles. And so it was, while paddling with friends through a meandering channel to visit a Tsimshian native village, that I imagined scenes from another era.

I could see sails billowing on the horizon. Drawing closer, I could hear creaking timbers and smell the pungent eighteenth-century fragrance of tar, hemp, and canvas. Upon the salt air wafted the lilting accents of British, Spanish, and American seamen. They came from the exploring ships *Discovery*, *Santiago*, and *Columbia*, captained by Vancouver, Perez, and Gray respectively.

In like manner, I could see high-prowed, cedar dugout canoes, 40 to 70 feet in length, being paddled by broad-chested, coppery-hued Tsimshians. Their sinewy muscles rippled in rhythm to the cadence of a guttural song. On every fourth stroke they gave a shout while striking the gunwales a resounding blow with their paddle looms. These Tsimshians were men of the forest, men of the coast, men of the sea. It was the time of first contact between Europeans and natives along this coast—mankind meeting itself from differing cultures.

My historical images blurred and vanished, however, when fishing boats intruded upon the timeless environment. Then the long channel passage was transformed into a maze of islands. Beyond them lay the Tsimshian village we sought.

In the failing evening light, we landed wearily on an island near the village and set about making camp. Thoughts of hot supper and a snug sleeping bag pervaded our minds. We felt a special sense of freedom, accomplishment, and camaraderie. We were at peace with ourselves and our environment.

Our reverie was rudely interrupted by the racing motors of two fishing boats heading toward us. A white-haired Tsimshian came quickly ashore, his broad face taut with anger.

"This is a reserve. You'll have to leave," he stated sharply. His angry words collided with our idyllic sense of being. Without hesitation, our group leader agreed we would comply. His navigation chart, he explained, didn't identify the island as a reserve. Had it done so, we would not have landed.

During the time we talked with the Tsimshian native, I thought back to the historical images occupying my mind while paddling the long channel. The billowing sails and dugout canoes had met centuries ago, and the resulting cultural impact sent shockwaves hurtling across the reaches of time into the present. My mental escapism had turned into a palpable truth: I was a product of history.

About the time we had gathered our gear, the white-haired Tsimshian was almost apologetic for making us leave. He knew we had landed innocently on the island reserve and meant no disrespect. I told him we enjoyed the environment and looked forward to visiting his village the next day. He regarded me for a moment, then turned to gaze at the distant village. He seemed to be deep in thought.

"Here I am," he mused while slowly turning toward me, "using a white man's law against you people trying to experience our way of life . . . how native people used to travel." He paused, wistfully regarding the irony of the situation, then shook his head when he saw I understood. His expression was eloquent beyond words.

Index

Acknowledgments

Serendipity plays a large part in creating books. This anthology is no exception.

Often, when getting involved with a new activity, there is a tendency to seek out and devour any and all information on the subject. Such was the case with me after my first sea kayak outing in the early 1970s. Upon inquiring at various bookstores, however, I was told there were no books on sea kayak touring.

By chance, I found a copy of *Folbot Holidays* by Jack Kissner in a used-book store. Although written by Kissner to promote his portable Folbot boats, the book was a useful compilation of techniques and equipment relevant to sea kayaking. Moreover, the illustrated trip accounts by Folbot users served as a guide for places to visit. But it was the feelings and moods expressed in these accounts that fascinated me most of all. As a novice kayaker, I found myself comparing my waterborne experiences with those related in *Folbot Holidays*. Without my realizing it, the foundation for *Seekers of the Horizon* had been established.

After a few extended wilderness sea kayak trips, I wrote about my experiences for various outdoor magazines. My writing led to an interview with Dr. Paul Kaufmann, author of *Paddling the Gate*. His book, a composite and poetic account of his many kayak trips on San Francisco Bay, had been well received by sea kayakers but was no longer in print. One question followed another and before I knew it, Dr. Kaufmann had given me permission to reprint his book. Then the idea struck me: Use Kaufmann's book as a starting point for an anthology conveying the spirit of sea kayaking through various adventures. Yes, an anthology similar in format to *Folbot Holidays*.

The road between my idea and the realization of this book became a wilderness journey unto itself. I am grateful to my fellow sea kayakers who believed in the project and took the time and effort to participate. I am also grateful to Carolyn Threadgill of The Globe Pequot Press for her confidence, encouragement, and advice from the outset. She made it all seem possible. I accord special thanks to Carolyn's colleagues, Bruce Markot and Margaret Foster-Finan, for their meticulous attention and care in skillfully editing the final manuscript.

Finally, I am indebted to the late Jack Kissner for his literary role model. His daughter Olivia J. Smith was kind enough to send me the original version of *Folbot Holidays* published in 1940. I thought it especially significant when Mr. Kissner concluded his acknowledgment page: "This being the first published work on Foldboat Sport in America, I dedicate it to the thousands of foldboaters to come." I like to think my anthology represents a passing of the torch for the current generation of sea kayakers. Perhaps someone in a future generation might discover it in a used-book store. Serendipity? Of course.

Will Nordby
September, 1988
San Anselmo, California